Published by Hawthorn Press, 1 Lansdown Lane, Stroud, Glos. GL5 1BJ, UK
Tel: (01453) 757040 Fax: (01453) 751138
E-mail: info@hawthornpress.com Website: **www.hawthornpress.com**

Drawings and cover illustration © Marije Rowling
Cover design and typesetting by Hawthorn Press, Stroud, Glos.
Printed on environmentally friendly chlorine-free paper manufactured from renewable forest stock.
Printed by Athenaeum Press Ltd, Gateshead.
Originally published in 2004
Reprinted 2009

Every effort has been made to trace the ownership of all copyrighted material and to acknowledge this. If any omission has been made, please bring this to the attention of the publisher so that proper acknowledgement can be made in future editions.
All stories (including puppet show story) are by Ann Druitt.

We are grateful for the kind permission of Sally Schweizer to use her work.
'The night before the birthday', from *Gateways: Poems, Songs and Stories for Young Children*, 1999, reprinted by kind permission of Wynstones Press.

British Library Cataloguing in Publication Data applied for

ISBN 978 1 903458 01 3

Contents

Foreword

This is a resource book, but also far more than that. Out of many years' experience of celebrating birthdays imaginatively and creatively in their own families, the authors have compiled a heart-warming book which is as practical as it is inspired. Fascinating historical and cultural perspectives are spiced with recipes, stories, songs, games, ideas for cards and gifts and, most importantly, a rich variety of different ways of approaching and celebrating birthdays at different ages – right up to three figures!

What comes through in this volume, above and beyond the wealth of down-to-earth ideas and suggestions, is a sense of the real meaning of birthdays: how they are milestones on a journey in which each of us, with our precious and different gifts, increasingly gets to grips with life and – hopefully – unfolds our full potential.

Diana Carey, co-author,
Festivals, Family and Food.

Authors' acknowledgements to Marije Rowling, our illustrator, for her enthusiastic collaboration, to our American proofreader, Paula Moraine, for her prompt and cheerful help and to Vigdis Wold for her research in Norway.

To our families – Oliver and Maria, Matthias, Francis, Laura; Roger and Anastasia, Francis, Thomas, Sophy – for being the inspiration behind years and years of birthdays.

It is not the years in your life but the life in your years that counts.
Adlai Stevenson

Introduction

Do you number your birthdays with thankfulness?
Epigrams Book II, Horace

We wrote this book for the many people who wish to find ways of bringing beauty, meaning and a touch of magic into the celebration of birthdays. We hope you will find within its pages some new ways of showing the special people in your life, young or old, how much they are loved and valued, along with ideas for sharing this joy with others. This is a book particularly suited to those who want to create opportunities for taking pleasure in simple, inexpensive things and unsophisticated pastimes rather than high-tech or lavish occasions. Our focus is on letting children enjoy being children and encouraging adults to enjoy being creative. Everything offered here has been tried and tested in busy households and we maintain that 'hand-made-with-love' is an ideal worth striving for, if not always achieved.

A birthday is a time of hope – of looking to the future. For the child it brings a sense of being special, of achievement and inner satisfaction; for the adult it can evoke a New Year mood of reviewing the past and speculating on the years to come. It is said that our bodies are completely renewed every seven years, therefore a birthday is also a time for saying goodbye to a particular stage in one's life, and the signal for completely new possibilities to arise. Such a thought encourages us never to lose sight of the particular individual who is being celebrated. While we world-weary adults often respond to a cocktail of clever, original and unexpected ingredients, young children, for whom the world is still new and constantly changing, enjoy and find support in anticipating familiar, trusted things.

Our advice throughout the book is to 'keep it simple'. Nevertheless, some of the preparation lists can appear more daunting than they actually are. Although you will discover that many of the projects can be adapted or simplified (or elaborated!), no one can deny that hosting a traditional children's birthday party, for example, does not entail a significant amount of work. It is also true that all this effort is worthwhile, for treasured memories of birthdays can last a lifetime.

A final word of thanks goes to our friends and extended families who have freely shared their experiences and tips, and also to Ann's mother who, without fail, served slices of bread and butter with the birthday jelly – why?? – and those long, narrow, chocolate-covered, wafer biscuits....

'he' and 'she'

To avoid the awkwardness of using both genders
we will alternate from chapter to chapter.

Chapter 1

WHERE DO BIRTHDAYS COME FROM?

You have no birthday because you have always lived; you were never born and never will you die. You are not the child of the people you call mother and father, but their fellow-adventurer on a bright journey to understand the things that are.
Richard Bach, *There's No Such Place As Far Away*

'Tell me about when I was born...'

Such a request can be the prelude to intimate moments of pure delight in the family as the well-known story of birth and early years is rehearsed. Very often it is the presence of friends or adult visitors at the meal table which prompts the question, as if the story had not only to be told but must also be witnessed by others. With each child's need to hear that he or she has their own story, with each child's instinct that that story is unique and deserves to be celebrated, we are reminded of what is developing in the young person: a sense of identity, an emerging awareness of their precious individuality.

There is an old Navajo tradition of the 'Laugh Day' which was given more significance for a child than their birthday. It was on 'Laugh Day' that the child was truly seen to respond to life, with a joy freely expressed. The person for whom the baby had first laughed was assumed to have a special relationship with the child and was therefore invited to become godparent. In this way it was laughter which began the development of a spiritual life.

Was this sense of individual identity and its importance always so vitally present? No, it was less pronounced in past eras and in tribal societies. In Western societies, however,

1

where tribal and family constraints (and sustaining traditions!) have been largely eroded, blurring racial, national and cultural boundaries, and where social and religious conventions governing the roles of men and women have relaxed, there is now a growing focus on individual autonomy. Of course we see tribal elements still surfacing in modern society in the herd instincts cultivated by fashion and the mass media, but on the whole we have grown more separate and distinct from one another. Parallel to this development, a day of personal tribute has become established to coincide with the birth anniversary. This is the Birthday that most of us feel we have the right to celebrate once a year.

Birthdays in the ancient world

When people began to record time and keep a calendar, awareness of a birth anniversary became possible. Time could only be plotted after close scrutiny of the movements of the sun, moon and stars. The Chaldeans, who lived beside the Euphrates in what is now Iraq, and the Egyptians, who settled by the Nile, were the first two cultures to become skilled in their observations of the heavens, to record them carefully on stone tablets and create the first calendars. The very name 'Chaldean' came to mean 'astrologer' or 'astronomer'. It is not surprising, therefore, that in these parts of the world we find the first records and celebrations of birth anniversaries. In the Old Testament, (Genesis chap. 40) the birthday of Pharaoh, King of Egypt, is mentioned. The celebration involved a feast for all the household, including slaves, and an amnesty for prisoners in the royal gaol. Another famous Egyptian birthday party was recorded by Plutarch: Cleopatra's magnificent feast in honour of Anthony, where the guests

received lavish gifts as well as the best food. Unfortunately, this was to be Anthony's last birthday for, within the year, after defeat by Caesar, both he and Cleopatra took their own lives.

In Egypt and Chaldea at this time records were certainly kept of royal or noble births, but it is unlikely that the common people were aware of their own natal day. Later, however, the Greek historian Herodotus mentions that, of all the days in the year, the one that the Persians celebrated most was their birthday. On such a day, those who could afford it gave a lavish feast and those with less means also celebrated but on a much smaller scale. The culinary skills of the ancient Persians extended to an unusually wide variety of sweet cakes; perhaps this was the background to the array of sweet party food offered at most birthday events today.

China's greatest teacher and moral philosopher, Confucius, is believed to have been born on 28 September 551 B.C. This is now known as 'Teacher's Day' and traditional ceremonies are held early in the morning at the Confucius Temple in Taipei. Everyone wears formal dress and there is music and dancing.

Birthdays in ancient Greece

It is most likely that the ancient Greeks took the idea of birthday festivals from the Egyptians or the Persians. They certainly kept birth records for taxation purposes but the birthday of a woman or a child was not significant enough to be celebrated. The important male head of the household, however, could hold a 'Genethlia' (a festivity for a living person on his birthday). When he died, his birthday would still be remembered with a post-mortem feast (a 'Genesia') after which his grave would be honoured with flowers, food, wine and other gifts.

Much more important than the birthdays of mere mortals at this time were the birthdays of the gods. Each deity presided over a particular day in the month which was kept sacred to them. The character of the god, or gods if the date was shared, would give a certain quality to that day. The third day of the month, for example, was dedicated to the stern god Chronos (who ate his children), the warrior goddess Athena and the god Ares who held sway over war, rage and carnage; these gods evoked terror rather than sympathy in the hearts of the people so it is no surprise that the third day of each month was considered very unlucky.

Anyone born on the fourth day of the month, however, would be destined for a busy life of hard work, for this was the day of Hermes the constantly active messenger of the gods, and the hero Heracles who had to complete twelve impossible tasks before he secured immortality.

Artemis, a moon goddess who brought prosperity and fertility to those who honoured her, was born on the sixth day of the month of Thargelion. The following day her twin brother Apollo, the musician-god of light, was born. The students of Platonism entering the Academy of Athens were, reputedly for centuries, only admitted on the seventh day of the month in honour of Plato's birth on Apollo's Day.

With the spread of the Roman Empire and the enslavement of the Greeks the character of individual gods went through a development. Over the centuries their connection with particular days waned and changed even as the calendar itself was modified. One feature of these beliefs that was not entirely lost was that of the personal *daemon*.

The Greeks used the term *daemon* to describe a good spirit who mediated between human beings and the gods, most especially between an individual and the god on whose birthday he was born. Such a spirit would attend a birth and thereafter be a watchful and protective presence over the course of that life. This supernatural but beneficent being became the *genius* of Roman times and as such was considered to be the creative force in the individual, watching over the development of his or her life until its end. From the moment of birth it formed the infant's personality. If the child was a boy, his protector was a 'Genius', while the protector of females was a 'Juno'. Such a tutelary spirit can be rediscovered in more recent times in the form of the guardian angel, the good fairy or fairy godmother, or the patron saint.

Birthdays in the Roman Empire

During the early years of the Roman Empire traditional celebration of the birthdays of the gods lapsed or was repressed. Apart from the practice of certain cities or states to honour the birthday of their patron or liberator, only the emperor's natal day was to be observed. The nature of the festivities themselves was also strictly controlled and usually involved grand parades and public entertainments held annually. Virgil, however, notes that Emperor Augustus had his natal day commemorated each month, following the style of the Greek gods. This was not so difficult to understand for he would have had the support of those captive slaves from the East who formed half the population of Rome and who had been used to celebrating a semi-divine king.

Fashions in imperial birthdays were certainly not stable, for the next emperor, Tiberius, banned all public spectacles on his natal day, whereas the later Emperor Caligula, who was renowned for his bizarre behaviour, punished those attempting to excuse themselves from his lavish festivities.

The Romans seem to have fully absorbed Greek ideals of democracy and commitment to individualism, albeit only towards the free-born male members of society. Greek artists had already begun signing their work, and the urge to put one's name to something was capturing the imagination even of Roman citizens without artistic talent. What could be easier than to put one's name to a date on the calendar and join in democratic alliance with the ruling gods for one day in one's own household, by celebrating one's own birthday?

Two thousand years ago it was becoming fairly commonplace for the wealthier citizens, merchants and government officials to keep their natal-day if the law allowed, and no doubt this practice spread throughout Europe to the far-flung outposts of the Empire as did so many of the cultural trappings of Roman society. The torch of individualism was passed to Europe and shines today as the candle on the humble birthday cake.

Celtic influences

Other attitudes widespread in pre-Christian times can be found to have a bearing on birthday customs in general, and some strange ones in particular.

The Celtic people, for example, reasoned that there must be a gap between the end of one cycle of time and the beginning of a new cycle i.e. between, say, the old year and the new one. This gap was thought to be a state of 'no time', never otherwise experienced by human beings on the earth but only after death, when they would share this mode of existence with shadowy beings from all the various corners of eternity. Such an abyss in the landscape of time was experienced by the Celts as highly dangerous, fraught with confrontations with goblins, demons and the needy souls of the dead.

At the close of the Celtic year, therefore, families gathered together to observe certain 'protective' ceremonies. Every fire in the village would be thoroughly extinguished and new fire would be ritually ignited. A great deal of noise was made to scare away the pestering spirits and bring human beings back to their normal senses. Charms were spoken and food offerings made. Slaps, pinches and other mild physical attacks would be exchanged in an effort to keep everyone's consciousness better anchored in the physical world until the moments of vulnerability had passed.

As the centuries moved on and people's consciousness evolved, the need for these practices diminished and such traditions only survived as harmless superstition or pleasing folk custom. It may well be that when people generally became aware of their natal date – the anniversary of which is, of course, the ending of one year of life and the beginning of a new – these types of transition ritual were incorporated into birthday observances.

This would explain such ceremonials as the 'giving of bumps' (see page 23) and ritual pinching or spanking; the blowing out of candles; the loud singing, clapping and raising of cheers; the playing of games that demand presence of mind; the offerings of gifts and food, and the reciting of such good luck charms as 'many happy returns of the day!'

The name day

With the decline of the Roman Empire in Europe and the rise of Christianity, however, birthday celebrations became less popular. Origen, an influential early Christian theologian, held that all objects of religious knowledge were to be found beyond the plane of history and he therefore frowned upon the fixing of a birth date for Jesus Christ. As a result, perhaps, or simply as a reaction to Roman rule, the church actively discouraged birthday festivities, concluding that they were pagan practices.

By the twelfth century, things had changed insofar as church authorities were in some places, habitually recording dates of birth. (Even so, two hundred years later, Winchester College was registering its students rather uncertainly as, for example, 'fourteen last Easter'.) It had become customary to give a child the name of a patron saint at baptism and by the fourteenth century this was well established in church ritual. Priests were charged with the duty of seeing that each child was supplied with a name from the Church Calendar of Saints, and the child would henceforth be expected to celebrate their 'name day' on the day of the year dedicated to the honour of their patron saint.

A popular choice seems to have been to give the child the name 'it brought in its fist' i.e. the name of the saint on whose day the child was born. If that was not possible, then the choice would be for a saint whose day lay not too far ahead in the year from the birth date. If the birthday, the baptismal day and the name day all coincided, this was considered to be especially fortunate.

In modern times, many members of the Roman Catholic and Greek churches still keep the name day as the prime day of personal celebration in the year. In such a way, religious practice has preserved the idea familiar to the ancient Greeks of a personal spiritual guardian who mediates between the individual human life and divine will.

(A calendar of Saints' Days is to be found on pages 205–208)

European birthdays

In 1694 an act was passed in England 'granting to His Majesty certain rates and duties upon marriages, births and burials...' The duty on births varied according to the rank of the parents. A duke paid £30 on the birth of his eldest son, and £25 for every other child. A bishop or a doctor paid £1 for every child, a 'gentleman' of moderate means paid ten shillings and every other person not receiving charity paid two shillings...The act itself had a very short life.

The foundation of the typical children's birthday celebration of modern times can be traced back a few centuries to Germany. There, middle-class families had become accustomed to holding a children's party on the occasion of an offspring's birthday.

Such parties would feature a birthday cake, with candles placed around it on the edge of the plate; also gifts, games and often a decorated tree, large or small, standing in the room or on the table. The cake might be layered, or baked in a ring mould and whitened with powdered sugar, or sometimes would be rich in fruit and nuts. Even in poorer families there was often a cake, and any candles by it would be lit first thing in the morning and extinguished either at sundown or after the cake was eaten. (Today it is still common for German families to eat the cake at breakfast.)

There is a Scottish tradition called the 'first-tooth birthday'. Upon the emergence of a first tooth, the child receives a bannock (a small flat loaf) in which a teething ring is hidden. The child plays with the bannock until it breaks apart. The family then eat the loaf and the child has the ring to bite on.

By the early nineteenth century such customs were creeping into England despite the fact that they were regarded as 'scarcely proper' by most sober and virtuous folk, who suspected that children would thereby be encouraged to give way to vanity and superficial ideals.

Nevertheless, by 1830 there was a report of a children's birthday party where 'ice creams, preserves and sweetmeats ornamented the supper table'. Rich plum cake was served and playthings distributed to guests. To the music of harp and violin, the happy group danced around a large tree which beamed with coloured lamps.

Another writer in 1865 described an evening dance on the grass to which all the servants and farm workers were invited. Games were played, a 'throne' was built for the 'King of the Day' who could choose a Queen and place a garland on her head. It was usual for all guests, including children, to drink the health of the birthday child in red wine and wish them 'a succession of happy new years'.

The giving of gifts to the birthday child (new things for a new year) and to the guests, was established among the well-to-do by the middle of the nineteenth century. Those less comfortably off either preserved a respectable and disapproving distance from these excesses, or celebrated in a quieter way. Paintings from around this time indicate that a birthday cake bearing candles was common to all but the very poorest in society.

The birthday party as a twentieth century phenomenon in Europe and U.S.A. developed more rapidly after 1918. By the 1950s the tradition of a child's birthday celebration was both accepted and firmly secured in the West, and from there its influence has spread to many other parts of the world.

Birthdays today

Many people are now quite accustomed to celebrating birthdays and the privilege is no longer just for the wealthy, the male, or even the adult. With the exception of some strict religious groups, most people agree that every child has the right to be the centre of attention on their special day once a year: to be crowned like a king or queen, to be garlanded like a god or goddess, to have their burgeoning ego-hood acknowledged, their uniqueness celebrated.

Many fairy tales indicate that we are all on a quest to become 'king', to rule our own kingdom (i.e. ourselves), to make wise decisions and to preside over a healthy and peaceful domain ever after.

The birthday has developed in Europe as a festival where both the singularity of the person and the universality of the human journey is addressed and supported, where the individual is celebrated and affirmed by the community. These rather weighty motifs are invoked in the simplest of ways.

What are the essential ingredients of a birthday festival? They are: a cake to share with those who are close to us, a candle on the cake and greetings, blessings or gifts from family or friends. Nothing more is required, everything else – flowers, decorations, games, dancing, entertainment – are loving elaborations of these three essentials which are needed to feed the whole of ourselves, that is our body, soul and spirit. Everyone requires nourishment on these three levels if they are to grow, thrive and fulfil their destiny.

✧ The **cake** represents the totality of life of which we each claim a part. Its substance is a gift of the sustaining earth which fulfils all our bodily needs so that we can step out energetically on our life's path.

✧ The upright **candle** reminds us of the light of our spiritual nature, our unquenchable individuality that offers moral direction and purpose, guiding us like a beacon through darkness so that our lives do not lose meaning, so that the light in our eye never fades.

✧ Along our path of life we meet many people. To these – our relatives, teachers, friends, colleagues, acquaintances and others we have never physically met – we owe most, if not all, our outer and inner progress. For this reason, it is necessary that these landmark anniversaries of birth are witnessed by such 'helpers on the path'. The **gifts** and sentiments they bring are no more than tokens of the valuable soul gifts they settle upon us during our life's journey. The love of family and friends is a warm garment for the travelling soul, their interest and regard beams towards us like sunshine on a growing plant, bestowing inner strength and vitality.

Rudolf Steiner (Austrian educationalist, philosopher and seer) kept a list of birthdays on the inside of a cupboard door. He felt it was important to join in people's birthday celebrations, explaining his views as follows: 'During the night following a birthday, individuals are closer to their guardian spirit than usual and are able to talk to it – in their sleep – as one person to another.'

A. Samweber, *Aus meinem Leben*

Chapter 2

THE CANDLELIT CAKE

So I supped, and was merry at home all the evening, and the rather it being my birthday 33 years, for which God be praised that I am in so good a condition of health and estate, and everything else as I am, beyond expectation, in all.

Diary of Samuel Pepys – 23 February 1666

The cake is a symbol of wholeness. It is a gathering together of all the fruits of the earth, a converging of the four elements – earth, air, water and fire; it is an offering from the four kingdoms of nature – mineral, vegetable and animal substances bound and fashioned by human will. Its roundness denotes eternity and faithfulness, reflecting both the Creator's boundless giving and the selfless endeavour of human beings. When divided and eaten together it becomes a symbol of the solidarity of the community who share it.

A possible origin of the candle on the cake can be found in the image of a primitive divinity – a nameless goddess of childbirth – believed to have originated in Crete. She is most often depicted kneeling and carrying a torch. A later custom connected with birth maintained the flame motif, as recorded by the historian Philochorus. He tells of women in ancient Greece who offered rounded honey-cakes lit with tapers at the shrines of Artemis, the moon-goddess who presided over fertility, to give thanks (or beg for) a safe childbirth. It is possible that this offering came to be associated with the natal day and began a tradition of birthday cakes, but there is no clear line of connection. However, the traditional British birthday cake, with its round shape and moon-white icing, might well be seen as an echo of an Artemis offering, especially when it is so often carried, glowing with candlelight, through a darkened room to the tea table. What we do know is that by Roman times the cake was central to such celebrations: Emperor Hadrian, for example, sent cake to all those guests who had not been able to attend his birthday party.

For a sure record of the custom of candlelit birthday cakes we have to look back to Germany in the eighteenth century (see page 5). From here came the 'Life candle', the extra candle on the cake 'to grow on' – sometimes larger, sometimes red – carrying the light of life on into the future after the other candles had been extinguished.

Most religions have reverence for the flame, often regarding it as the gateway to a higher world. Indeed, to see young children watching the flame of a candle, one could easily imagine that they gaze upon the wonders of another world. Through recent centuries, the candle flame has woven its own special magic to link together two worlds – earthly and divine – with prayer and wish, and to give us the customs that now accompany the candlelit birthday cake. These customs usually indicate that the cake candles have power to grant a wish. The wish is made silently, and silently it rises to higher worlds on the smoke from the candles. If the candles are blown out all in one breath, the wish is more likely to be granted.

The birthday candles have always been identified closely with the birthday child – hence one candle for each year of life – and are not, therefore, to be blown out by anyone else. Only the birthday child may lay claim to her own life's light. A candle that fizzles out is a disappointment; one that is blown out by the celebrant as 'a deed' is a potent reminder of the decisiveness and the autonomy of the ego.

> …Our birth is but a sleep and a forgetting
> The soul that rises with us, our life's star,
> Hath had elsewhere its setting,
> And cometh from afar…'
>
> W. Wordsworth,
> *Intimations of Immortality, Canto 5*

With the passing of years the candles on the cake increase in number and their cumulative radiance highlights the individual's growing empowerment. The birthday child, with identity confirmed, is born into a new year with its unknown events and unheralded demands and challenges. Every year will call forth something new; every year will build our biography. The little birthday flame throws its light much further than the cake, and each one of us holds promise far beyond what is yet known.

In Norway the cake has traditionally been offered first among an array of sweet delicacies, whereas in Britain and the U.S.A. it is usually the last item to be served. The candles are allowed to burn for a while but at the moment of blowing them out the company gives their full attention and approval. Likewise for the first cut of the cake. The birthday child does this, if she is old enough to handle a knife, and will then be honoured with the first slice.

Basic recipe

This recipe can be made in any shape or size simply by increasing or decreasing the ingredients in proportion. It is especially suitable for novelty cakes where cutting and shaping are required. The pieces of cake can be fixed together with butter icing.

Variations

- Add chocolate chips
- Replace 50g of flour with ground almonds and use almond essence in place of vanilla
- Blend 1 tbsp cocoa powder with 2 tbsps hot water. Cool slightly and beat in with sugar and fat
- Add 1 tbsp Instant coffee powder
- Replace vanilla with juice and zest of an organic orange or lemon

Butter icing

You will need:
125g soft butter (preferably unsalted)
250g icing sugar
2 tbsps milk
Flavouring (or food-colouring) of your choice

Cream butter with half of sugar. Beat in remaining sugar with milk and any flavouring e.g. almond, vanilla or coffee essence; the juice and zest of an organic orange or lemon.

Chocolate flavour: Blend 2 tbsps cocoa powder with 2 tbsps of hot water. Cool and add to the icing with a little milk.

Carrot cake

A delicious, moist cake which can be made a few days in advance. The cake will be about three centimetres high, but the slices are filling, especially with our cream cheese frosting. Two cakes sandwiched together would make a substantial feast.

You will need:
4 large eggs (separated)
150g soft light brown sugar
200g finely grated carrots
200g ground hazelnuts (or almonds)
50g plain flour

You will need: (for round sandwich cake)
250g softened butter or margarine
250g caster sugar
4 large eggs
250g plain flour
2 level tsp baking powder
2 tbsp hot water
4 drops vanilla essence
2 x 20cm cake tins
Baking parchment

Grease tins and line base with parchment. Cream fat and sugar together until light and fluffy; sift flour with baking powder.

Beat in eggs one at a time, adding a little flour with the second, third and fourth egg. Fold in remaining flour with a metal spoon. Add hot water.

Turn mixture into prepared tins and bake on middle shelf of preheated moderately hot oven (Gas Mark 5, 190°C/375°F) for approximately 25–30 minutes or until cake springs back when lightly pressed. Cool on wire rack.

Level one of the cakes if necessary and sandwich them together with butter cream.

Tip: For novelty cake reduce baking powder to ¹/₂ tsp.

1 level tsp baking powder
Juice and grated rind of 1 organic lemon
Round cake tin (22cm diam.) lined with
   double layer of baking parchment

Beat together egg yolks and sugar until pale
   and creamy. Add lemon rind and juice.
Stir in nuts and carrots. Fold in stiffly-beaten
   egg whites and flour sifted with baking
   powder.
Spoon into prepared cake tin and bake in
   preheated moderate oven (Gas Mark 4,
   180°C/350°F) for 3/4–1 hour, or until cake
   springs back when gently pressed. Leave
   to cool in oven.
Dust top of cake with icing sugar or use
   cream cheese frosting.

Cream cheese frosting

You will need:
200g full fat soft cream cheese
30g softened butter or margarine
150g icing sugar sifted with 1 level tsp
   cinnamon

Decoration: Dust cinnamon lightly in the
centre of the cake and strew strands of
orange or lemon zest, or shavings of dark
chocolate, around the edge.

Gluten-free 'Dream cake'

A luxuriously rich cake made without flour,
more suitable for teenage and adult parties.
The meringue is best made in advance.

You will need: (for meringue base and
topping)
4 egg whites (not too fresh)
200g sugar (50:50 granulated and icing sugar)
200g roughly-chopped hazelnuts
Round cake tin (22cm diam.) with
   removable base
Baking parchment

Method:
Spread nuts on shallow baking tray and roast
   in fairly hot oven for a few minutes until
   pale gold in colour. Cool.
Whip egg whites until stiff. Add half of sugar
   and whip further. Fold in other half of
   sugar. Fold in nuts.
Line base of cake tin with baking parchment
   and spread on half of mixture. Spread
   second half on any other lined baking sheet.
Dry in very low oven, with door ajar, until
   crisp. This may take several hours.
Carefully remove, keeping the paper. If
   meringue is not dry and crisp right
   through, return it to oven, base uppermost.
Store meringue base on its paper. Crumble
   second half of meringue into small chunks
   and store in an airtight container.

You will need: (for the cake)
100g butter
100g caster sugar
4 egg yolks
125–150g dark chocolate
3 heaped tsps powdered gelatine or agar★
500ml litre double cream
★ Agar flakes can be used instead of gelatine.

Optional: 1 tbsp coffee powder

Optional: melted or grated chocolate for
decoration

Method:
Prepare cake tin with meringue base in place
   and sides lined with baking parchment.
Melt chocolate over basin of hot, *not boiling*,
   water. Whip cream until fairly stiff.
Sprinkle gelatine into 125ml of very hot, *not
   boiling*, water. Stir until dissolved.
OR: Sprinkle 3 rounded tsps.agar flakes over
   125ml cold water and bring to simmer
   over medium heat without stirring.
Simmer 3–5 mins, stirring occasionally until
   flakes dissolve.
Remove from heat. Stir until lukewarm.

Beat butter and sugar until creamy.

Add egg yolks, coffee powder and chocolate.

Add gelatine *or* agar. Fold in cream immediately, leaving mixture streaky.

Fill cake tin with mixture and level the top. Press crumbled meringue firmly into top of cake.

Decorate with grated chocolate or drizzled or piped melted chocolate.

Chill until ready to serve.

Cakes for special birthdays

I woke that day feeling unusually terrible, not just plain terrible but fancy terrible, terrible with raisins in it. Oh yes, it was my birthday.
Dorothy Parker

Some birthday parties are big occasions and demand a lot of preparation. Here is a rich fruit cake that can be made up to twelve weeks in advance and decorated with almond paste and royal icing. (It is also perfect as wedding cake or Christmas cake.)

(For ingredients see quantity chart on next page)

Preparation:

Grease cake tin, line base and sides with two layers of baking parchment extending 4cm above rim.

Tie layers of newspaper on outside of tin and stand tin on thick newspaper on baking sheet.

Sift dry ingredients together. Halve cherries.

Method:

Cream fat with sugar until pale and fluffy. Beat in treacle/molasses. Add eggs singly, alternating with a tablespoon of flour. Stir in remaining flour and ground almonds.

Fold in dried fruit and nuts, adding vinegar and milk. Stir mixture thoroughly. (More liquid can be added if necessary to achieve a soft dropping consistency.)

Turn mixture into prepared tin and smooth top with back of teaspoon, creating a slight depression towards centre of cake.

Bake in preheated oven as directed. After $2^{1}/2$–3 hours, protect top of cake with double layer of baking parchment.

Test at appropriate time by inserting a knife blade into centre of cake. If it comes out clean the cake is cooked, if mixture adheres to the blade return cake to oven and test again at 20 min. intervals.

Leave cake in tin for 30 mins. before turning out on wire rack to cool. Leave one layer of paper on the cake.

When cold, cover top of cake with baking parchment, wrap in aluminium foil and store in cool, dry place.

Almond Paste

Cover cake with almond paste at least one month before the party. Home-made paste tastes good but may stain the icing. Shop-bought standard white marzipan is easier to use.

Method:

Level top of cake and spread with apricot glaze (see below).

Sift icing sugar on work surface.

Roll out half the marzipan to a square or circle 1cm thick and 1cm larger all round than the cake.

Turn cake over on to paste. Keeping knife blade upright, trim paste to fit cake.

Turn cake topside up and glaze sides.

Special cake

You will need:

For a round cake size:	18cm	23cm	28cm
For a square cake size:	15cm	20cm	25cm

INGREDIENTS

Butter	120g	240g	340g
Caster sugar	60g	120g	180g
Soft brown sugar	60g	120g	160g
Black treacle/molasses	1/2 tbsp	1 tbsp	1 1/2 tbsp
Eggs	3 medium (approx. 160g in the shell)	6 medium (approx. 300g in the shell)	8 large (approx. 500g in the shell)
Plain flour	100g	200g	220g
Self-raising flour	80g	160g	220g
Mixed spice	1/2 tsp	1 tsp	1 1/2 tsp
Cinnamon	1/2 tsp	1 tsp	1 1/2 tsp
Nutmeg	1/4 tsp	1/2 tsp	3/4 tsp
Ground almonds	40g	80g	100g
Blanched, chopped almonds	60g	100g	160g
Currants	180g	360g	500g
Sultanas	180g	360g	500g
Raisins	80g	160g	260g
Mixed peel	60g	120g	180g
Glacé cherries	60g	120g	180g
Cider vinegar	1/2 tbsp	1 tbsp	1 1/2 tbsp
Milk	1/2 tbsp	1 tbsp	1 1/2 tbsp
Time required before testing	3 hrs	3 1/2 hrs	4 hrs
Oven temperature	Gas mark 1 140°C 250°F–275°F	Gas mark 1 120°C–140°C 250°F	Gas mark 1/2 120°C 225°F
Position in oven	2nd shelf from bottom	2nd shelf from bottom	1st shelf from bottom

Almond paste

	500g	1 kg	1.5 kg

Royal icing

Powdered egg white	8g (2 x heaped 5ml tsps)	12g (3 x heaped 5ml tsps)	16g (4 x heaped 5ml tsps)
Water	90ml	135ml	180ml
Icing sugar approx.	450g	675g	900g
Glycerine (omit for piping)	1 tsp	1 1/2 tsp	2 tsp

Roll out remaining marzipan to approx. 0.5cm thickness. Cut 4 identical rectangular strips to fit sides of cake and come level with top.

Position strips carefully, allowing edges to meet closely (at corners of a square cake) but not overlap. Avoid pressing marzipan with fingers; instead, use palette knife to smooth and bind edges.

Use sharp knife to trim excess and keep a neat join between top and sides. Do not handle cake at this stage but leave on board to dry for 24 hours or more.

When marzipan is firm, place on baking parchment in a tin and leave for a few days before icing.

Royal icing

Ingredients: (see quantity chart on page 14)

The following method (using a food mixer) gives a light, easy-to-handle icing suitable for both a quick, single coat, or a more professional three-coat finish. All equipment must be clean and *grease free*.

Method:
Reconstitute egg white with the water, making a smooth paste. Leave to stand for 20 mins.

Pour solution into bowl of food mixer. Add sieved sugar. Use beater attachment on slowest speed for 12–20 mins. or until mixture is matt and forms a soft peak.

Add glycerine during the beating. When icing is ready, transfer it speedily to an airtight container and store (not in the refrigerator).

Allow to rest for 24 hours. Before use, stir briefly to disperse air bubbles. Use icing within 8–10 days.

For a smooth professional finish, royal icing should be applied in three or more coats with an icing ruler. Ideas for formal piped decoration are to be found in specialist books.

One layer of 'rough' icing takes little time and expertise:

Method:
Ice the cake evenly. While icing is still soft, press tip of a palette knife on the surface and draw it sharply away to create a peak. Repeat this all over cake.

Tip: Other interesting effects are obtained by using the knife (or other tool) in different ways.

Apricot glaze

You will need:
250g apricot jam
3 tbsps water
1 tsp lemon juice

Place ingredients in small saucepan and heat gently. Pass through a sieve and return to pan. Bring to boil and simmer until mixture becomes syrupy.

Apply glaze with a brush while warm. Store unused glaze in a screw-top jar in the refrigerator.

Two useful motifs for birthday cakes

The year clock:

Mark out a circular cake with the numbers of a clock face. Point the hands of the clock e.g. to six o'clock for a sixth birthday. Numbers and hands could be piped on the frosting with a contrasting colour or made out of marzipan (Roman numerals could be used).

The parcel:

Make a square cake and cover with royal icing, butter icing or whipped cream.

Lead a water-and-grease-resistant gift ribbon centrally from base of one side to base of opposite side and secure beneath cake.

Repeat for other two sides, allowing ribbons to cross at centre of cake. Attach bow of same ribbon to crossing point.

Tip: Use well-washed empty food cans of suitable size to make miniature birthday cakes.

Kransekake
(Scandinavian pyramid cake)

This is called the Queen of Norwegian Cakes and is used only for gala occasions, such as a 50th birthday or important wedding anniversary. It is a very rich cake and small servings will suffice. (The graduated 16-ring tins are available in specialist kitchen shops.)

You will need: (for a 16-ring cake)
780g blanched almonds
800g icing sugar
4 (large) egg whites (at room temperature)
1 tbsp white flour
Semolina or rice flour for dusting the tins

Grind almonds in blender at high speed, small portions at a time.

Sift sugar, mix with almonds and return both briefly to blender.

Beat egg whites until stiff and add to almond mixture a little at a time. Reserve about one fifth of egg white.

Knead dough briefly and add flour. Mix until dough is soft but not sticky, yet firm enough to shape. (Dough that is too moist will rise too much and be difficult to remove from tin. Remedy this by adding flour. Dough that is not moist enough will not rise satisfactorily and results will be hard and dry. In this case, add some of the reserved egg white.)

Grease tins well with unsalted butter or light cooking oil and sprinkle generously with semolina or rice flour. Shake off excess.

Roll portions of dough into 'sausages' to fit the tins. Cut ends with a knife, moisten one end with egg white and butt ends together to form a circle.

Place on baking sheet in centre of moderate oven (Gas mark 2, 150°C/300°F) for 20 mins. or until lightly golden. Do not over-bake.

Cool quickly, in a draught if possible. When nearly cool, remove carefully and place on cake rack. Use pastry brush to remove excess flour.

Icing

You will need:
250g icing sugar
1 standard (size 3) egg white
1 tsp glycerine

Sift sugar and mix with other ingredients. Beat well.

Use piping instrument or bag to decorate each cake with a zigzag pattern, making sure the pattern reaches well over the edges of each ring.

Stack rings, one on another, while icing is
    soft and can act as adhesive.
Decorate pyramid with flags and/or other
    novelties.

Tips:
- Sometimes the cakes are smaller, but
  seldom less than eight rings.
- When serving, remove rings one by one,
  starting at base.

Chapter 3

BIRTHDAY TRADITIONS

In Therevada Buddhist tradition, the birthday of the Buddha is honoured on the full moon day of the month of Vaisakha (April – May). It is a three-day festival (known as Vesakha Puja) with processions, flowers and lanterns. Candles are lit and caged birds set free in memory of Buddha's compassion. In Japan the Buddha's birthday is celebrated on April 8th. The festival is called Hana Matsuri. Sweet tea is poured over the statue of Buddha in the temple, as a reminder of the sweet-smelling heavenly water that is said to have bathed him at the moment of birth.

The day of birth

Among Orthodox Jews the rules of the Sabbath may be lifted for a woman in labour. For example, she may be permitted to ride in a taxi, but her husband will have to walk.

The event of a new birth is a time for celebration and thanksgiving in most parts of the world. Family and friends visit the mother and the new baby to wish them good luck and happiness. Gifts are offered, usually food, clothes, toys or money, and religious prayers or custom-led domestic rituals are enacted for the infant. An orthodox Jewish family may pin a red ribbon to the crib to ward off the 'evil eye'; in Bali, the placenta is taken and solemnly buried; in the ancient world it was a custom to place the new-born immediately upon the ground. 'Man alone at the very moment of his birth', wrote the learned Roman, Pliny the Elder, 'cast naked upon the naked earth…'

In the face of great mysteries, communities have always evolved rituals or symbolic or sympathetic acts in order to meet the event rightly when commonplace words or deeds are inadequate. The appearance of a new individuality in the world is accompanied by joyful wonder and solemn responsibility.

✧ At a Hindu birth, even before the umbilical cord is cut, the Jatakarma ceremony takes place. This is a special purification ritual in which offerings are made. A little while after the birth the baby is given a sweet and holy welcome into the world. A little honey is put into the child's mouth and the sacred syllable 'OM' is traced on his tongue with a golden rod.

✧ A Muslim father will whisper the great Call to Prayer (Adhan) into his newborn's right ear. These will be the first words the child hears spoken. A second prayer (Iqaama) is whispered in his left ear. A drop of honey or date juice may also be placed in the baby's mouth.

✧ On the day of birth in a Sikh family, the parents present friends and relations with boxes of sweetmeats. In return they receive new clothes, money and cloths for turbans. The words of the Mul Mantra, the basic teaching of Sikhism, are whispered in the baby's ear. Soon after the birth, the child is taken to the temple where the great prayer of remembrance (Japji) is recited and honeyed water (Amrit) is prepared – a few drops for the baby and the rest for the mother. The holy book (Guru Granth Sahib) is opened at random and the first letter of the first hymn on the page will become the initial letter of the child's name.

✧ A baby born into the Jain religion will usually have the first letter of his name determined by astrologers according to the time, date and place of birth.

✧ According to Jewish tradition, the birth of a boy is especially welcomed in the expectation that he will say memorial prayers for his parents after their death.

A girl is born a Jew, but a boy needs to confirm this with circumcision, which usually takes place eight days after the birth. Long ago it was the custom to plant a tree when a child was born – a cedar for a boy, the fragrant cypress for a girl. At the time of a marriage, branches would be cut from such trees to support the bridal canopy.

✧ In some parts of Europe an apple tree would be planted at the birth of a boy and a pear tree planted for a girl. The ancient practice of 'wetting the baby's head' (literally by pouring water), stemmed from archaic rites relating to fertility and growth.

✧ The first celebration for a newborn Chinese baby comes, traditionally, one month after the birth. It is known as the Fullness of the Month and the guests, members of the immediate family, bring symbols of happiness (red eggs), of longevity (white eggs), of prosperity (acacia incense) and of beautiful children (flower seeds). On the day of birth, a Chinese baby is traditionally considered to be aged one. The child will be endowed with another year on each New Year's Day, so a child born on the last day of a year will be two years old the next day! It has been a tradition to hang a portrait of the Mother of Heaven in the bedroom during the pregnancy, to guard the mother and child. At the 'Fullness' ceremony this would be removed and tied to a paper balloon. A lighted taper within the balloon ensured that the Mother of Heaven was carried back to the starry sky, accompanied by the heartfelt gratitude of the family.

Krishna, the 'blue god', was born at midnight of the August full moon. The Hindu festival of Janmashtami celebrates the birthday of this well-loved god. There is a legend attached to the birth:

Krishna's mother was a princess but his uncle, the king, was jealous of her newborn son and secretly vowed to kill him. The gods warned Krishna's mother and told her to send the child across the river to be brought up by a cowherd. The river was in high flood and too dangerous to cross. Krishna's father put the child down on the bank while he thought of what to do. The infant touched the water with his foot and immediately the torrent subsided and a path divided the waters and allowed the child to be taken across.

Family traditions

There is no single, right way to celebrate a birthday; each family has its own traditions which developed over the years – perhaps even through generations. Sometimes they are drawn from a parent's own childhood, sometimes they are taken up very consciously in the early years of the family or have arisen quite spontaneously within the routines and idiosyncrasies of family life. Minor actions innocently initiated by an adult may be taken up by the child as a significant ingredient of the birthday event; a feature introduced for one child's birthday may well be anticipated by a sibling when his own special day draws near.

All such 'traditions' once established, become an essential feature of the birthday (or of particular birthdays) and woe betide the parent who forgets or attempts to make changes!

Birthday traditions will not of their own accord become simpler, rather the reverse, and it is not difficult to imagine that traditions generated with enthusiasm can, in certain circumstances, become a burden. Any custom that is elaborate or time-consuming to prepare, may be difficult to achieve in times of family crisis or even if the parent is having an 'off' day. Faced with a large fried birthday breakfast and the indigestion which will surely follow, a parent may heartily wish that he had established a boiled egg as the regular birthday fare. Wagner composed the Siegfried Idyll to awaken his wife Cosima on her birthday: history does not relate whether she insisted that he compose something new for the occasion every year thereafter... Changes can be made, of course, but tact, compensatory planning and advance warning may all be needed to avoid disappointment or hurt feelings on the day. Sensitivity is also required to assess whether a child is outgrowing certain traditions and would be embarrassed by them, although it can be a surprise when a custom you may consider too babyish is, in fact, still valued and vigorously defended.

We include here a collection of birthday traditions, some from our own families, others enthusiastically reported to us by friends and families from many different countries.

Food traditions

Most Western families have adopted the candlelit birthday cake as the central feature of a birthday. Family rituals concerning the cake differ widely:

- It is always served in the afternoon.
- It is on the table, candles alight, when the birthday child comes to breakfast.
- It is always served with ice cream.

- At a baby's first birthday the guests are given a cake to share but the baby has his own miniature cake, probably plainer, with reduced sugar.
- A cupcake with a lit 'number candle' is brought to the child as he wakes up; for a double-digit birthday two cupcakes and two candles are used.
- The cake remains unseen until 'Happy Birthday' is sung, followed by clapping and a hearty Three Cheers.
- The cake, with candles ablaze, is floated down a stream to meet the party.
- The windows are darkened and lights put out while the candlelit cake is brought in and cut. If the candle sparks, it means another gift is on its way.
- The number of candles remaining alight after the big 'Huff and Puff' indicates the number of girlfriends or boyfriends the child or young person will have. The candle-blowing is crowned with loud applause from the guests.
- As the first slice of cake is cut, the child has a wish; alternatively, all the people in the room may have a wish.
- The slices of cake are served with the silver cake server that was used at the parent's wedding.

Other food traditions include:

- An edible birthday path on the eighteenth birthday (see page 29).
- *(From China)* Noodles are served to promote a long life. Often these are particularly long noodles and the child has to stand on his chair while eating them to appreciate their length.
- The person celebrated eats all meals off the family's best china and has all cold drinks served in a wine glass.
- A stack of birthday pancakes are served, crowned with a candle and flowers. Each pancake has the child's age painted on it in food colouring.
- A special 'fruit-of-your-choice' pie is always part of the birthday meal.
- *(From China)* Shou-hsing, the god of long life is the patron of birthdays. He is the second brightest star in the sky, Canopus, and is portrayed as an old man with a pure white beard and a very large bald head. He holds in his hand a peach, the fruit of immortality. Therefore, a Chinese child might find a peach on his plate on his birthday, especially on his tenth birthday.
- *(From Nepal)* Rice yoghurt is painted on the forehead of the birthday child.
- The child is taken out on an errand on the Saturday morning nearest to his birthday. Everything is made to seem like an ordinary day. When he returns at lunch time all the guests are there for a birthday meal.
- *(From Tibet)* To mark important social occasions such as birthdays, a small amount of 'tsampa' (roasted barley flour) is thrown in the air to express good wishes for the happiness of all concerned.
- The birthday child is served breakfast in bed on a tray covered with a special birthday cloth, accompanied by flowers and a candle.
- Birthday breakfast always begins with half a grapefruit in a special dish reserved for these occasions.

Some 'awakening' birthday traditions

- The child is awoken by singing and the gentle playing of musical instruments outside his door.
- The child finds a 'fairy' present under his pillow (usually something of little cost but undeniably beautiful, e.g. a feather, a shell, a tiny crystal or polished stone).
- The child is greeted by a number of kisses equal to his age (see page 174).

- The child finds balloons tied to his bed or floating under the ceiling (see page 49).
- *(From Argentina)* The child has his earlobe pulled – eight times if he is eight years old.
- The child has a little butter rubbed on his nose to help him slide gracefully into his next year.
- *(From Ireland)* The child's hands and feet are held by four family members who suspend him, face upward, a little way off the ground. Then they lower him *gently* to give him little 'bumps' to his bottom, one for each year of his life. *(This custom can cause injury.)*
- The child's whole family is up by 6 a.m. to watch him open his presents. Then they all sit down to a special breakfast together.
- *(From Mexico)* Plenty of food and drink is made the night before in case the birthday singers arrive to welcome in an adult birthday at cock-crow.
- When the child gets dressed he finds a 'fairy path' (see page 28) leading from his bedroom door to the breakfast table.
- When the child wakes up he finds a golden string tied to the bed which will lead him on a trail through the house to the hiding place of a birthday surprise.
- As the child leaves his bedroom he passes through streamers hung across the bedroom door – one for each year of his life.

Decoration traditions

- A birthday ring (see pages 131–138) is hung above the child's chair or the birthday table (see page 25).
- A chair-of-honour is decorated with leaves, flowers, balloons and a coloured cloth.
- Balloons decorate the rooms and are tied at the entrance of the dwelling to announce the party.

- Helium balloons, one for each year of the child's life float in his room when he wakes. In the evening they are released, filled with wishes, to fly to the heavens (see page 49).
- A large bouquet of fresh flowers has pride of place on the birthday table. A birthday star wand (see page 138) stands among them.

Gift traditions

- The child receives a new pair of socks or shoes to assist his 'next step' in life.
- *(From Japan)* New clothes are given at every birthday to dress the 'new person'.
- Every year the child receives a new book.
- A few 'fairy presents' of small cost but great worth are found among the gifts on the birthday table.
- *(From Germany)* The Birthday Mannikin, a bearded elf invisible to all, has placed a pretty trinket, gift-wrapped, in the child's pocket, a chocolate button under his plate, a cookie in his toy box and a posy of flowers in his outdoor shoes.
- The child's family hides all his gifts and help him to hunt for them by calling 'Warm!' when he approaches a hiding place and 'Cold!' when he moves away.
- (From Denmark) Gifts are piled quietly around the child's bed before he wakes.
- One of the gifts that the child opens is labelled 'A surprise for all the family'.
- The gift of a ring or necklace is given by the parents on the 'coming-of-age' birthday to symbolise their eternal bond with their child.
- The number of gifts is often matched with the number of years of the anniversary.

Growing-up traditions

- At each birthday the child's height is measured and marked on a particular door of the house (see page 154).
- The child has his photograph taken with his birthday cake each year. When he is eighteen his mother will present him with these arranged in an album, then he will see them for the first time.
- The child poses for his birthday photo every year in the same place: beside the tree that was given as a seedling on the day he was born.
- The child has his palm painted on his birthday and he makes a print of his hand on a piece of absorbent art paper to compare with the print of the previous year. Or textile ink is used to put a hand-print on a piece of linen.
- On his thirteenth birthday the child is taken on a special outing to mark the transition to teen years.

Other birthday traditions

- The child always tidies his bedroom the night before his birthday, and folds his clothes neatly on a chair (see page 174).
- On the morning of his birthday the child shows the family how he jumps into his next year by jumping out of bed.
- *(From Norway)* A flag is flown from the window on a family birthday.
- One of the child's parents takes him for a birthday run around the block – a lap for each year. Later, while sitting at the meal table, each person gives the child a birthday wish: 'I wish you sunshine', 'I wish you a rosy apple', 'I wish you a good sleep tonight'....
- The child's birthday is in the winter-time, so every year his family make a 'Snow-Child' and he can choose one of his hats or scarves to dress it with.
- The child's family take him on a day trip or weekend camping trip to explore new areas of the country nearby. He brings a friend with him.
- *(From Lithuania)* The birthday child is hoisted into the air on an elaborately decorated chair.
- *(From China)* On a first birthday, four items are laid out in front of the baby: a piece of bread, a silver coin, a book and a flower. The one the baby first picks up will indicate whether he will be healthy, wealthy, wise, or nature-loving as an adult.
- In some families the Name Day (see page 5) is very important and can be like a second birthday. Having two parties is also a common practice: one for family (more often on the birthday itself) and one for friends at the weekend.
- Many families maintain a tradition of ease and comfort for their birthday child, someone else does his chores and he is waited on hand and foot.
- *(From the West Indies)* A birthday celebration will often last all day, with streamers, lanterns, songs, lots of flowers and maybe even a magician to entertain the guests.
- *(From Holland)* Some birthdays are traditionally more 'valuable' than others. Decade birthdays are known as 'Crown' birthdays, half-decade birthdays are 'Half-Crown' birthdays.
- *(From Norway)* It is common for birthdays of 50, 60 and 70 years to be celebrated in formal style with open house for friends, neighbours and colleagues. Speeches are made and responded to, eulogies (amusing or solemn) are read or even sung. The Kransekake (see page 16) is served, decorated with flags.

Birthday table and 'throne'

A birthday table makes a charming and practical focus on this special day. Family tradition prefers to use the same piece of furniture every birthday: a coffee table, chest or sideboard would be suitable.

A festive 'birthday cloth' covers the table which bears cards, presents, flowers and maybe the birthday cake. In some countries the cake appears at breakfast time, in which case the birthday child (or adult) waits outside the room while the family gathers around the table. When the cake candles are alight, a little bell is rung to give the signal for the door to be opened and the birthday song to begin.

The family dining table could also become a birthday table with one carefully decorated place setting and the best china. Surround the plate with seasonal flowers, leaves or berries, add a birthday candle and a card and, as a regal touch, arrange a birthday 'Throne'. This is easily done by throwing a cloth or muslin veil (see page 211) over the chair and adorning it with stars, flowers, streamers or balloons.

If there's a throne, then there ought to be a crown: cut a grand one out of gold card (see page 26) or make a garland of flowers (see page 27).

Birthday tree

A fresh or gold-painted branch stands on the birthday table. It bears small gifts, ribbons, sweets or biscuits. Sometimes it bears only ribbons – one for each year, but the last one waits to be tied on by the birthday child himself.

Birthday crown

A birthday crown can make a child feel special, (some genuinely dislike wearing anything on their heads, so don't *insist* that it is worn...).

The head can be measured discreetly a few days before the birthday. For a 'queenly' effect, drape pastel coloured muslin (see page 211) over the head before crowning.

You will need:
Birthday crown pattern page 213
Stiff card 14cm x 60cm in gold or preferred
    colour

Scrap paper approx. 18cm x 60cm (join two
    pieces together if necessary)
8 paper clips and stapler
Scissors and glue
Sequin 1cm diam. in child's favourite colour

Fold scrap paper in half bringing short sides
    together.
Transfer (see page 210) crown pattern to
    folded scrap paper and cut it out.
Place paper pattern on stiff card and secure
    with paper clips. Cut round pattern.

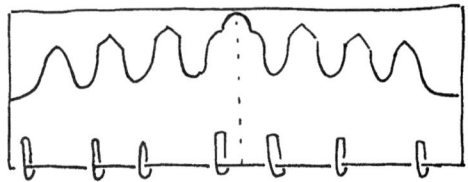

Glue sequin to top centre of crown.
Staple A to B, overlapping to fit child's head.

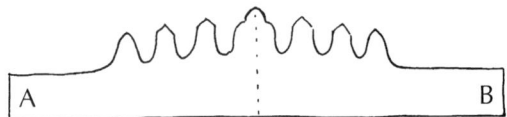

Tip: See also Coronets on page 93.

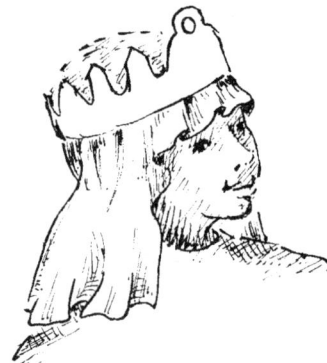

Birthday garland

A simple plait in raffia or cloth makes the base for a birthday garland which can be used repeatedly. Decorate it with ribbons, feathers, leaves, berries, fresh or dried flowers. All items are threaded into the plait and removed when no longer needed.

You will need: (for a head garland)
3 lengths of cotton fabric (8cm x 80cm)
Or, 26 strands of natural raffia approx. 80cm long
Scissors and large darning needle
Optional: Pinking shears

Fabric garland

(The strips of cotton fabric may be torn or cut, preferably with pinking shears.)
Sew strips together at one end.
Begin plaiting, taking care to fold in and conceal the cut edges of the fabric.
Work fairly loosely until plait is about 50cm long.
Sew all ends together to join the circle

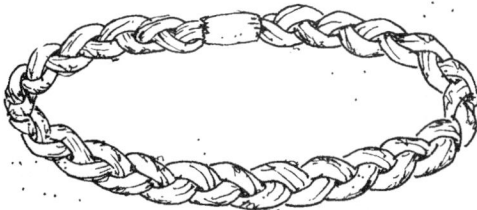

Raffia garland

Take 24 strands of raffia and tie together in a knot at one end.
Divide strands into three groups of eight and make a simple, but *not* tight, plait.

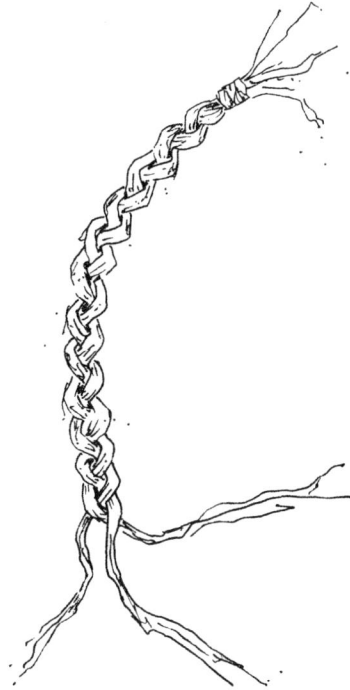

When the plait is about 50cm long, tie ends tightly with a single raffia strand.
Trim both ends of plait and join by binding neatly with a single strand of raffia. Sew in loose ends with darning needle.

Birthday paths

A fairy path

Each birthday is a milestone on the path of life and this theme can inspire family birthdays for young and old.

Pathways leading from bedroom to birthday table can be created with a trail of rose petals, streamers or little shells, star sequins, glitter dust or chocolate.

For those extra special years, the birthday fairy may be in generous mood and one might find, say on a seventh birthday path: seven small packages, wrapped in the seven colours of the rainbow, each containing seven of the same kind of thing, e.g. 7 balloons, 7 seeds, 7 marbles, 7 cherries, and so on.

A rhyming path

Time and enthusiasm can make the path more elaborate: mark the path with a piece of wool or string decorated with balloons and streamers along its length.

On separate pieces of paper write out a short rhyme for each year of the child's life, e.g. 'When you were one, life was such fun', or 'At the age of seven we camped in Devon.'

Attach these rhymes to the string at regular intervals together with a tiny wrapped gift.

Edible paths

We shall describe this as for an eighteenth birthday but it could be adapted for other anniversaries.

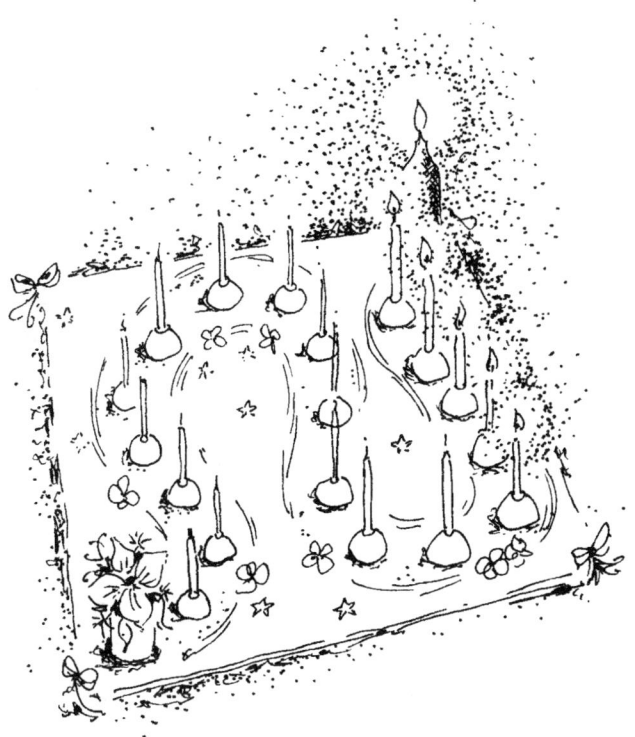

You will need:

Large cake board (or thin wooden board covered in baking foil) approx. 45cm square

18 cake candles from the larger end of the range

18 candleholders

1 freestanding, long-burning candle

(Try to harmonize colours of candles and holders)

18 small identical cakes, large enough to bear a cake candle with its holder, but small enough to fit comfortably along the path. Large chocolates or marzipan could possibly be used instead of cakes.

Quantity of royal icing (see page 15) using one small egg white.

Piping bag or instrument with a not-too-fine nozzle for piping lines

Sugar cake decorations, e.g. silver and gold balls, hundreds and thousands, sugar flowers

Icing sugar for dusting

4 bows of gold ribbon approx. 0.5cm wide

Very small glass vase of flowers

Taper

Optional: Gold star sequins

Pipe two lines of icing on the board to indicate serpentine path leading from one corner to its diagonal.

Dust whole board with icing sugar. Sprinkle hundreds and thousands within borders of path and fix sugar flowers at points along borders with dab of icing.

29

When all the candles are alight and all the memorable words spoken, then the flames can be blown out and the cakes shared among the guests.

For a simpler display the cakes and candles can be arranged along a broad ribbon down the centre of the table.

If you have agile fingers, dispense with the cakes and model a figure or small scene for each year. Set a candle in a rosette of icing beside each scene. Buy prepared modelling icing or use the recipe on page 127.

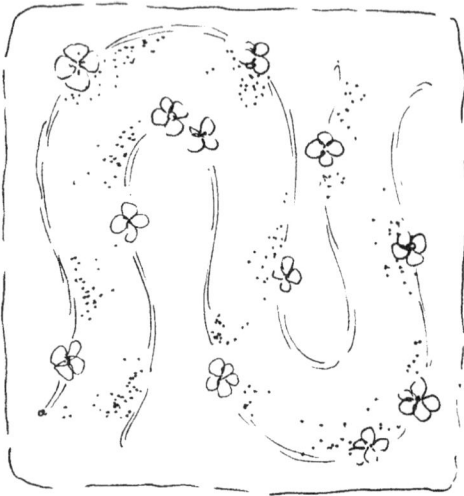

Arrange candles with holders, one in each cake. Place cakes at equal intervals along path without disturbing sugar dusting.

Set large candle at beginning of path and small vase at the end.

Fix bow of ribbon to each corner of board with dab of icing.

Cover holes of star sequins, if used, with dot of icing and distribute them over space outside of path.

On the special day itself light the large candle. After the guests have gathered and the right moment has come, use a taper to light the first cake candle from the large candle while saying a few words about what happened to the eighteen-year-old during the first year of life. Pass on to the next candle and describe something of the second year of life, and so on.

The spoken contributions should not be too long, for the cake candles have to keep burning right through to the eighteenth year. There should be enough time to pick out one or two landmarks in the year, or some choice quotations, which need not be too important or too serious.

Alternatively place a small box (see pages 167–168) by each candle containing a gift with some sort of connection with that particular year: a silver coin as a late present from the tooth fairy, perhaps, or an item 'made from the same wood as your favourite climbing tree' and so on.

Chapter 4

EXCEPTIONAL BIRTHDAYS

'I'll spend it like I spent my first day – quietly.'
Grandma Moses, just before her 101st birthday

Birthday shared

A birthday is the one day in the year when the individual can expect to be celebrated. If two members of your family share a birth date, therefore, it is important to hold the idea of two celebrations, rather than two people sharing the celebration. This will mean more work for the parent but it will pay dividends by increasing security, morale and self-esteem, and reducing the risk of jealousy among family members. In the case of twins, separate birthdays may become an issue as they grow older and develop their own individuality. Two celebrations may mean two different cakes, two differently decorated birthday tables or meal places, two sets of invitations and so on, but there are ways in which one can avoid twice the work. The same basic cake mix can be used, for example, but with different flavourings (see page 11), different decoration and different candles. It may be possible to share the parties or outings; the main meal celebration could also be shared but the responsibility for choosing the menu for main course and for dessert could be divided; the celebratory meal might be separated into a festive breakfast and then a later event at teatime. Selecting personal-choice menus can lead to weeks of mouth-watering discussion!

With adaptability and the necessary tact, a parent can ensure that both birthdays receive the honour due to them. If the parent organising the day is also one of the birthday people, it is even more important that this last point is not overlooked.

Birthday at Christmas

The people we know who were born on Christmas Day all tell us that they missed out on feeling that this was *their* special day; their birthday seemed to have no place of its own. The following suggestions may go some way towards avoiding this:

✧ Create a space for the birthday at a particular time on Christmas Day. It could, for example, be quite practical to delay the opening of Christmas presents until after lunch and enjoy a birthday breakfast. If cake is not palatable at that hour, serve it with due honour later in the day – but it should be a birthday and not a Christmas cake. (Likewise, avoid using a Christmas tablecloth for the birthday meal, or Christmas paper for the birthday presents.) Try to reserve the same time of day for the celebration each year so that it gains strength as a sacred family tradition. This will help to uphold the importance of the individual to the family as a whole.

✧ Friends may not be free to join a party on Christmas Day, so choose a convenient date not too long after the birthday on which to celebrate with others: a date, perhaps, of particular significance to the child e.g. the baptismal day or name day. If the chosen arrangement is faithfully adhered to each year, it will contribute a healthy stability and rhythm to the child's life.

✧ We have heard of a half-birthday being held for a Christmas child on 25 June, with a half-moon shaped birthday cake at both winter and summer celebrations! Half-glasses of drink were served; eggs, olives and peaches etc. were halved. Gifts came in half-kilos or half-dozens, (even half a box of chocolates), or half presented by one person and half by another. (The novelty of this would be fine for an adult, but many children would fail to appreciate the mathematical joke and might well feel that they had been cheated out of the 'whole'.)

Birthday at New Year

As New Year is traditionally a time for prophecy, wrap symbolic charms (e.g. ring for marriage, thimble for industry, coin for wealth) or rhyming 'fortunes' in cooking foil and insert into the birthday cake.

Leap year baby

The only person we have known who was born on 29 February is now seventy years old and cannot remember ever feeling disturbed because his birthday appeared only occasionally on the calendar. In fact, we suspect he enjoyed the added celebrity factor in his life and the freedom of choice of celebration day that it brought. This supports us in the belief that any 'deprivation' experienced by, say, a Christmas child, arises from feelings of being pushed into second place by the festivities of Christmas, and of the family not giving the time and the full attention that a birthday anniversary might deserve.

Birthday fever

If a child wakes up on the morning of the birthday with a fever, or an upset stomach, one might pause to ask whether this has happened as a result of over-excitement in anticipation of the event. Some children are disposed to react in this way but it could be worthwhile to explore avoidance tactics. These might entail limiting the hectic or competitive games, replacing them with a creative activity, or offering an outing with a best friend instead of a party. It is better to avoid placing any burden of decision-making upon such a child, for this easily creates anxiety.

Most children are more able to make preferences known if the parent is readily available to listen. Reassurance can be given to the vulnerable younger child with a 'preparatory' story (see page 182).

A child with a fever is not ready for a birthday party, despite what she might say! Arrange another date and allow the child to have the necessary rest and quiet to recover. The special day can still be celebrated, depending on exactly how ill the child is:

✧ Prepare a birthday bed – perhaps on the settee in the living room or in the child's own bedroom or parents' room. A fairly tidy room with soft lighting will create a more restful atmosphere. Decorate the bed with ribbons and/or crêpe paper streamers, and drape a silk scarf over the pillow. There could be a birthday table, with a cloth and a vase of flowers. A candle or several candles could stand here but will need adequate dishes to catch the wax and very careful supervision.

Tip: If the fever is high, avoid strong smelling flowers (e.g. lilies), and the rasping of balloons.

✧ If the child can sit up then a birthday crown or wreath (see page 26) can be offered, although a sick child may prefer her favourite doll or soft toy to wear it instead. Most of the birthday food will have to be left for another day but a prettily arranged plate of mixed fruit slices, served on a tray with a lace cloth and the best crockery, will make the patient feel special. A vegetable broth sprinkled with fresh herbs and fingers of dry toast, followed by a jelly made with real fruit juice (see page 127), or rice cakes smeared with honey, could all be part of a sick child's birthday meal. Serve only small portions and wait for more to be requested.

✧ Even if the child is out of sorts she will appreciate an undemanding game or activity to mark the unique date in her year. Suitable activities for the very young could include blowing soap bubbles (with a parent holding the soap mixture), threading beads or making simple paper chains (using a glue stick). Older children may enjoy practising skills such as paper folding, knitting, knotting, crochet or traditional string games. Some of the craft projects in this book would be suited to these circumstances. Such quiet, deeply absorbing and satisfying occupations are more restful and healing than the range of entertainments that technology can offer.

✧ Before bedtime anyone would enjoy the birthday wash! Prepare a china or glass bowl with warm water fragranced with a natural flower essence or bath milk, and float a few tiny flowers or petals in it. Use a freshly laundered washcloth and towel and massage the clean skin with soothing body oil. A fever can dry the skin quite severely, so a lip salve and skin food is helpful as long as it is not too sticky. Something easy to overlook is that a fever often makes the five senses hyper-sensitive, so that an artificial perfume, the

smell of cooked cabbage or fish, the sound of a paper bag being scrunched up or even the feel of synthetic fabric can be an unwelcome irritation.

✧ A child who is ill can still appreciate having a story read or told her at any time, but bedtime on the birthday is an opportunity to tell or retell a birthday story. This should be the last event of the day, after the child is tucked up in the bed in which she will spend the night.

Birthday in hospital

If someone has been hospitalised it is usually because they are extremely unwell, or because there is some acute anxiety about their health. These circumstances do not lend themselves to an exuberant celebration but the birthday can of course be acknowledged with flowers, cards, bottles of mineral water, fruit and so on, depending on the needs and circumstances of the patient.

Thoughtfulness and consideration for the individual are paramount; in one case visits may be better restricted to one or two people spending a couple of hours at the bedside just quietly 'keeping company', while in another case the patient might be cheered by many short visits from a number of friends and relations. Some people could find it tiring having to answer the same questions from a string of well-meaning friends; others might enjoy all the attention.

✧ If conditions allow, a birthday cake may be a welcome break in the routine of hospital food, and a good gossip about office or family news could be just the thing to over-come the isolation that being in hospital can impose; but beware of burdening a patient with news of worrying events.

✧ There is little space in a hospital locker for birthday gifts, but it is nice to have something to unwrap. The following things are useful to a patient and make good gifts: accessories such as face and hand cream, packs of personal tissues, a new facecloth or toothbrush. If the patient is not too ill they might welcome something to occupy the time, a new novel or magazine, a book of crossword puzzles or brain teasers, a pack of cards and a book of patience games. More substantial gifts could include a dressing gown, slippers, pyjamas or, for someone who is not in great discomfort, the visit of a hairdresser or manicurist.

✧ It is possible to create a lively birthday celebration in, for example, an orthopaedic ward where there are many long-stay patients who do not feel particularly ill or fragile. These patients have usually created a little community among themselves, and a birthday will be of general interest and shared anticipation. In these circumstances it would be appropriate to bring a cake large enough to be shared out, and maybe a 'lucky dip' basket of wrapped chocolates and small presents or novelties for the benefit of all the occupants of the ward, not forgetting the nurses. If the birthday is for a young child in a long-stay ward, ask the nurse whether the child could be given a tray or basket containing a garden of dry moss and stones in which little ducks, hedgehogs or other small animals or even tiny elves (see page 157) are living. With the agreement of staff, a child could also be offered a performance of the birthday puppet show (see page 118). Hospital staff often welcome such events; even the appearance of a choir or string quartet to entertain the patients may be possible, but careful liaison with the authorities is necessary and their guidance must be accepted.

Birthdays away

> By the Births and Deaths Registration Act 1874 and the Merchant Shipping Act 1894, commanding-officers of ships trading to or from British ports must, under a penalty, transmit returns of all births occurring on board their ships to the registrar-general of shipping.

A birthday may fall during the family's summer holiday, away from home in an impersonal hotel or on a primitive camp site, or even on an extra-long car journey; but with a little forethought the specialness of the day can be maintained.

Camp site

Balloons and crêpe paper streamers come out of the suitcase and are pinned or pegged up around the tent, buttercups are gathered for a birthday bouquet or birthday wreath (see page 27), and soap bubbles blown for lots of wishes to shimmer their way up into the land of hopes and dreams. Discussion over the menu: will it be sausages and spicy beans or pancakes, or barbecued fish, or...?

A cake appears, thankfully intact, from the boot of the car and someone has bought plastic windmills and stuck them in the ground by the birthday throne (a grand title perhaps, but the least-wobbly camping chair is now arrayed with fresh bracken and a cushion of dried grass).

The birthday song brings smiles and waves from other campers, and the breeze wants to be the first to blow the candles out... is it time yet to open another parcel from the birthday pockets? (see pages 37–40)

Alpine camp

A rock garden created on some mossy ground, a few tiny vases brought with us 'just in case' nestle among the rocks, fragments of stone spell out the significant initials and a date, and an appropriate number of tea lights flicker softly in the twilight as the last story is read before bedtime. It has been a happy day – a long walk interrupted with a festive picnic. Presents have been opened and the favourite gift was a length of rope to hang as a swing on the nearest sturdy tree....

Seaside camp

A middle-aged parent sits with eyes closed while forty birthday cake candles are fixed to forty shallow shell 'dishes', and forty pretty pebbles are arranged in a circle with daisies and feathers and any other not-too-dirty beach treasures. There's lots of suppressed grumbling by the garland threader over the lack of seashells with holes in them, but soon it's all done and the birthday song is sung as a signal for middle-aged eyes to be opened.

Cake and ice cream is being devoured when someone spots an unusual shell sticking up out of the sand. It is unearthed immediately and its large size and wealth of mother-of-pearl tell of incredible journeyings across oceanic continents from far, far distant lands... or a short bus ride from the up-market gift shop in the next village...

Surprise birthday pockets

This is a handy and versatile item, well worth the effort of making it. We have designed it to fit the back of a car seat to enliven a birthday that has to be spent journeying, but it could also be used in a tent, a hotel or at home. The idea is to provide the birthday child (or adult) with little surprises to unpack from the pockets all through the day.

- If the birthday child is able to read a map, the pockets could be marked with the names of certain places en route.

- If the birthday child can tell the time, the pockets could be marked with chosen times of the day.

- A treasure hunt or 'I Spy' game could be played at every stop or at certain moments on the journey: for example, a white pebble or a pink petal must be found, or one must spy a dog with fur of two colours or see three people together eating ice creams. Only when such a task is completed can the surprise be unpacked.

Pocket surprises could include small puzzles, a book, sweets to share, a special snack, a kaleidoscope, gummed paper chains, threads or string for knotting or finger crochet, wool and short knitting needles or other simple handcraft which does not include tiny items such as pins, needles or beads which might get lost in the car.

You will need:

Cotton canvas (or thick denim) 41cm x 55.5cm

Cotton fabric for pockets 46cm x 60cm

Thread in matching colour

Elastic 5mm wide x 11cm

Wooden dowelling 1.5cm x 38cm

Cotton tape in matching colour approx. 1.5cm wide x 80cm

For pockets to be used in a car, add:

2 lengths of elastic 5mm wide x approx. 60cm

To make backing piece:

Prepare canvas by neatening all edges with pinking shears or by over-sewing.

Fold under, press and sew 1.5cm hem on three sides, leaving one of the short sides.

Fold under, press and sew a 4cm hem on this short side as shown below. This becomes the top edge.

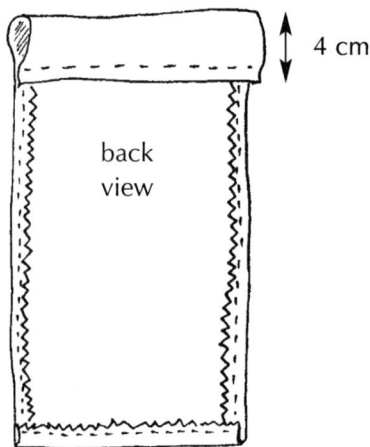

To make pockets:

Cut three panels from cotton fabric as described below:

Panel A (2 bottom pockets) 18cm x 53cm

Panel B (4 bottom pockets) 15cm x 47cm

Panel C (6 top pockets) 13cm x 60cm

Neaten all edges.

Fold, press and sew 1.5cm hem along one long side of panel A.

Thread 38cm length of elastic through hem and secure on each side with stitches.

Fold and press 1.5cm hem on other three sides of panel and mark centre of panel at top and bottom with a pin.

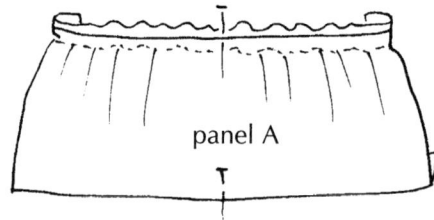

panel A

Measure distances of 17cm and 31cm from bottom of backing piece and mark lines lightly with pencil or tailor's chalk as indicated. These will be base lines for pocket panels B and C respectively.

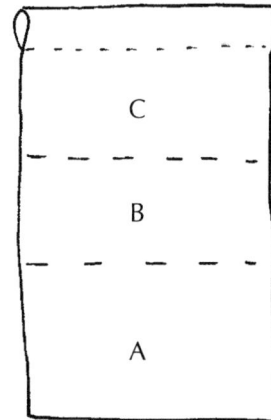

Mark centre of bottom edge of backing piece, and pin panel A to backing piece with centre points matching, as shown:

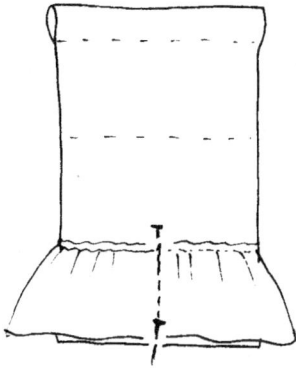

Sew along vertical centre line on panel A to secure it to backing piece. Pin and then sew sides of panel to edges of backing piece.

Take up excess fabric on bottom edge by making four pleats, one at each side of pockets as shown and sew base of panel to the backing.

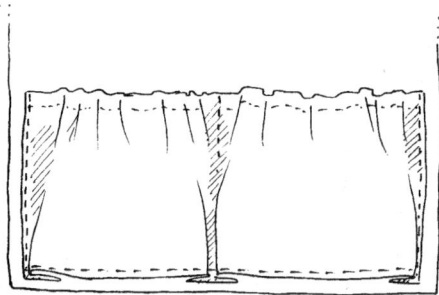

Proceed in the same way with panels B and C, dividing panel B into four pockets and panel C into six pockets.

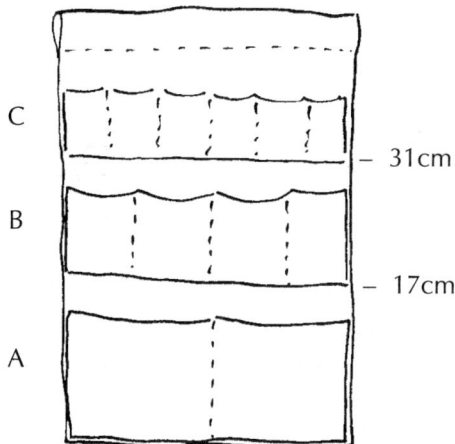

An alternative pleating arrangement for top pockets is illustrated:

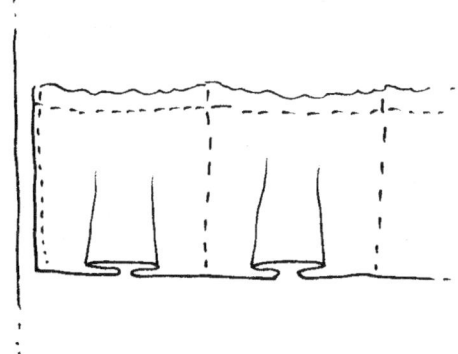

Cut cotton tape into two equal lengths, find centre of each length and sew firmly (with strong thread) to backing piece as seen below.

Sand ends of dowel and insert into top hem of backing piece. The surprise birthday pockets are now ready to hang on a wall or in a tent.

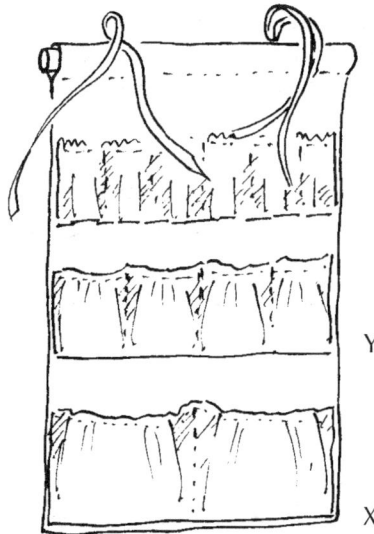

For pockets to be used in a car:

Sew one end of each 60cm length of elastic to reverse-side of backing piece at positions X and Y.

Similarly, sew other ends to opposite edge of backing piece.

Position pockets to face back seat of car and slip elastic over front seat tying tapes around headrest supports.

Fill pockets with treats and fun: and *Bon Voyage* to everyone!

Tip: Younger children may find the waiting for presents, which are visible in front of them, simply too difficult. In this case, the adult can produce small wrapped surprises at regular intervals from a secret store in the front of the car.

Camp at Khatmandu

He's sitting on a mountain with his rucksack at his side. Today he is 21 years old. At the bottom of the rucksack is a family-size matchbox 6.5cm x 2.5cm covered in gold paper that has been travelling with him for three months. There is a label on the outside that reads 'A Do-it-Yourself Birthday Kit – to be enjoyed with a Friend'. Inside are the following, wrapped in small pieces of tissue paper and clearly numbered with permanent ink:

1. A small birthday badge
2. Small plastic spinning top with red label marking one edge, blue at opposite side.
3. Balloon
4. A different balloon
5. Letters (of metallic alphabet confetti) to spell HAPPY BIRTHDAY SON.
6. Small piece of blu-tack
7. Birthday cake candle (not too small)
8. 2 tissue-paper crowns of different styles
9. Miniature streamers from a party-popper
10. 1 small 'roll-out' party hooter
11. 3 waterproof matches
12. 1 polished semi-precious stone
13. 2 small indoor firework 'sparklers' (bend wire to fit in box)
14. 2 sugar-flower cake decorations
15. A joke
16. A riddle
17. Small birthday card with personal poem
18. A very small present (on this occasion, an antique silver, 'lucky' threepenny piece)
19. Gift for a friend (perhaps a friendship bracelet)
20. 2 general knowledge quiz cards
21. Small jigsaw 'brainteaser'
22. Banknote
23. 2 small chocolate 'half-sovereigns'
24. 2 large and 2 small tiddly-winks, plastic lid (approx. 4cm diam.) with a low rim for a 'goal' and a copy of the diagrams below
25. Large chocolate 'sovereign'

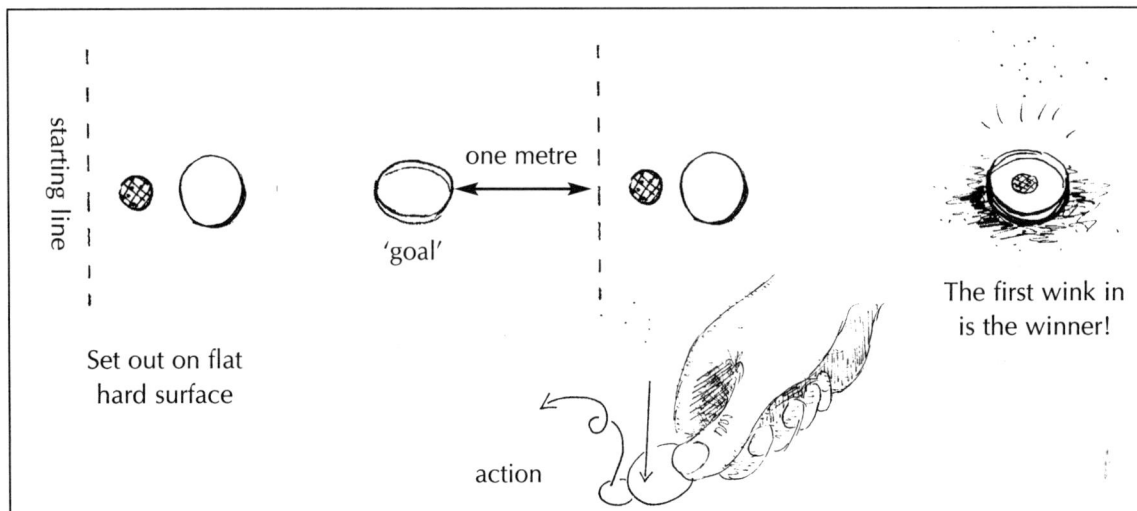

starting line

one metre

'goal'

Set out on flat hard surface

action

The first wink in is the winner!

On thin paper, folded and placed on top of the carefully packed items is a list of instructions:

Instructions for
DO-IT-YOURSELF BIRTHDAY KIT:

Remove drawer of matchbox – empty out contents
Place matchbox on nearby flat surface
Arrange contents in numerical order
Open and fix (1)
Open (2) – choose colour and twirl
Winner opens (3)
Ditto to open (4)
Deal with (3) and (4)
Open and decipher (5)
Arrange (5) neatly on surface around matchbox
Open (6) and place on top centre of matchbox
Open (7) and fix with (6) to centre of matchbox
Spin (2)
Winner opens (8) and chooses
Put on (8)
Open (9) – place around neck, ears, shoulders
Open (10) – use three times to announce next step
Open (11) – use appropriately and economically
Sing 'Happy Birthday'
Open (12) – hold tightly and wish
Open (13) and share
Open (14) and share
Spin (2)
Winner opens (15)
Open (16) and share
Address (7) at one blow, if possible and appropriate
Open (17) – read
Open (18) – express gratitude and delight
Give (19) to friend
Say 'Don't mention it'
Open (20) – give one to friend
Share your knowledge of the world
Open (21) – solve in one minute or give to friend
Open (22) – pocket
Give (23) to friend to open and share
Give up on (21)
Open (24)
Practise for the 'International Tiddlywympics'...
Winner opens (25)
Good luck! xxxxxxxxx

This basic idea can be adapted to suit individual circumstances. Use as **many** of the items as you wish and, of course, add or substitute inspirations of your own. Boxes of different sizes could also be used if the occasion allows, e.g. a shoe-box would be easy to fill for a student away at college, even a large carton from the supermarket could present an irresistible challenge....

We have heard of a youngster sent away to university with a birthday package in a zipped bag. The bag was secured with a combination padlock to ensure a call home on the birthday!

Long-lasting birthday chain

> I starts to get young at the age of sixty, and then it's too late!
>
> Picasso

This chain offers many days of amusement for adults of any age, but it becomes more impressive with every year that has passed. Let us take, as example, a forty-ninth birthday: the chain will have forty-nine presents, individually wrapped and including a message, tied along a length of colourful string. Each parcel is dated, the first one for the birthday and the others for each day following. The chain might emerge, parcel by parcel, from a decorated box or it could be hung around a room or up a flight of stairs. One parcel is opened each day.

A calendar of festivals and special days can be used to inspire a gift and an explanatory or humorous message e.g. 3 February in the Christian calendar is dedicated to St. Blaise, patron saint of sore throats; the obvious gift for that day would be a packet of throat lozenges or some sage leaves. A little doll would be more appropriate for 3 March – the Japanese festival of Doll's Day.

An insight into the working life or hobbies of the recipient could generate more ideas for gifts e.g. a soothing bath sachet for the end of a stressful week, a glitzy hairclip for a Saturday night, and so on.

This chain takes time to assemble but if two or more people share the preparation it reduces the work and increases the fun. The parcels need not be costly: even two or three matches can 'light up your day'!

Another idea for a special adult birthday is to take her shopping to choose as many items (under an agreed price) as she has years.

Eightieth birthday

✧ On the special occasion of a granny's eightieth birthday, a low table was prepared with flowers and birthday cake. When the guests were comfortably seated, the first candle (representing the first ten years of granny's life) was lit, and she told everyone where she was born and a few details about her first ten years. The second candle was lit and after gentle prompting she remembered that during the next ten years they had moved house and she had begun her first job. With the third candle she recounted her marriage and motherhood, and as the candlelight grew everyone found themselves within a very moving experience of eighty years of living history. The whole process took no longer than fifteen minutes.

✧ Well before her mother's eightieth birthday, a daughter contacted as many of her old friends as possible and asked them to send a written recollection with, if possible, a photo and their personal greetings. Together, these memories made a very special book.

In Japan, a 99th birthday is called the 'white-haired'. It is an alphabetical pun: the character for 'white' is the same as the character for '100' except for one missing line.

Centenary anniversary

Many people remember the sense of achievement they had when they became 'two figures' at the age of ten. How much more impressive is the moment when someone comes into three figures. The need to honour the day and celebrate the achievement is usually very strong within the family of, or among those close to the centenarian.

The form given to a celebration may be governed entirely by circumstances and the stamina and capacities of the celebrant. We offer here a few thoughts on creating a respectful and meaningful festivity, with the minimum of stress on the elderly birthday child.

The comfort of the 100-year-old is paramount. She needs to be seated in a suitable chair, in a warm, draught-free zone. No one can more fittingly grace a birthday throne (see page 25) than a person whose years are crowned with the wisdom of a century of history and the trials and triumphs of ten decades of life experience. So throw a beautiful cloth over the chair, place fresh flowers nearby and try to prevent the immediate area from becoming too noisy or too crowded.

Such a birthday creates its own need to recollect the past and one could build on the example given above for an eightieth birthday, lighting a candle for each decade. We suggest that the narrative of the life could be prepared well in advance by someone uncovering the details of the biography over a number of conversations. The highlight of each decade would then be related to the company on the day, allowing the celebrant the freedom to sit back and listen to her life-story unfolding, or participate in its telling, as the mood dictates.

We heard recently of a family who gathered in the shell of a building, which seemed to them to be a very appropriate location, to share their spontaneous offerings and recollections of a father who would have been one hundred years old on that day had he lived.

Their experience suggests that another way of gathering important life memories together at this time might be to ask the guests to bring something with them of the person's contribution to their lives e.g. a memory; an anecdote; a letter; a piece of advice or skill passed on that made a difference to a life; a present given once and still treasured; an object or photograph that holds dear memories; and so on. Such offerings could include sentiments expressed in poetry or music, painting or sculpture. They would be shared by all assembled and, in the process, a larger, fuller and deeper biography would emerge out of the way that one life touched and affected so many others.

It might be felt appropriate to record the event somehow and create a document (especially useful if the celebrant is hard of hearing) which could serve as an ongoing reminder of the joys of that special day. In time it may become an heirloom offering the great-grandchildren a unique and intimate insight into their own history.

Birthday of someone who has died

> Nothing was born; nothing will die; all things will change.
>
> Alfred, Lord Tennyson:
> (Juvenilia) *Nothing will Die*

When a member of the family, or someone very close to the family has died, it may feel appropriate to mark her birthday anniversary in some manner. Such an occasion needs to be approached with sensitivity and how it is actually arranged will, of course, differ according to particular circumstances. Nevertheless, a festive event on this day can be very helpful to those concerned, generating real joy in remembrance and lessening the sense of emptiness that can arrive with the date on the calendar.

The quality of the occasion may be quite different when it is shared by adults alone, or when children are involved. It is possible for adults to celebrate a quiet and solemn festival of remembrance, lighting a candle and exchanging memories or reading something together; it is not easy for children, however, to sustain solemnity. Children will participate well in an activity – picking flowers or gathering petals to take and place on a beach or a hillside, in a park or somewhere else connected with the person who has died. They could engage in collecting small stones to spell out a name in the sand at low tide, or in building a small cairn of pebbles or rock at a lonely place, or in making an earth candle in the garden (see page 98).

All these activities are meaningful in a simple way and create a sense of occasion, which will certainly be heightened for children if there is, in addition, special food involved. So this could also be a day for a picnic, or the sharing of a decorated cake.

There will come a time, perhaps sooner, perhaps later, when such a celebration will change, will be moulded by the passing of years, and will eventually need to be relinquished to take its place in the many-coloured patchwork of family memories. See also **Centenary anniversary** (page 43).

44

Chapter 5

PARTY TIME

Children's parties are a pleasant way of inculcating a feeling of hospitality in the child and of improving his manners. They teach him to consider others rather than himself, and when the child is no longer very young, he may learn a valuable lesson when he perceives that without order and method not even a party can be a success. The mother who makes of her child's party nothing but an opportunity for a show of ostentation does her child an injury…

Lady Troubridge, *The Book of Etiquette*, 1931

The preparation for a birthday party of any kind gives rise to certain questions:

✧ **WHY** have a party?

✧ **WHEN** to have the party?

✧ **WHICH** type of party?

✧ **WHERE** to have the party?

✧ **WHO** to invite?

✧ **WHAT** to eat/ to do/ to give?

✧ **HOW** to prepare a traditional party programme?

Let us take these one by one:

WHY have a party?

For children of one and two years, a party is an occasion for older siblings and adults who are close to the child to celebrate the day and share their delight in this younger member of the family who is, for the most part, unaware of the cause of the festivities.

The older the child grows the more aware he becomes that the party is celebrating him, that he is special, that each birthday marks a new step taken on life's path and, most important of all, that he values having people around who lovingly acknowledge and confirm all this. The only essential reason to hold a birthday party must surely be to express the love and pride felt towards the child (or the adult), and to bear testimony to his unique place in the world. An adult party is a good way to give someone a well-earned treat and show him he is appreciated. A party for an older relative also affords the chance for a scattered family to come together.

An adult who arranges a birthday party for himself has a wonderful opportunity to demonstrate his appreciation and affection for friends and/or family.

WHEN to have the party?

Aim to have the party on the anniversary day. If this is not possible, choose a time soon after the birthday, rather than before. For an older schoolchild, a family celebration on the day and a party or outing with friends within a week is often a satisfactory compromise. If a party has to be cancelled, try to fix another date immediately even if it is a month ahead.

WHICH type of party?

This could be discussed with a child of seven years or more but do not burden him with too much decision-making. It is a good idea first to ask yourself what sort of party you are prepared to offer, or indeed, would like to offer. If you feel that your circumstances make it too difficult to manage a traditional party then opt for something easier to arrange which your child would also really enjoy. It is much better to be clear and firm over this than attempt something that you cannot see through. The mood of a birthday depends a lot on a happy and comfortable organiser.

The choice of party is usually one of the following:

✧ A **traditional birthday party at home** with games and/or activities and a light meal with birthday cake. The company may include extended family and godparents and/or a number of invited friends of the birthday child.

✧ An **outing** to an activity centre or place of interest or entertainment, with family members and/or invited friends. This may include a meal at a restaurant, a picnic, a barbecue, or a meal at home on return. (The creative experience within the social group is the aspect of a birthday outing that needs most attention.)

✧ A **traditional birthday party at a hired venue** with games and/or dancing. Refreshments could be finger-food, a hot/cold buffet, or a barbecue, and would include a birthday cake.

✧ An **adult party** held in the afternoon or evening with finger-food or a hot/cold buffet, or an informal dinner. The birthday cake is cut and served later with coffee or other hot drink.

✧ A **themed party**, where the guests arrive in appropriate fancy dress and the decorations, games, food, prizes and so on are chosen accordingly.

Tips: Themed parties can mean a lot of extra work and expense (also for the guests), and may go right over the heads of young children. Parents often come to regard them as competitive endeavours. A themed children's party can miss the essential point of the birthday, which is to celebrate the child for who he truly is.

Some parents defer such parties until the child is *really* asking for one, and those who wish to avoid a commercially-driven motif will select a general theme such as: the rainbow, the fairy tale, trades, the seasons or the seaside. (Keep in mind that a child dressed as a pirate is likely to act as a pirate!)

Older teenagers and adults can have great fun with a themed party, for they are more able to contribute their personality and their humour to the event.

✧ A party organized, or contributed to, by a **professional entertainer**:

Tips: Choose the entertainer with care, especially for parties with young children. Entertainers who are loud and use a lot of 'hype' can prompt children into over-excited behaviour. Clowns can often have the same effect and, at close quarters, small children are frequently frightened by them. Instead choose an entertainer with a gentler approach and fairly ordinary appearance who uses skill to capture and hold the attention of a young audience.

Be guided by personal recommendation from someone whose judgement you respect and make sure that the entertainer is experienced with the age group of your party.

Puppeteers who use high drama or quirky monsters in their performance can expose sensitive children to nightmare material. Unsophisticated puppets and a few props, a careful choice of colours and mood, a meaningful story line delivered in a tranquil way, these will give wholesome freedom to a child's imagination. A fairy tale presentation offers time to dwell upon beauty and grace, upon the light and the shade in life, with the essential reassurance that life and the world are ultimately all for the good. This is the

soul-care that every child needs but which can sometimes be very hard to find.

Different temperaments

Bear in mind that children's temperaments differ* and arrangements for the party must take this into account. Here are some brief suggestions for responding appropriately to different temperaments:

✧ Fay is a bright, slender little chatterbox and wants to invite everyone in the world to her party, to dress up and play *lots* of games. (She may also change her mind a few times.)

Tips: Limit the number of guests to about eight. Guide the dressing-up into charades or acting out a story that is told by an adult. Plan a well-organized balance of lively and quiet games alternately, with no waiting around in between.

✧ Melanie is quiet, intelligent and observant and more sure of what she does not want at her party than what she does want. She is likely to ask for her few close friends as guests and may well choose a creative activity or an outing in preference to games. She may need some help to come to a decision.

Tips: Avoid major surprises and make sure she is consulted over the menu. End a party for the under-tens with a folk/fairy tale (lasting about ten to fifteen minutes) or a puppet show. Maybe Melanie will have a headache or be critical of the party as soon

---

* For more on the temperaments, see: *Lifeways*, Gudrun Davy and Bons Voors, Hawthorn Press, 1983

as it is over, but this will be her way of reconciling the extra-special things in life with the mundane, domestic routine. Offer her warmth, sympathy and another story before bed.

✧ Brenda is quiet, gentle in her movements and faithful to her routines. When questioned about her party plans, she may want to repeat aspects of the one the year before. She will have particular ideas about food for the meal but will be happy to be guided on other issues.

Tips: She will prefer little surprises to big ones, so plan the details of the party with her and offer those things that are, in essence, already known to her, e.g. a picnic at a familiar place, a game or type of activity with which she is already comfortable. Include her favourite food on the menu, (do not be tempted to make it 'more interesting'), and do not rush the meal. Encourage her to invite more than one guest and end the party with a puppet show if appropriate.

✧ Roxanne is robust and resourceful and tends to 'organise' her group of friends. She has very clear ideas on the party programme and you may feel she is demanding too much of you.

Tips: Tact and the art of compromise may be necessary to arrive at a programme which is mutually acceptable. This is the moment when it really helps to know what you are prepared to take on. If you do not want more than ten guests, for example, avoid excuses such as 'There is only room for ten at the table', because this child is likely to have already calculated that the table upstairs and the bench from the porch would solve such problems. Use a statement that cannot so easily be set aside, e.g. 'I do not feel comfortable with more than ten guests in a

room of this size'. Roxanne enjoys winning an argument and she also enjoys winning party games, so guide her into a judging or refereeing role occasionally and include some non-competitive and/or team games in the programme. She might enjoy ending the party with a piñata original (see pages 80–81).

WHERE to have the party?

This book deals primarily with parties that take place at home. This could mean either home of a child whose divorced parents have joint custody or even, perhaps, the larger or more convenient home of a willing friend or relative. One may still consider the party to be 'at home' if that is where a meal is eaten after time has been spent on a pleasure trip.

Hiring a venue

It is often easier to influence the ambience of a party held at home, but sometimes a hired venue is the only answer to specific party problems, especially the question of handling an unavoidably long guest-list.

Tips: Book the venue well in advance. Check if supervision and/or catering is provided. Confirm all arrangements in writing and make contact again a few days before the party. Enlist the required number of helpers well in advance.

An outdoor party

A party with a picnic or barbecue can be very popular with older children and teenagers. Younger children lose concentration and tire easily when outdoors for too long, but could enjoy half-an-hour or so of outdoor games.

Tips: Inform guests in advance that the party will be outdoors but plan a rainy-day alternative. One can still have lots of fun with a picnic indoors.

If helium balloons are to be released make sure these are biodegradable latex ones. Foil/mylar helium balloons and ribbons should not be released.

WHO to invite?

This question is often only solved with a compromise between the number of guests your child, for example, would like to invite, and the number that you think you can manage. We have collected a few suggestions on this:

Establish a tradition of allowing the birthday child as many guests as he has years (i.e. a five-year-old has five guests) and discontinue this practice at the maximum number that you and your living accommodation can cope with (i.e. perhaps the eighth or tenth birthday). Thereafter do not exceed that number until the child becomes a teenager, when such issues are dealt with on a more individual basis.

If your custom is to have a sit-down party or tea or birthday meal, do not invite more guests than can be comfortably seated around a dining table. A meal is a social event and something of this quality is lost if the guests are divided between two tables.

Similarly, if indoor games or activities are planned, relate the number of guests to the size of the games room or the area of work surface available.

Try solving the problem of numbers by having two events e.g. a family celebration on the day and a party with friends at the weekend; or one party for school friends and one for neighbourhood play-mates. (This will usually mean two birthday cakes.)

Simplify the party concept: engage a few helpers and invite the whole class to an informal ball-game at the local park. Serve only savoury nibbles, cake and a cold drink.

Invite only the girls/boys of the class.

Tips: Keep child guests to a minimum for birthdays of one to three years. Children of this age have few social skills and can be overwhelmed by large groups. (Their tendency to be fiercely protective of their own toys and personal space, while plundering those of other children is not a recipe for a harmonious celebration.)

Many families agree that, for the under twelves especially, smaller parties are qualitatively more satisfying and more fun.

For an outing, limit the number of guests to about six and include one or two adult helpers.

Other points

- Children under nine years usually mix easily with children they do not know.
- Invite parents with children up to three years. Offer the option of staying at the party to parents of children of four to five years.
- If possible, invite only the relatives with whom your child feels comfortable. By the age of nine most children are clear on their preferences; older children are prey to censure by their peers and can be painfully embarrassed by the idiosyncrasies of others.
- Keep the social entity of the class in mind and avoid, for example, inviting all but one of the boys/girls in the class.

WHAT to eat ? (see pages 125–129)

WHAT to do ? (see pages 67–123)

WHAT to give?

A birthday party is intended to give the birthday child and his guests a happy and satisfying time together. Anything more than this could be considered a bonus, but some conventions have grown up around the birthday party that cannot be entirely ignored after the age of five or six: the prizes and the party 'take-home' bag. Some parents feel that these engender a materialistic, 'what's-in-it-for-me' attitude, but there are many ways of minimising such an effect while at the same time giving genuine pleasure. A carefully chosen but inexpensive prize will award a child the recognition he deserves just as well as a more costly item.

The essential point is that gifts presented to the guests have parity with one another. Here are some suggestions:

Crafts

bead necklet / bracelet kit
paper chain kit
ball of variegated wool and 10mm knitting
    needles
beads / sequins
glitter-glue / dust
coloured, carded fleece
origami paper
coloured beeswax / plasticine
pencil sharpener
petit-fours baking tins
rainbow pencil
pack of coloured paper / card
wax crayons / chalks
drawing pad / notebook

novelty eraser
lengths of narrow ribbon
felt squares
gold / silver ballpoint pen
embroidery thread

If you have had a craft activity at the party, the guests may appreciate a kit to take home to practise this further. It could be a complete kit or one key item to get them going e.g. decorative sprinkles for cake-making, origami paper for Bell-catchers (see page 95) or Candleboats (see page 103)

Games

rainbow string for string games
yo-yo / marbles
lightweight ball / frisbee
mini kite / balloon
dressing-up finger ring / crown
bubble mixture
false moustache / face paints
spinning top
conjuring tricks / pocket puzzles
shuttlecock / skipping rope

Novelties

Note: Bells and small items are not suitable for children under three

bell on a ribbon
party popper
bells on elastic for wrist/ankle
pretty shell
tiny purse / box
Japanese water flowers
polished stone
lavender bag
biscuit cutter
small crystal
small items jewellery
'stained glass' window stickers
candle

bath pearls / bubble bath
'confetti' alphabet / stars etc.
jumping beans
small glass / china animal
small address book
stickers
decorative hairclip
pack of novelty tissues

Treats

chocolate gold sovereigns
seasonal fruit
decorative cake sprinkles
gingerbread man
home-made fudge / coconut ice
sugar mouse
small home-made cookies
sugar flowers
Japanese rice crackers
liquorice stick
home-made toffee apple
mini jar of honey / jam
marzipan novelties
unshelled nuts

Seasonal

Spring:
    packet of seeds
    small pot of spring bulbs
Summer:
    windmill (pinwheel)
    sand castle flags
    floating candle
Autumn:
    bulbs to plant
    dried apple rings
    wheat straw decorations
Winter:
    bird food
    festival decorations
    star cookies

(See Gifts pages 151–162 and Activities pages 91–113 for more ideas of simple gifts to make at home.)

✧ Prepare some extra **prizes**, just in case, and wrap them, or use a treasure chest (see page 68).

✧ Prepare **take-home** gifts also for the birthday child, his siblings and any teenage helpers. These gifts can be presented in a paper basket (see page 98) or lidded box (see pages 170–171). Alternatively, place them in the centre of an opened paper napkin or squares of giftwrap, gather the four corners together in a bunch and tie with ribbon or decorative string.

✧ Younger children may enjoy a **lucky dip** before they go home: place the party bags or individual gifts in a decorated box, with an opening in the lid just large enough to allow the child to retrieve his parcel. If dry sawdust or wood shavings are available, make a traditional 'bran tub' by decorating a large box or other container and burying the gifts.

✧ Take-home gifts could hang as decoration from the ceiling or from a mobile or, if the contents of the take-home packages are all the same, the children might enjoy a hunt for them just before leaving the party.

HOW to prepare a traditional party programme?

In many parts of the world the birthday has now become the major personal festival of the year, hopefully bringing a glow to the heart and, perhaps more important, to that inner space where seeds of personal growth and understanding are nurtured. For many children, their expectations of this festival are embodied in the party, therefore it seems right to pay attention to the total nourishment of the child on this occasion in particular – not just food for the body but for the soul and spirit also. How can this be achieved?

Most festivals around the globe, whether religious or secular, involve food, flowers and fire; and a birthday party is no exception. The body needs food, the soul hungers for beauty and our spiritual search for meaning in life, for enlightenment, is always fuelled by the spark of enthusiasm. From the wonder that shines in a young child's eye as he gazes at the moon or the candles on a cake, is born the endeavour to secure his own true place in the world.

So let us have special food, candles and flowers at a party. Let us have beauty for the eye and for the ear, harmony of decorations and companionship, quality rather than quantity. All this nourishes the child's developing soul. Folk tales and fairy stories, puppet shows and simple 'magic' tricks that allow the child to live in a quiet state of wonder and delight, will support and strengthen his spiritual development.

Suggestions

One to two years: Keep the party small and *quiet*. Try not to disrupt the child's routine but arrange the party around it: this will usually mean a lunch party or a tea party, and one and a half hours is a tolerable length of time for this age group. Serve refreshments to adults and children (see page 126). Allow time for the birthday song, the blowing out of candles (see page 10), the unwrapping of gifts, and perhaps some photographs. Have toys available to occupy the children (see page 70). Two-year-olds may enjoy a simple ring game (see page 70) to end the celebration.

Tips: Avoid balloons and keep all decorations out of reach.

Three to four years: Limit the time to under two hours and use the indications above as a guide. Offer a cold drink to any adults who are staying and then organise the un-wrapping of gifts. It is possible to include a ring game (see pages 71, 73) or an organised activity (see page 92–93). Allow 20–30 minutes for the meal (see page 126). Children of this age have a short attention span and tire easily, so two or three games (see pages 70–74) could be quite enough. End the party with a short story (see pages 181–182) and perhaps with a lucky dip.

Tips: Supply crayons, paper and a few toys for shy guests. Plan in toilet breaks.

Five to six years: Allow two hours for the party and half-an-hour for the meal (see page 126). Make an introductory game (see page 72) and unwrapping of gifts the first items on the programme, followed by 20–30 minutes of organized activity (see pages 93–96). Play four to six games (see pages 74–76) and end with a puppet show (see page 118) or a ten-minute story (see pages 181–182).

Tips: Ask a helper to occupy a shy guest with a suitable game / book / activity. Avoid pressurising a reluctant child to join in but observe him closely to see if he is unwell. Plan in toilet breaks

Seven to nine years: Follow the format for the previous age group but allow two and a half hours for the party. A few active games (see pages 77–81) before the meal and an activity (see pages 96–100) and/or up to six games after the meal. End with a quiet game, and a story (see pages 181–182) or puppet show (see page 118).

Tips: Do not be shy of setting some rules of behaviour if it becomes necessary. Noisy children can often be quietened if an adult whispers to them; over-boisterous children may react well to being given a responsible task. Plan in toilet breaks.

Nine years and above: For the lower end of this age group three hours is sufficient for a traditional party. Follow the format for the previous age group but offer drinks and nibbles first if the children have come straight from school. Nine-year-olds may enjoy a story to end the party (see pages 181–182). Ten-year-olds may feel that they have grown out of such things, so end the party with a couple of quiet games. Teenagers may need as much as four hours to complete all the social interaction they require.

Tip: Consider whether it would be better for a younger child in the family to be with a friend or baby-sitter during an older sibling's party.

Before the party

✧ Keep in mind that what you do for one child may also be anticipated by a sibling, and beware of making any promises regarding the party that cannot be kept.

✧ If the birthday child is eager to be involved in the preparations then encourage him, according to ability, to help with: cutting out and colouring invitations (see page 57); making paper chains, pompoms (see page 94), crêpe streamers (see page 133); cutting out and decorating cookies; shaping bread rolls; decorating paper plates; making name cards for the meal table; garnishing the plates of food. Bear in mind that small children (and some larger ones) have a short attention span and may not always finish the task they begin. Be tolerant, and never press a reluctant child to help with the preparations.

✧ There should be a minimum of two adults present at a children's party or outing. Ensure that there is at least one adult for every four or five children. Invite helpers who you know you can work with and explain their tasks as fully as possible before the day. An older sibling might take on specific tasks e.g. pouring the drink, clearing the table, supervising some games, keeping a time check on the proceedings. Arrange for helpers to arrive half-an-hour early if possible.

Before the meal

✧ Greet each guest personally on arrival and place gloves/scarves etc. in coat pockets before putting them away.

✧ Make sure children know where the lavatory is. Children of three to five years will be helped by a toilet routine before games and before or after the meal.

✧ Presentation and unwrapping of gifts needs to be the first event of the party. Late arrivals can offer theirs at the meal table after the cake has been served.

✧ Young children, especially boys, need to run about at times. If weather permits, have some outdoor play/games before the meal.

After the meal

✧ A puppet show and quiet games are best placed indoors after the meal.

✧ Games that need setting up in secret e.g. *Hunt the matches* (see page 86), need a position in the programme after the meal, an outdoor game, or another activity that takes place away from the hunt area.

✧ Prepare extra games but do not try to fit absolutely everything in. Allow yourself time to round off the party without rush. Be firm about pick-up times for it is better for a party to be ten minutes too short than ten minutes too long. Overtired children are not happy children.

✧ An only child may appreciate having a friend to stay on for some extra time after the party.

End of the day

✧ Some children ask for 'sleep over' parties. Many parents find that these are not always an experience they wish to repeat with groups of children and perhaps it is better, in many ways, to aspire to end the party satisfyingly. For a child of eight or nine years, having a friend to sleep over after the party can be a relaxed and happy time as long as the following day is not a school day.

✧ At the end of a busy day with many unusual events and experiences, children may need some help to settle back into the routine of daily life. A simple task such as tidying up the birthday gifts, or a quiet conversation about the day that has gone or the day that is coming may be all that is needed to relax an excited child as bedtime approaches. A child who bursts into tears over the slightest thing is not usually a discontented or unhappy child, rather one who is trying to relax in his own way. Patience, cuddles and bed is usually an effective cure.

✧ The unwrapping of one last present could be reserved for when the child is ready for bed, but before the bedtime story.

✧ Small children are often too exhausted to cope with anything more demanding than a story. In this case, the 'circular' structure of *George goes to market* (see page 188) is ideal for rounding off the day.

Checklist for a traditional birthday party

While the list below may seem daunting, it is intended to be comprehensive and a guideline to cover every eventuality. Of course you should only select the things you wish to use, and make the party simpler if you wish. You do not have to feel you are orchestrating a military manoeuvre!

Three months before

- Decide on the type of party (see page 46).
- Visit, select and book a hired venue, if required. Book an entertainer/puppeteer (see page 47) and confirm these arrangements in writing.
- Consider giving a simple puppet show to the party with the help of a friend.
- Do you wish to make some decorations / prizes / take-home gifts / a piñata (see pages 80–81)? If so, start now.
- Leave some simple items to work on later with your child.

Four weeks before

- Make a guest list (see page 49)
- Observe your child and see what they like to do best. This may help you plan an outing or activity for the party.
- Prepare invitations (see page 57).
- Plan teenager's surprise trail (see page 111) and book helpers (see page 53).
- Settle on the style of the birthday cake and its decoration; make and freeze the basic cake, if appropriate.
- If a story will be needed for the end of the party (see pages 52, 181), choose it now and read it through several times before the birthday to become thoroughly familiar with it.
- If you are giving a puppet show, prepare all the puppets.

Three weeks before

- Mail the invitations.
- Book the helpers / babysitters you will need (see page 53).
- Make a list of guests' home telephone numbers / parents' mobile phone numbers, as needed, in case of problems. Display it near the telephone.

Two weeks before

- Decide on the party programme and the menu.
- Make a list of items to prepare and / or to buy: food; decorations; prizes and take-home-gifts (see pages 50–51); materials and props for activities, games, puppet show; first aid for accidents (see page 56); camera film, if applicable.
- Do the necessary shopping.
- Plan treasure hunt with tasks (see page 83) and make clues.

One week before

- Confirm bookings of venue / entertainer.
- Finish any non-food items that you wish to make yourself.
- Rehearse the puppet show and / or practise a chosen craft activity with your helper.
- Plan simple treasure hunt trail (see page 74) and prepare clues.

Two days before

- Check that you have everything you need for the party: cake decorations and candles; food for adults and children; drinks; decorations for room and table; cutlery; crockery and glasses; table cloth and napkins; equipment, materials and patterns for activities; clues and treasure for treasure hunts; props and prizes for games; treats for the piñata (see pages 80–81); props, script and puppets for puppet show; story book; take-home-gifts.
- Do last-minute shopping.
- Make and / or decorate the cake.
- Clear a space for guests' coats etc. and decide on work surfaces for activities.
- Check that all the arrangements are made for a teenager's surprise trail.
- Prepare copies of the party programme for each helper.
- Warn neighbours (or invite them) if the party is likely to be noisy late at night.
- Prepare outdoor areas and clear them of hazards.
- Wrap prizes, take-home-gifts and treasure for the treasure hunt.
- Allow time to share some preparation with the birthday child (see page 53).

One day before

- Blow up balloons (avoid balloon decorations for children up to three years).

- Lay out materials and equipment for activities.
- Clear the activities/games room of all unnecessary furniture and breakables.
- If the guests include children under four, take appropriate safety precautions with stairs, electrical cords and plugs, curtain cords, medicines and cleaning fluids and outside gates and pools.
- Remind yourself of first-aid procedures for stings, nosebleed, choking, fractures, sprains (have a packet of frozen peas in the freezer), and concussion.
- Prepare an ashtray outside for smokers.
- Set up the puppet 'theatre' if possible and cover it with a light cloth.
- Place loaded camera in a convenient and safe position.
- Prepare and store as much of the party food as possible.
- In the evening, decorate the house (keep decorations out of the reach of young children), and fold napkins (see page 147).
- Decorate the birthday child's chair and place for breakfast (see page 25).
- Prepare the birthday table (see page 25).

On the day

- Give each helper a copy of the party programme when they arrive.
- Complete as much food and drink preparation as possible early in the day. Keep bread items fresh under a damp cloth.
- Mark the entrance of the party with a few balloons.
- Remove a young child's favourite toys to a safe place.
- Position the prizes, treasure chest (see page 68), lucky dip (see page 51), and take-home gifts in convenient places; cover them if necessary.
- Lay out materials and equipment for activities on the chosen work surface, if possible.

- Hide clues and treasure for treasure hunts, and hang up the filled piñata (see pages 80-81).
- Arrange props for games/puppet show in a convenient place and in order of use.
- Arrange outdoors play equipment and play corner for young children, if required.
- Block off all out-of-bounds areas and see that pets are comfortably housed away from the party area.
- Place matches and candles out of reach of young children and check that all candles are in stable and non-combustible holders. **Do not leave burning candles unattended.**
- Lay the table and decorate the birthday child's place.
- Complete the garnishing of food.

The day after

- Send a thankyou card to all helpers and a take-home gift to any guest who was not well enough to come.

Tip: Record details of the party in a notebook reserved for the purpose. If there is (or will be) more than one child in the family, this may prove a very useful reference for future parties. Things to record could be:
  - name and age of child;
  - guests;
  - descriptions of cake, menu, activities, games, prizes, contents of take-home gifts/piñata;
  - story/puppet show/magic tricks;
  - details of entertainer;
  - gifts received.

Note also what did and did not work well, and what was especially popular.

Chapter 6

INVITATIONS AND CARDS

Children love colour and decoration, and it is no breach of etiquette for their cards or letters of invitation to parties to have pretty designs upon them... If the children are old enough to write their own invitations they should do so, since it teaches them the importance of social duties...

Lady Troubridge, *The Book of Etiquette,* 1931

Tips:

- Invitation cards are not really necessary for pre-school children.

- If invitations are not for the whole class of school friends, we recommend that they are sent by post, addressed to parent and child together. Invitations handed to selected friends in a classroom are likely to cause upset.

- An invitation should clearly state: the date and place; the arrival and departure times; requests to bring e.g. bike, sunhat, overall, swimwear, rain gear, soft shoes etc.

- In addition, ask to be informed of any dietary requirements or allergic condition.

- Include a telephone number or e-mail address for reply.

Some ideas for unusual invitations

St. George's Road
Friday, 18th May, 18…

Miss and Master Johnston present
compliments to Miss Bell, and request
the pleasure of her company to a pic-nic
at Bothwell Castle on Thursday next,
the Queen's birthday.

Carriages leave at 11 o'clock

(Reply – declining)

Hill Street
Saturday, 19th May 18…

Miss Bell presents compliments to Miss
and Master Johnston, and regrets that
indisposition (from which she cannot
expect to be sufficiently recovered by
Thursday) makes her decline their polite
invitation.

The Gentleman's Letter Writer (19th century)

Balloon invitation

Inflate a plain-coloured balloon and tie a
  string around the opening in such a way
  that it can easily be removed.
Write the invitation on the balloon with a felt
  tip permanent marker pen.
When the ink is perfectly dry, deflate the
  balloon and mail it.
Put your address on the back of the
  envelope, in case the balloon bursts.

Mystery invitation

Write invitation on decorated notepaper but
  leave a generous space for each of the
  figures e.g. time and date of party, etc.
Dip point of cocktail stick into fresh lemon
  juice and write in missing figures with
  juice. (Do not make figures too small.)
Leave until completely dry.
Add an ink postscript to invitation suggesting
  that the use of a medium-hot iron will solve
  the Mystery of the Missing Numbers….
(Especially suited for nine or ten-year-olds.)

Puzzle invitation cards

The details of the party will become clear only when the puzzle is completed.

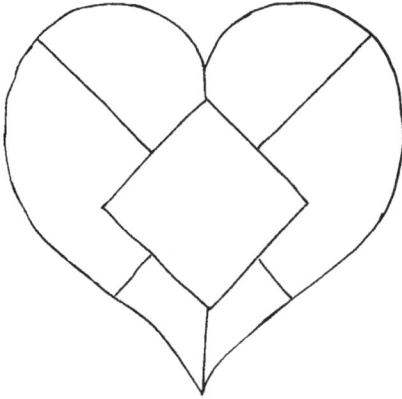

You will need: (for each design)
Strong card (postcard size)
Pencil, ruler, pen, scissors or craft knife

Plan the shape of the invitation and cut the card accordingly.
Write the message on the card.
Draw cutting lines lightly with a pencil on the back of the card. Cut along the lines.

Tip: Address the envelope before cutting up the puzzle

Coded invitation

To Maxine								From Ted	
Y	T	T	O	Y	O	W	I	U	R	I	U
O	E	H	N	T	F	O	R	S	I	M	M
U	D	D	W	H	M	T	T	E	N	M	E
A	T	A	E	E	A	O	Y	P	G	I	L
R	O	Y	D	E	Y	F	A	L	Y	N	O
E	M	P	N	I	F	I	T	E	O	G	V
I	Y	A	E	G	R	V	M	A	U	C	E
N	B	R	S	H	O	E	Y	S	R	O	T
V	I	T	D	T	M	T	H	E	S	S	E
I	R	Y	A	H	T	H	O	B	W	T	D

RSVP   **Tel:123456**

The words of the invitation are printed in a block, reading downwards from the left hand top corner. Other versions could be invented by changing the direction of reading.

Invitation with a personal touch

If you enjoy playing around with words, arrange the invitation to highlight the name of the guest or birthday child. Capital letters could be coloured and decorated:

a waRm

welcOme awaits you

at Betty's birthday party

6pm on WEdnesday , 5 January

R.s.v.p.

we do hope That you can come.

Come

to A

LighT-hearted

birtHday

fEast

foR a

mystery mIss

at seveN o'clock on

JunE seventh

Birthday cards

Birthday greetings were first commercialised in Britain in 1850, in the form of cards. Today there are cards to suit all birthdays and all tastes. Nevertheless, there is still a place for the unique and personal gift of a handmade card.

Suggestions for creative card-making

Explore art and craft shops for decorative paper and card. Indian, Chinese, Japanese and Thai papers are rich in colour and texture. Score textured card on the *inside* to make a cleaner crease.

✧ ✧ ✧

Finely grate wax crayons – blues and reds, *or* blues, greens and yellows, *or* yellows and reds – and sprinkle liberally over one half of a sheet of drawing paper approx. 20cm x 20cm.
Fold clean side of paper over gratings.
Place folded paper on white scrap paper and press with a medium hot iron until wax melts. Open up the paper.
Cut out a symmetrical form, e.g. a daisy or butterfly, across the fold so that the colours are mirrored on the two halves of the form.
Glue form to folded card.

✧ ✧ ✧

Paint a miniature picture, or free composition of colours, in watercolour on a good watercolour paper torn into a small square or rectangle.
Mount this on stiff white or coloured card.

✧ ✧ ✧

Consider sewing a design on card, or sewing a collage of ribbon or cloth.

✧ ✧ ✧

✧ ✧ ✧

Almost cover one side of folded card with a textured paper.
Make two parallel cuts (2cm long, 1cm apart) with a craft knife through the paper and one layer of card.
Through this cut one can thread the stems of pressed leaves or flowers, the quill of a beautiful feather or simply a length of sheer ribbon to tie into a bow.

✧ ✧ ✧

Use a craft punch with a small design to decorate the vertical edge of a strong coloured card.
Glue paper, tissue paper or ribbon in a contrasting colour behind the perforations.
Punch a hole across the crease 1cm from the top of the card and draw through some interesting threads or fibres to match the colours of the card.
Knot fibres at base of card.

✧ ✧ ✧

Experiment with a wide variety of materials to use in collage work. Exclusive designs are possible with split cardboard, an empty teabag and a gold pen...

✧ ✧ ✧

Use a pen with coloured ink to practise creative writing on coloured card, e.g.

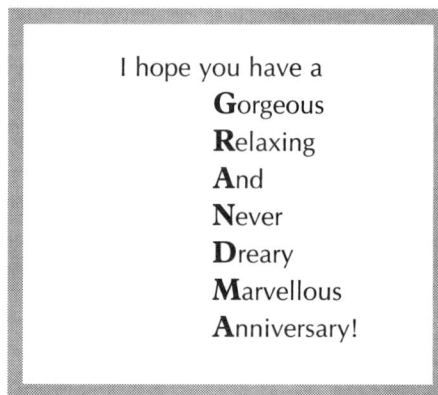

> I hope you have a
> **G**orgeous
> **R**elaxing
> **A**nd
> **N**ever
> **D**reary
> **M**arvellous
> **A**nniversary!

I wish you a
Lovely
Abundant
Unendingly
Radiant and
Amazing
Birthday!

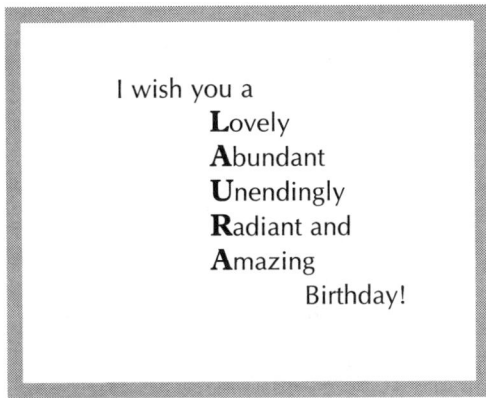

Or send a bouquet of everlasting flowers:

Sweet pea	tul**I**ps
Orchid	ro**S**es
Poppy	p**A**nsies
Honeysuckle	**B**ay
Iris and	g**E**ntian
Erica	ph**L**ox

(Try spelling out the birthday child's name with a bunch of *living* blooms, using the initial letter of each flower.)

✧ ✧ ✧

Compose a poem where the first letter of each line makes up the name of the recipient. This could become a card that is treasured for years – or maybe just a piece of cheerful doggerel to raise a smile:

And may this day
Not see a cloud, may
Dew drops glitter and
Robins sing loud, and
Ever-cheerful may you be
Wherever you are, whatever you see!

Sunrise birthday card

Offer the birthday child the privilege of bringing the sun up on this important day!

You will need:
Two pieces of lightweight, pale coloured card: 18cm x 26cm and 14cm x 14cm
Pair of compasses
Ruler, pencil and scissors
Coloured pencils or crayons
Glue and one paper fastener

Fold larger piece of card in half as indicated below. Draw thin pencil line vertically down centre of card and another line horizontally across centre of card.
Mark point **x** 1.5cm below point where lines cross.

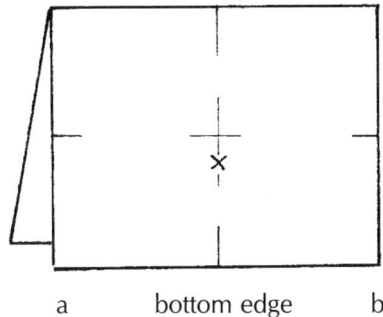

a   bottom edge   b

Using compasses, with point x as centre and shortest distance to edge **a-b** as radius, draw semicircle above horizontal centre line:

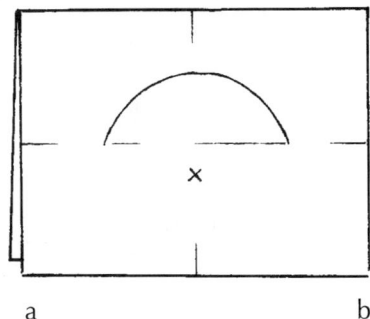

a   b

With same radius, draw circle from centre
of second piece of card, and another
circle from same centre but with radius
increased by 1.5cm.

Cut along perimeter of larger circle to create
a disc.

Divide disc in half with faint pencil line.

Use coloured pencils to draw golden yellow
sun in centre of one half of disc, and
moon and stars gathered in other half.

Surround moon and stars with deep blue
and sun with light blue, allowing colours
to fade and mingle across centre line.

Draw a 'birthday banner' in sunny half as
indicated. (Omit banner for children too
young to read.)

Draw a scene around, but not inside,
semicircle on first piece of card. Open up
card and cut away shaded area indicated:

a   b

Fold back of card down. With point of
compasses push hole through both layers
of card at point **x** and then through centre
of disc.

Press paper fastener through front of card,
then through disc and finally through
back of card. Open out fastener.

Dab glue between back and front of card to
secure corners **a** and **b**, making sure that
disc turns freely.

Flower with a message

Write a message in the centre of the flower and use it as a greetings card, or glue it to the lid of a box (see pages 170–171).

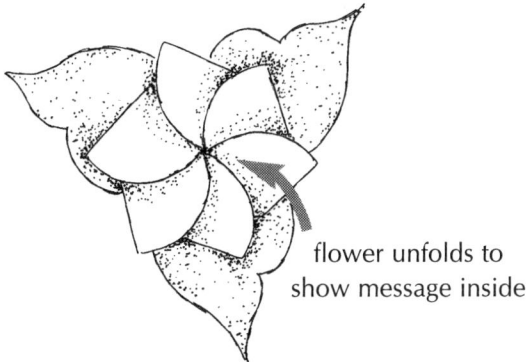

flower unfolds to show message inside

You will need:
Coloured writing paper or thin card
   10cm x 10cm
Green paper or card 8cm x 8cm
Ruler, scissors, glue

Transfer (see page 210) leaf pattern to green paper and cut out.
Transfer flower pattern to paper or card.
Cut out flower along solid lines and score all dotted lines with back of scissor blade.
Fold points **a** and **b** upwards and towards each other so that line **xy** lies in a valley.
Repeat process for each petal as flower takes shape as indicated below:

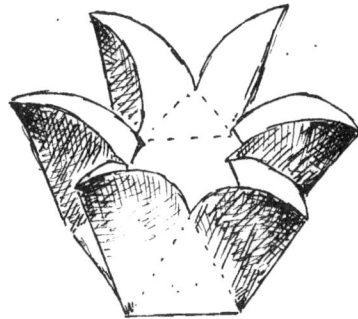

Gently push petals down in clockwise direction, closing flower.
Fix flower to leaves with dab of glue.

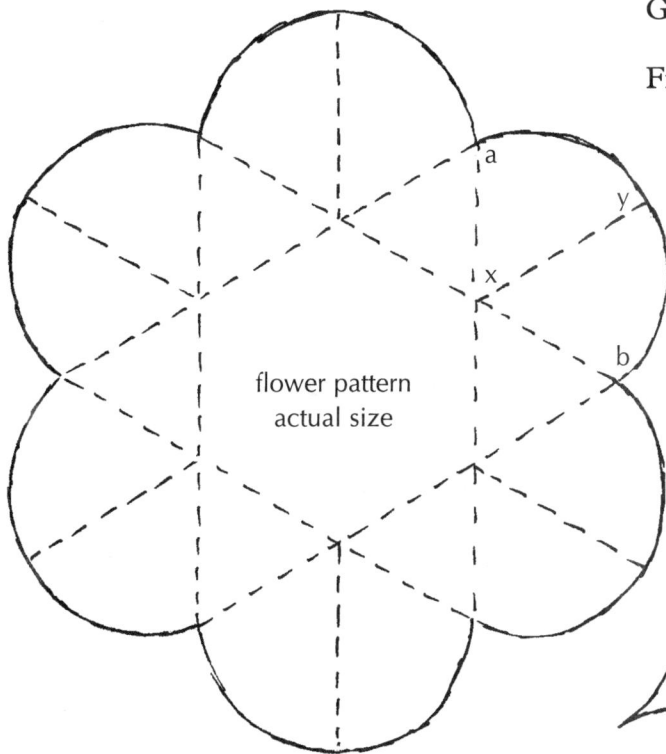

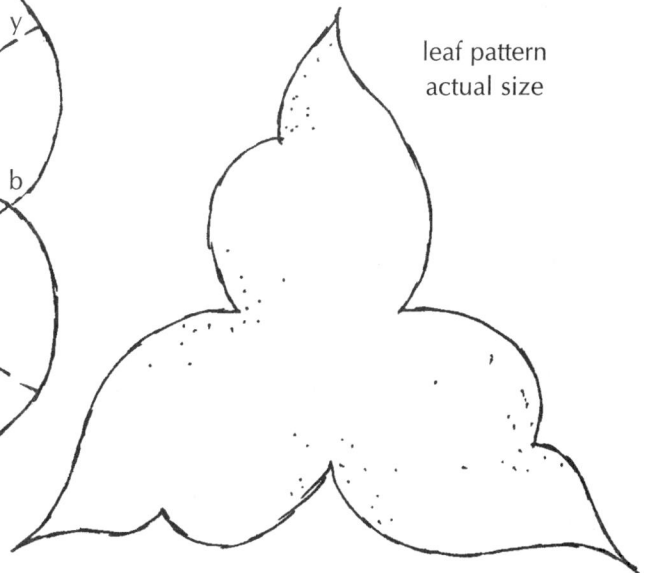

a
y
x
b

flower pattern
actual size

leaf pattern
actual size

Flower birthday card

A child who can handle a craft knife would find this card simple to make. Younger children will enjoy colouring in after an adult has done the cutting. The design can easily be adapted to create a smiling sun, a Valentine rose, or a shining Christmas star.

You will need:
Flower card pattern, page 214
Piece of white or pastel lightweight card
   21cm x 15cm
Craft knife and cutting board
Coloured pencils or crayons

Fold piece of card in half, bringing shorter
   edges together. Open out card.
Transfer (see page 210) top half of flower
   pattern to card directly above crease.

With craft knife cut along marked flower
   outline. **Do not cut along dotted line.**
To complete flower, fold cut-out petals along
   crease to lie flat on top of card.
Draw around their outline lightly with pencil.

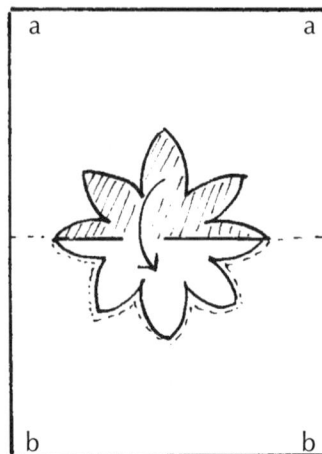

Unfold petals and colour flower, allowing
   space for a golden yellow centre.
Fold corners **a** back and down to corners **b**.
   (Alternatively, fold corners **a** forwards and
   down to corners **b**.)
Write a greeting across card below flower.

Add other messages to inside of card. Fold
   top half of flower down when placing card
   in envelope.

Envelope

There may be times when a handmade
greetings card needs a handmade envelope.
Take this opportunity to experiment with
interesting paper, or even cloth.

You will need:
Sheet of paper (see diagram below)
Pencil and ruler
Scissors and glue

Measure and cut sheet of paper to
   appropriate size for your card, as below:

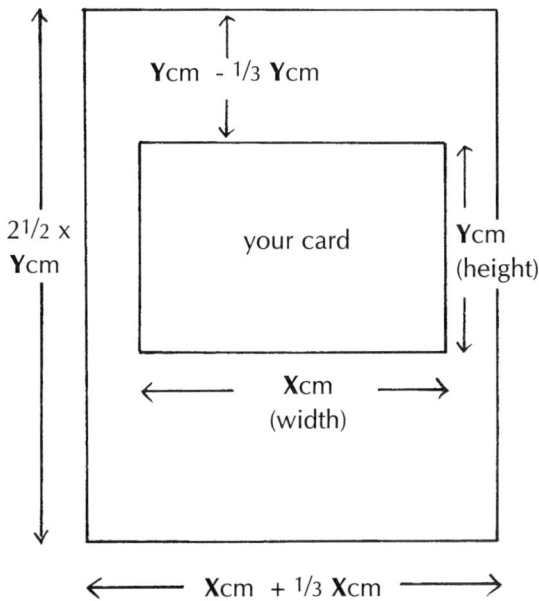

Mark points **o** (distance **o** to **f** is always the
same) and cut away shaded area:

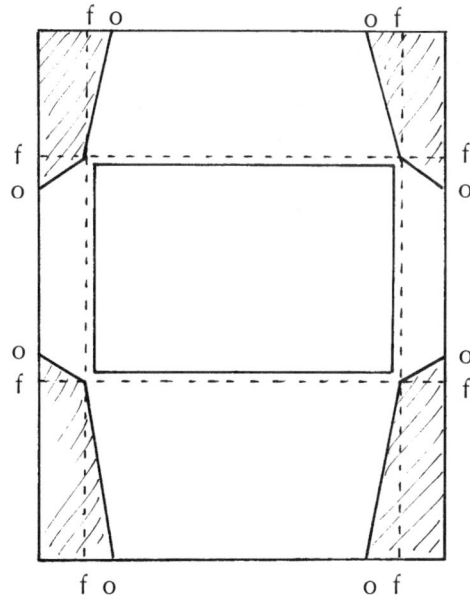

Position card as indicated and mark lightly
   around edge with pencil.
Using ruler and scissor blade, lightly score
   folding lines (dotted lines) leaving narrow
   space around card.

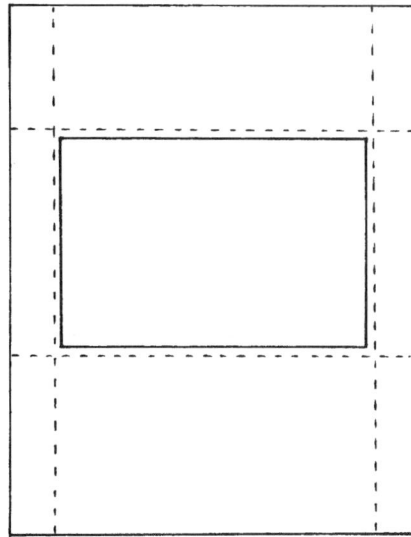

Fold side flaps in and bottom flap up. Secure bottom flap to sides with thin line of glue on inside of edges **o-a**.

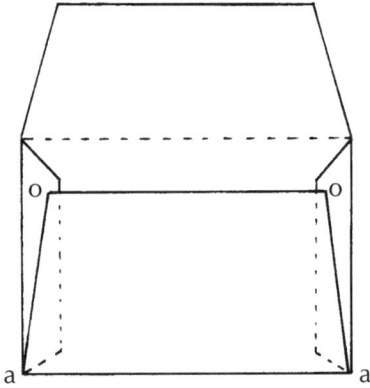

Tip: Re-use cellophane wrappers from commercial greetings cards for chic envelopes. Draw a line around edge of front face with glue stick and sprinkle with glitter. Add sticky label for recipient's name. (This envelope is not suitable for mailing.)

> A wanderer is man from his birth.
> He was born in a ship
> On the breast of the River of Time
> Matthew Arnold, *The Future*

Optional: Before folding envelope, use craft punch to punch small design in corner(s) of front of envelope or along edge of back flap. Line envelope with tissue paper of a strong colour before folding in flaps. Make lining 3mm smaller overall and glue only along line **a-a** before folding. After folding, but before gluing envelope, secure lining with small dabs of glue where necessary. (This envelope is not suitable for mailing.)

Chapter 7

PARTY GAMES

Games should be under the charge of a sprightly young lady who knows a number of games, shows how they ought to be played, and peremptorily insists on the order in which they shall be played. A whimsical youth who interferes with her directions must be ignored. No time should be wasted between one game and another. Musical Chairs, Brother I'm Bobbed (especially with boys), General Post, Blind Man's Buff, Puss in the Corner, are always favourites...

Advice on 'Juvenile Parties' from *Jack's Reference Book*, 1915

Since classical times the occasion of a birthday has been honoured by games. The birthday of a Roman Emperor, for example, might have been celebrated with chariot races or other tests of skill that brought entertainment and enjoyment to the people. In present times, party games have been scaled down a little but they remain for the most part tests of skill, which entertain family and friends and allow them the opportunity to take pride in the progress of someone dear to them.

In this section we have included just enough examples of games to indicate the type suitable for each age group. There are many excellent party-game books available but the art lies in choosing which games to play when. Games are fun, they can be exciting, but who can say exactly when excitement begins to run wild? Seasoned parents may enjoy swapping the near-death experiences of past parties but they are also quick to pass on tips for avoiding them. We include some below:

Preparation

- Plan the order of games, alternating a lively one with a quieter one. Arrange for most of the games to take place before the meal; a quiet game after the meal followed by a story or simple puppet show (see page 118) should ensure that the party ends peacefully.
- Prepare a few more games than you intend to use, and plan a rainy-day programme if appropriate.
- Respect the birthday child's preferences when choosing games and keep to your plan (a deviation on the day will only work if the child is really enthusiastic about it).
- When choosing pencil and paper games it may be necessary to consider the need of a child with dyslexia. Arranging for teams of two may be helpful.
- Buy or make the required number of prizes, plus one or two more.
- If necessary, tactfully remind the birthday child in advance that she will not be the winner of every game.
- Engage one helper for every six children.
- If the party has a theme, adapt the names of the games accordingly.
- Write out the order of games (including all 'props' needed) and give each helper a copy.
- For a mixed age group, plan an activity/toy corner for very young children under the supervision of an adult or responsible teenager.
- Collect all the props needed for the games and store them in a convenient place.
- Clear all breakables from the games room.
- Make available an old blanket or other cloth to protect carpet or floor during messy games.
- Familiarise yourself with the games' rules and learn the words of any action song or circle game by heart.
- Prepare any treasure hunt trail and prepare the clues.
- If there are going to be treats or prizes awarded, prepare containers tagged with each child's name, to care for such trophies.

Prizes

- Parties are about having fun with your friends but if prizes become too important feelings of jealousy, rejection and unhappiness can easily arise. Children have plenty of opportunities to experience and cope with such feelings in the hurly-burly of daily life without having them mar an occasion which had promised so much enjoyment. Play down or eliminate individual prizes for the under-sevens, and keep prizes modest for older children (see pages 50–51).
- Where possible, award group prizes for sharing, or an equal prize for winner and runner-up in a game. For team games, both sides can be rewarded with a dip into a basket of popcorn or other tasty nibbles.
- If prizes are to be awarded, ensure that every child goes home with some sort of trophy; keep in mind that prizes can also be given for the most skilful/graceful/original/entertaining way of playing the game.
- Avoid offering a choice of prize as many children find this too stressful and want to change their minds later. Instead, slip the appropriate prize into a 'treasure chest' (a decorative box) and then present it each time for the winner to open.

On the day

- Remember to hide any 'treasure' needed for treasure hunt or surprise trail.
- Keep games short i.e. five minutes for the under-fives, increasing to ten minutes for eight-year-olds. Repeat a game only once, *if* the majority beg for it. Abandon any game which is causing children confusion or unhappiness.
- Start the next game promptly to avoid any waiting around which makes children tired and disagreeable.
- Explain any rules very clearly and slowly, making sure that they are understood.
- Do not press any child to join in if she appears to be more comfortable as an observer.
- Discreetly manipulating a party game in order to allow each guest her own 'winning moment' is not a mortal sin.
- Younger children who cannot understand the games may, nevertheless, like to join in and imitate. Remove them to the toy corner only if they actually disrupt the game or are likely to get hurt.
- If one child's bossiness or boisterousness affects the social harmony, try appointing her to a responsible role e.g. refereeing a game, dealing with props, handing out snacks.
- Allow the birthday child to start off as many of the games as possible. She might also like to present the prizes.
- If a sibling shows signs of jealousy, take an opportunity to remind her of her next birthday and ask her to think about which games she would like to play. Follow it up later that evening or the next day.

To make teams

For two teams: ask the children to stand in a circle and number them 1,2,3,4,5 etc. Even numbers make one team, odd numbers make the other. For three or more teams: number the circle 1,2,3, 1,2,3, or 1,2,3,4, 1,2,3,4, or 1,2,3,4,5, 1,2,3,4,5, and so on. Children with the same number make a team.

A tasty way to choose teams for a game following the birthday meal: colour pieces of white marzipan red or green with food colouring and hide them inside croissants or covered tarts. Those who find red marzipan in their tart make up the red team, the others join the green team.

Music

Many games demand some kind of musical accompaniment. While recorded music appears an easy option, this does have the tendency to lower concentration levels and encourage unfocused behaviour. Some kind of live music will bring a calmer atmosphere to a party: younger children will play happily to an adult singing a nursery song or beating a rhythm on a tambourine. If there is an older child who can play simple tunes fairly confidently on an instrument, then all the better. She will gain the admiration of the company and could be given a prize at the end of the party.

> For a simple dance-game nothing beats The Muffin Man. Movement is the grand secret of entertaining children.
>
> Advice on 'Juvenile Parties'
> from *Jack's Reference Book,* 1915

Games for age one

No organised games but provide rugs, cushions, soft dolls, light rattles, small building bricks etc. Young siblings or guests may enjoy singing a birthday song (see pages 174–180) while moving in a circle around the birthday baby, who is held in the arms of a parent.

Games for age two

No organised games but free play with toys. (Remember that a two-year-old has not yet learned to play socially or share toys.) However, most will enjoy playing *Ring-a-ring-a-roses* or other simple circle songs. A sandbox, well-supervised paddling-pool or pull-along toys will keep them occupied outdoors.

Ring-a-ring-a-roses

> Ring-a-ring-a-roses,
> A pocketful of posies,
> A-tishoo! A-tishoo!
> We all fall down.

This traditional rhyme has a single verse, but try one of these as second verse to help you back on your feet:

> A-tishoo over the mountains,
> A-tishoo over the sea,
> A-tishoo over the chimney pots
> And up jump we!

> Chickens in the barnyard,
> Fishes in the sea,
> We all jump up with a
> One, two, three!

Games for age three

Simple games based on imitation will be popular: circle games, action songs or rhymes, or follow-my-leader, (peg sheets / blankets close together on a line outside and weave the children in and out). Most of these could be repeated at least once.

Free play with dolls and dressing-up is fun but do not expect this age group to be good at sharing their toys. (For this reason it may be practical to keep the birthday child's favourite toys out of sight.) Have some picture books available and a table prepared for activities such as colouring, modelling dough, cutting and gluing; supervise the activity but intervene only when needed.

Outdoor activities could include sand and water play, a game of catch with a large, light ball, or bubble blowing, where each child has a loop but an adult holds the jar of bubble mixture.

Making houses or tunnels with cloth and pegs is also appealing but supply muslin cloths (see page 211) or sheets of a light colour as most three-year-olds prefer not to be in a dark space, (nor do they like to be blindfolded in games).

Other suitable games:
Ring-a-ring-a-roses

Here we go round the mulberry bush

ENGLISH TRADITIONAL

Here we go round the mul- berry bush, the mul- berry
bush, the mul- berry bush. Here we go round the
mul- berry bush, on a cold and fros- ty mor- ning.

Chorus:
(Children and adult(s) hold hands and dance
in a circle)

> Here we go round the mulberry bush,
> The mulberry bush, the mulberry bush,
> Here we go round the mulberry bush,
> On a cold and frosty morning.

Verses:
(Adult(s) mime the action, children copy –
or perhaps prefer to watch)

> This is the way we wash our face,
> Wash our face, wash our face,
> This is the way we wash our face,
> On a cold and frosty morning.
>
> This is the way we wash our hands...
> This is the way we clean our teeth...
> This is the way we brush our hair...
> This is the way we eat our bread...
> This is the way we have our rest...
>
> (and so on)

Games for age four

The first phase of a four-year-old's party could be filled with 'let's pretend' free play. So have dressing-up clothes available, together with light cloths and pegs for houses, 'cooking' equipment, dolls and trucks. Prepare an activity table as well, with wax crayons, paper, glue, scissors etc. Plan a few non-competitive games with simple rules. Circle games and action songs or rhymes are very popular.

It is often the case that the receiving and opening of birthday gifts is a hurried and confused affair taking place just inside the front door. *Spin a bottle* (see below) is a good game to start with as it makes space for each gift to be acknowledged and admired by all. If the adult mentions each child's name once or twice during the game it will ease the social blend.

Suitable game from previous pages:
Here we go round the mulberry bush, page 71

Toad in the hole

Cut the top flaps from a large cardboard box and place the opening on the floor. Cut a hole (radius 10.5cm) in the side of the box. Decorate the box with crêpe paper. Each child stands in turn at a measured distance from the box and is given three 'toads' (lightweight balls). The task is to see how many toads can be helped to jump into the hole.

Hide and seek

One child hides, the others search. The finder hides for the next game.

Hunt the slipper

An everyday item is hidden and searched for. The finder hides the item for the next game.

Pat the pan

One child is blindfolded and given a wooden cooking spoon. The others make a circle around her at a distance of approximately 1.5–2 metres. A metal basin or cooking pot that will sit comfortably upside down on the floor is quietly placed somewhere in the circle with a small present hidden beneath it. The blind child's task is to move around, tapping the ground with the spoon until it strikes the pan and the prize is won. Younger players might be allowed to lift the blindfold occasionally, and help can also be given by calling 'warm' or 'cold'.

Spin a bottle

Collect the birthday gifts, unopened, in a large basket as the guests arrive. When everyone is present, the children sit in a circle on the floor. Place an empty glass bottle on its side in the middle of the circle and spin it. When it stops turning, the child to whom the neck of the bottle points may offer the birthday child her gift to unwrap.

Adam he had seven sons

A- dam he had seven sons, seven sons had he, they

would not eat, they would not drink, but they all walked just like

me, all walked just like me.

Adam he had seven sons

Follow-my-leader games are always popular with this age group. The children either walk in a circle together with the adult, or follow the adult in single file weaving through the house, garden or park.

As the text indicates, the adult chooses different ways of walking for the children to copy: skipping, long strides, tip-toe, stamping, hopping, hands-on-head, and so on. The new way of walking would begin at the point in the music indicated by *.

Ma and Pa's old clothes

Prepare an item of adult clothing for each child playing, (half women's clothes, half men's clothes). Accessories such as clip-on earrings or a rucksack could also be included.

Divide the children into Ma's team and Pa's team. Place the clothes neatly in two piles near each other and at a distance from the teams. Each child must run to the appropriate pile and put on one item of clothing.

Only when they have finished dressing (i.e. buttons and zips fastened and so on) may they run back to their team and release the next player. The first team to finish the task is the winner.

Simple treasure hunt

Choose similar 'treasures' for each child, or choose two of the same treasures for each pair of children. These could include: small pack of wax crayons/chalks, glitter-glue pen, small novelty soaps, hair accessories, sheet of stickers, pretty shells. Wrap two treasures in each parcel, reserving a piece of the wrapping paper. Stow the parcel in its hiding place, ensuring that it is only partially concealed. Give each pair of children a piece of wrapping paper from 'their' treasure, explaining that they may only touch the parcel if their paper is a true match. (Select boldly differing wrappers.)

Surprise trail

(an imaginative follow-my-leader obstacle course)

Note: Bells and small items are not suitable for children under 3.

The children walk behind a leading adult. First they are giants taking giant steps towards a bench. Then they are as small as mice and crawl beneath the bench to nibble some raisins. Who can manage this without touching the bench?

Moving on they become gnomes, carrying pretend sacks on their backs. Digging in the sandbox, they each find a 'treasure' (perhaps a shell or a crystal).

Next they skip to the banks of a stream (a blue cloth) to catch a ball thrown by the adult from the far side; they throw it back and hop across the stream as little croaking frogs. If they can each now attempt a somersault they receive a gold star on their forehead.

Transformed into butterflies, they make their way – arms flapping – to a place where they blow soap bubbles. Maybe one of the bubbles leads the way to a magic bush where golden bells grow on coloured ribbons, and maybe there are just enough bells for each child to pick one...

Tip: Many variations on this idea are possible, also for indoors.

Games for ages five to six

Ring games are still popular for this age group and, in addition, they really enjoy organised games. Their social skills are developing and most will cope with very simple team games. Obstacle courses can now become more demanding: walk a narrow plank road (on the ground), hop or hobble in a sack, carry a tablespoon of water, and so on.

Let their achievement be sufficient reward and allow any player to repeat a turn to 'get it right'. Plan for six or seven games. Children over five years need to know everyone's name, so a naming game is useful.

Suitable games from previous pages:

Naming game

All stand in a circle with an adult. The child on the right of the adult is encouraged to say: 'My name is …, and I would like X to stand by me'. Then child X and adult exchange places. It is the turn of the child now on the right of the adult to say: 'My name is …' etc. The adult and another child exchange places and so on until each name has been spoken enough times.

Animals in the cave

Spread out an old bed sheet or other large cloth on the floor. Give each pair of children the name of an animal (include a helper if necessary to keep the numbers even). Split up the pairs and space the children evenly around the sheet. Ask them to hold the edge of the cloth firmly with both hands.

Practise making a 'cave' (raising the sheet to billow in the air) a few times. Then call out the name of an animal. The two children must run through the cave to swap places before the cave collapses.

Any child caught by the sheet must find her place as best she can.

Sardines

One child hides, the others search. Anyone finding the child joins her (quietly and secretly) in the hiding place. The first (or perhaps the last) child to discover the hidden one becomes the next to hide.

Pass the parcel

A present (individual or for sharing) is wrapped in many layers of gift-wrap, each layer tied with ribbon or yarn. Hide a surprise between each layer e.g. a tiny 'treasure', a few nuts or raisins, a piece of candy. Include more than enough layers to enable each child to experience at least one surprise.

The parcel is passed around the circle to the sound of music, singing, clapping or tambourine. Each time the accompaniment ceases, the player who is holding the parcel may unwrap one layer.

Ring dances

Ring dances have been developed by many social and tribal groups in the past to strengthen the solidarity of the community. The form of the ring has an almost talismanic mystique as something that cannot or should not be broken, (hence the widespread use of rings in marriage ceremonies).

Among traditional ring games are some that feature one player on the outside of the ring who must pursue and try to catch anyone leaving the ring. Some sources feel that these games are a relic of rituals enacted in ancient times to portray the struggle between good and evil. We have not included this type of ring game because for a birthday to be a success most people agree that the children need to be kept in 'good spirits'!

Making the birthday cake

WORDS AND ACTIONS: SALLY SCHWEIZER   SONG FROM RUSSIA

A To- day it is our (name)'s birthday, let us make him a birthday cake.
                                                        her

B Oh but look how thin it is.   Oh but see how small it is.
       Oh but look how wide it is.   Oh but see how tall it is.

C Birthday cake,   Birthday cake,   Tell us who you wish to take.

D (Spoken) Oh, I like you all the best, but our (name of chosen child) more than best.

Instructions:

A: Birthday child in the centre as the 'cake'. Others make a circle and move to the left.

B: Standing still but making appropriate gestures. e.g. palms together, hands to floor, hands out wide, stretch up high.

C: Stretch arms towards birthday child.

The birthday child fetches the chosen friend.

Spoken by all the children:

D: 'Oh, I like you all the best, but our (name of child chosen by Birthday child) more than best.'

The two children stay in the middle of the circle as the whole song with all the actions is repeated. At D each of them fetches someone. Gradually the 'cake' gets bigger and circle smaller until all are in the birthday cake and all dance.

Games for ages seven to nine

Most seven-year-olds will enjoy energetic team games, relay races, games of fantasy and any game which involves the unravelling of a mystery. A treasure hunt now means following a trail of picture clues or riddles. *Hunt the slipper* leads on to *Hunt the thimble* and the mysterious difficulty of perceiving the obvious. Unravelling a tangle of strings (see below) makes a perfect party opener.

Some individual prizes are appropriate, also prizes for gracefulness, originality, good humour etc. Group prizes could be given to the winning *and* the losing team. Plan for up to ten games and move quickly from one game to the next.

Suitable games from previous pages:
Spin a bottle, page 72
Toad in the hole, page 72
Ma and Pa's old clothes, page 73
Naming game, page 75
Animals in the cave, page 75
Sardines, page 75
Pass the parcel, page 75

Tangle of string

This is useful as an introductory game because the children have to deal with one another at close quarters.

Prepare a string for each partygoer. The string should be 10 metres long, or longer. Use felt-tip pens to mark one end of each string clearly in a different colour. Tie these ends to a chair leg so that they are not lost.

Then create a glorious tangle of strings! If the strings are long enough one could lead them all over the house tying up door handles, furniture, banister rails and so on.

Optional: Tie a small gift or treasure-hunt clue to the far end of the string.

The coloured ends of the string are untied in readiness for the game and each child makes her choice of colour. All strings will need to be wound into balls as the untangling proceeds.

Variation A: Cut only half as many strings as there are children at the party. Tie one end of each string to a chair by the entrance of the games room. Create a tangled web across the room and around the furniture and lead the other ends of string back out of the room and tie them also to the chair. Invite each guest to untie an end for herself and to wind up the string as she goes. As the web is unravelled they will discover someone at the other end who can partner them in the next game, e.g. *Take your partners,* (see page 86)

Variation B: The final end of the string could be tied to a pillowcase containing items for dressing-up. A new game would then ensue in which each child takes on a character in a fairy-tale and follows the action as it is narrated (see pages 181–182).

Hunt the thimble

One person places a thimble where it is not actually hidden, but camouflaged or in a place where no one would think of looking e.g. among a pile of cutlery, on an adult's finger or head, or sitting on the flower bud of a sturdy plant.

I-spy

An adult thinks of an object in the room and says: 'I spy with my little eye, something the colour of... (e.g. yellow).' The first child to guess correctly may choose the next mystery object.

Older children may like to play this game with letters e.g. 'I spy with my little eye, something beginning with… (e.g. W for window).'

Picture treasure hunt

Children hunt in pairs and are given a colour to follow. The clues on their trail are pictures on a card of the appropriate colour. Each picture indicates the hiding place of the next clue. The prize is shared between the pair. (Each pair of children follow a trail that could be slightly different or completely different from the others.)

Variation: Nine year-olds may enjoy a trail of riddles instead of pictures, e.g. 'Very near a pretty blue, you will find a useful clue.' This might lead to a flower, a sweater or a ball as the marker of a further clue.

Ball tunnels

Two teams of 6-8 people stand in a queue with legs wide apart to make a tunnel. Each team has a ball which must be rolled back through the tunnel to the last person who will pick it up and run to the front of the queue. The winning team is the first to return their original leader to the front with the ball.

Potato race

Divide the children into two equal teams. Two baskets, each containing about 2kg of washed potatoes, stand on one side. On the other side, about 20 steps away, there are two empty baskets.

One player from each team must carry the total content of a basket (using their hands only) to the waiting empty basket. Any dropped potatoes must be picked up before proceeding further.

A point is awarded to the team whose player first achieves the task. The next two players repeat the process, and so on until each player has had a go. The team with the most points wins.

Potato polo

Knot a piece of string very tightly around a potato. Attach it to the waist of a player so that the potato hangs behind her just above floor level. Do this for every player. Stand players on a starting line and place a sugar cube or small building block on the floor behind them. Who will be the first to move the cube over the finishing line by hitting it with the potato?

This game is best played on a smooth surface. Alternatively, make this a team game; the winning team is the one which gets all their cubes over the finishing line first.

Flip the kipper

Prepare in advance a fish shape (at least 18cm long) for each child, cut from medium-weight paper. Decorate the fish individually, or invite the children to colour their own at the party. The race begins as the children fan their fish from starting line to finishing post with the help of a folded newspaper.

This could become a relay race: The first player fans her fish from A to B, then runs back to hand the newspaper to the second player, who fans the fish from B to A. Play continues until each member of the team has had a go. The first team to complete wins.

Dragon race

Organise teams of five or more children and line them up behind a starting mark. Every player kneels and takes hold of the ankles of the child in front. This makes a 'dragon' and the leader is the 'head'.

At a signal the race begins. Any dragon which disintegrates on the way must stop for the count of five. The 'head' may roar to increase the dragon's speed. The winning beast is the first one to pass the finishing post still intact.

Dunking the donkey's tail

This game offers the spectators a little merriment.

Tie a pencil to one end of a string (approx. 1.4m long). Tie the other end around the waist of each player so that the pencil becomes the end of a donkey's tail hanging down to knee height. Three wide-necked glass bottles each approx. 18cm tall are placed on the floor. The three 'donkeys' must manoeuvre their tails into the bottle without using their hands. The first one to succeed wins.

To make this a relay race, have one 'donkey' and one bottle for each team. As soon as a tail has been dunked in the bottle, that donkey may return to their team and tie the tail on the next player who then becomes the donkey. Play continues until one team wins.

Musical folds

Each player is given a page of a newspaper. Music is played while everyone dances. When the music stops, the players must fold their paper in half and stand on it. Then the dancing continues. At the next pause the paper is folded in half again, and so on. Standing on it becomes increasingly difficult. Anyone stepping off their paper during the pause leaves the game.

King's treasure

The children make a circle around a 'king' (or 'queen') who sits blindfolded and very still on a throne (wooden chair) holding his sceptre (a folded newspaper) in one hand. The children take it in turns to be 'thief'.

The thief tries to get hold of the treasure (a wooden box containing two marbles) which lies beneath the chair. If the king hears the thief he is allowed one swipe with his sceptre. If he touches the thief then she must return to her place and allow the player on her left to be thief. If the thief manages to evade the swipe and steal the treasure, then she becomes queen (or king) and the old king joins the circle. The game finishes when everyone has had a turn as thief or king.

Tip: To make the thieving easier, remove the marbles from the box.

Catch the cat

All players but the 'cat' are blindfolded. The cat moves about the room ringing a small bell. The others, guided by the sound, try to catch her. The player who succeeds in doing so exchanges her blindfold for the bell.

Chocolate game

Players sit in a circle on the floor or at a table. A gift-wrapped bar of chocolate, a knife and fork, a hat, scarf and gloves are placed before them. Each player takes a turn throwing a die or dice. The first person to throw a six puts on all the garments and begins to open up and eat the chocolate, *one square at a time*, using knife and fork *only*.

The other players continue without pause to throw the dice. When another six comes up the garments and cutlery must be surrendered immediately to the new player.

The object of the game is to eat as much chocolate as possible before the next six is thrown. A player may choose to cut one square at a time from the bar and place it in a bowl (using knife and fork only) for later consumption or exchange for a preferred delicacy.

The piñata

The piñata is a popular tradition in Latin America, and could be used as a grand finale to the games. It is best played outdoors unless sufficient steps are taken to protect the furnishings in the home from damage.

Traditionally, the piñata is made in the form of an animal but a well-decorated round form is both functional and festive. Make it at least one week before the party.

Hang the piñata from a branch of a tree some way out of the reach of the birthday child. Give her a stick or a length of wood that is fairly strong and long enough to reach the piñata.

The birthday girl is then blindfolded and has to try and hit the piñata hard enough and often enough to cause it to break and shed its contents on the ground or into the hands of the other children. Some say the children keep what they manage to catch and the rest is shared out; some say it should be a free-for-all.

A less boisterous way of opening the piñata (more suited to indoor parties) is to use the option of a trapdoor which can be opened by pulling on a ribbon. This method enables the piñata to be used again in the future.

You will need: (for a piñata original)
Large balloon
Paste (made from 1 cup white flour and 1
   cup water)
Newspaper
Crêpe paper, approx. 1m square
15 crêpe paper streamers in 3 different
   colours, approx 2.5cm x 60cm each
String, scissors and glue

For piñata with trapdoor, add:
Pencil, glue and craft knife
Circle of tissue paper 14cm diam.
Large darning needle
Narrow ribbon, 1 metre length
Large button and bead or small bell
Sweets, nuts, tiny toys or novelties

Blow up balloon and knot string around its neck. Hang balloon from hook or line to give access from all sides while working.

Tear newspaper into strips (approx 12cm x 6cm) and soak them in paste. Cover balloon with strips (overlapping by approx. 1cm) but leave a small opening at the top. Allow 24 hours drying time.

Repeat this procedure twice more, using strips of crêpe paper. Allow to dry thoroughly. Pierce balloon and remove. Use scissors to enlarge top opening to approximately 14cm diam.

Decorate piñata by gluing streamers to inside of top edge. Overlap them to strengthen rim. Pierce rim in two places (directly opposite each other) and attach two lengths of string for hanging.

Fill with sweets and/or novelties.

For piñata with trapdoor

Draw a circle (12cm diam.) on base of piñata and cut it out carefully with craft knife. This will be the trapdoor.

Glue tissue-paper circle to inside of door so that paper overlaps edge evenly.

Thread darning needle with ribbon and take it through centre of door from outside to inside.

Thread on button and return needle through door so that button is lying flat, as shown above. Attach bead or bell to the two ends of ribbon.

Apply glue to inside edge of trapdoor hole.

Carefully push trapdoor into the piñata's cavity and withdraw it again gently allowing tissue paper to adhere to inside edge, thus making trapdoor once again an integral part of piñata.

Decorate and finish piñata as described above.

Blind man's buff : The *blind man* is chosen by lot, such as drawing the shortest broomstraw from a bundle held by the chest. He is blindfolded and led to the centre of the room.

The host says: 'How many cows has your father got?' The *blind man* answers: 'Three!' 'Then turn around three times, and catch you may.'

The game then is to avoid being caught by the *blind man.* A good deal of fun is made by touching him on the head, arms, back, legs etc. As soon as one is caught, that one becomes the *blind man.* This game can also be played in the gardens and fields.

Dr. A.W. Chase:
Recipes or information for Everybody 1874 (U.S.A.)

Games for ages ten to twelve

Children of this age are developing strong individual tastes which are, nevertheless, significantly influenced by peer pressure. Their choice of games for the party (indeed, the whole concept of the party) may undergo a radical change. If games are wanted, then word games, memory games, games of skill and quizzes are popular.

Suitable games from previous pages:
Spin a bottle, page 72
Chocolate game, page 80
Piñata, pages 80–81

Pass the parcel with quiz and forfeits

(see page 75)
Played with a general knowledge quiz question between each layer. If the player fails to answer correctly, then apply a forfeit, e.g. reciting Ring-a-ring-a-roses backwards, or standing on left foot with right foot on left knee and both hands high in the air for the count of ten.

Tangle of string

(see page 77)
Here the trophy at the end of the string is the first clue to a fairly complicated treasure hunt (see page 83).

Human knot

One person leaves the group and everyone else stands in a circle holding hands. By twisting, turning and stepping, the circle ties itself into a complicated knot without releasing hands. The person outside is invited to untangle the knot using spoken instructions only.

Charades

Two players go out of the room. They choose a word with two parts e.g. cup-board, win-dow, wood-worm. They return to the room and each mimes one part of the word. (The syllable may be used phonetically e.g. 'board' could be mimed 'bored', 'doe' could become 'dough'.) The audience has to guess the word. If they fail to guess, the players then mime the whole word.

Art gallery

Prepare a photocopied sheet for each player bearing on it a *very simple* shape or scribble. The players have to turn the shape/scribble into a picture without obliterating the original line. Supply a variety of art materials. The pictures are displayed and judged, and prizes are awarded for beauty, originality and technique.

Funny fables

An adult chooses a short but well-known fable or fairy story and writes it out in advance leaving gaps for adjectives.

The players sit in a circle and take turns to suggest an adjective (of any kind) which the adult then writes into the story. The completed story is then read out. (The children at the party would be even more delighted if a story was invented to include *them* as main characters.)

Word search

One player leaves the room. The others agree on a word. The player is called in and asks questions in turn to each of the others who must bring into their answers the word previously agreed upon. The hidden word has to be guessed by the questioner.

Fashion parade

One player (the judge) stands and looks carefully at the others as they file past, taking note of what they are wearing. Then the 'fashion models' go out of the room and, in three minutes, each of them exchange one item of clothing. They return to the room and file past the judge again. If the judge guesses which child has given away which item of clothing, the judge receives one point. If, in addition, the judge guesses the name of the child with whom the item was exchanged they receive a further point. If the guess is incorrect, then the judge loses a point which is given instead to the child who was wrongly named. The winner is the player with the most points. This game needs an adult to keep a scorecard.

Blind man's breakfast

Nobody wins in this game but it is fun for those watching. Two people, both blindfolded, sit opposite each other and are both given a spoon and a bowl of popcorn (or cooked spaghetti or muesli for a *very* messy game). They are to feed each other... (Use large towels to protect clothing if necessary, and have a mirror handy.)

I went to town

One player thinks of an article that can be bought in a shop. She says: 'I went to town and I bought something...' and then she gives one clue e.g. rectangular/white/tiny/expensive. The other players ask questions but they may only be answered with 'Yes' and 'No'. The one who first guesses correctly thinks of the next article.

Four-ball dribble relay

Each team stands behind a starting line and is given four tennis balls. The first players dribble all the balls together to a marked line. They leave the balls just over the line and run to the back of their team, touching a second player as they pass. The second player then collects the balls, dribbling them back to the team for the third player to take over, and so on until the race is won.

Problem relay

Each member of the team must get herself to a marker and back while holding a balloon between her knees and a marble in a spoon between her teeth. The first team to complete the task wins.

Treasure hunt with tasks

This hunt is an outdoor game suitable for a small garden or park. It could also be played in a larger space or adapted for indoors. If notes are kept of the names of children and their team colour, clues, trail etc. then the hunt could be adjusted for a future occasion without too much difficulty.

Procedure:
Decide on the trail, clues and tasks for each pair of children at the party. Assign a different team colour to each pair.

Write clues very clearly, on paper of the team colour, and number them boldly.

Place clues 2–5 in separate plastic 'zip' bags for protection and add a stone to each bag to prevent it blowing away.

Lay the trails one by one, checking that all markers and clues are in stable positions and will not be obscured.

Hide the treasure (see page 68) where it is visible yet not obvious enough to be spotted during the hunt.

Choose the teams by inviting the birthday child to draw names from a hat. The first name to be drawn will partner the birthday child and the following two names will make the next team etc.

Give each team a plastic bag containing a few sheets of plain paper and a crayon or felt tip pen.

Define the area boundaries of the hunt and explain the rules to the players. Check that these are understood.

Tell the teams which adult is 'in charge'.

Assemble the teams at the starting point and give them their first clues. (Keep a compass handy.)

Check that the adult in charge knows their task (see clues below) and has clue 6 and 7 for each team.

Rules:

Stay within the hunt boundaries at all times.

Keep the correct number order when picking up clues.

Stay with your partner at all times.

Place clues one by one in your 'team bag', together with the results of your task, before looking for the next clue.

Give this bag to the adult in charge to check before getting your final clue. You will be sent back to repeat a task if it has not been carried out properly.

Do not touch any clue that is not of your team colour.

Anyone not observing the rules will be out of the game for three minutes.

Tips:

Prepare the whole scheme *well in advance*.

Allow up to two hours to lay the trail.

Engage a helper as trouble-shooter and another to keep a check on the visibility of markers and clues.

Choose paper streamers that do not lose colour when wet.

Keep the different coloured markers and clues as separate as possible.

Below are examples of a set of six clues. The framework of these could be used for a hunt with five teams. For example, clue 1 would give each team a different direction to head for at the start and therefore a different object to draw when they pick up clue 2.

As long as the different streamers and different parcels are kept well apart the teams will not rub up against each other too much.

Clue 1

Walk a straight line to the North (South, East, West, Northeast) and you will find the next clue.

Clue 2

Draw a picture of a leaf of this tree/bush/plant (or a picture of this gate/shed door/window…)

To find clue 3 look for a red/blue/green/yellow/purple streamer.

Clue 3

Tear the streamer into 16 pieces all the same length.

To find clue 4 look for a number four (twigs laid out or pushed into the soil in the form of the Roman numeral IV) near the…

Clue 4

Gather four different coloured stones / leaves /
petals / twigs / objects from the ground.
To find clue 5 look for a red / blue / green /
yellow / purple parcel hanging from a tree /
bush. (The parcel could include a morsel of
refreshment.)

Clue 5

Without speaking, multiply the number of
candles on the birthday child's cake by 5;
add 5; divide by 5; subtract 5. Take the
answer to the adult in charge and they will
give you clue 6.

Clue 6

Sit under or on a certain tree / bush / wall /
seat / piece of grass and write down twelve
words you can make from the word
TREASURE. Take these to the adult in
charge to check if they are correct. If you
have fulfilled all your tasks you will be given
the clue to the treasure!

(The treasure could be a communal treat of
some kind, shared only when all the teams
have completed their tasks. Alternatively,
each pair could receive a clue to their own
treasure in which case the treats should all be
fairly similar.)

Clue 7

This could be a riddle or a brainteaser; if the
treasure were hidden beneath a garden chair,
for example, the clue might be the following:

My first is in ice and also in cream
My second's in hedges but not in stream
My third is in armour and and and in hand
My fourth is in island but not in the sand
My last is in rowdy and roaring and rill
My whole is a place where I like to sit still
(Answer: CHAIR)

Alternatively, make the riddle out of five
questions with one-word answers. The initial
letter of each answer would spell the word
CHAIR.

Games for teenagers

Teenagers are very unpredictable with what
they want to happen at a party, but many
enjoy the horseplay that can arise from silly
games or even games designed for younger
children. The single gender party often
demanded by nine- to twelve-year-olds
begins to go out of fashion, and games where
couples make a team become more popular.

Suitable games from previous pages:
Chocolate game, page 80
Piñata, pages 80–81
Pass the parcel with quiz and forfeits,
    page 82
Tangle of string, page 82
Treasure hunt, page 83
Blind man's breakfast, see page 83
Four ball dribble relay, page 83
Problem relay, page 83

Who am I ?

This is a good introductory game for a
teenage party. A label bearing the name of a
famous person or fictional character is
attached to each guest's back as they arrive.
They must discover who they are by asking
questions. Only one question may be asked
at a time before moving to another person
for the next question. All answers must be
given in the form of 'Yes' or 'No'.

The names could be arranged as famous
couples: Adam and Eve, Jack and Jill,
Anthony and Cleopatra etc. When all the
names are discovered, perhaps *Take your
partners* could be the next game.

Take your partners

This game is best played outdoors or in a fairly large room. Players choose partners and stand side by side in a circle. One couple starts the game by crossing the circle together (e.g. they walk across holding hands), the next couple then crosses the circle, but in a different manner.

The couples must always touch each other while crossing and find ever more ingenious ways of getting from one side to the other as the game goes on. If the group is small then play could go round the circle two or three times. The game stops when ideas run out. The last couple to cross could be given a prize.

Hunt the matches

Hide a known quantity of matches separately around a room. Invite the guests to search for them. A prize goes to the one with the highest total. Hide at least twelve matches per guest. Set a time limit or keep the game going until the last match is found.

I remember Charlie

One of the party leaves the room. Everyone remaining is given paper and pencil and asked to describe the absent person. Make a check list of a dozen points – hair colour, eyes, jewellery, shoes, etc. Exchange lists for marking.

Top model

Organise teams of four or five and select one player from each team. At a signal, the others in the team dress the chosen player in as many of their clothes and accessories as are possible within three minutes. There are no dress rules, and shoes have been known to make a most becoming hat.

Prizes are awarded for the number of dress items received, attractiveness and originality.

Straw suckers

Two teams stand in separate rows, boys and girls alternating if possible. Each player has a drinking straw. A small piece of tissue paper is given to the first person in each row. They now have to suck the paper to the end of their straw and pass it to their neighbour's straw. No hands allowed on the tissue paper.

Musical poetry consequences

Distribute pencils and paper. Decide on a simple song that everyone knows, e.g. *Twinkle, twinkle little star.*

Players write a rhyming couplet at the top of the paper to fit the first two lines of the song, e.g. ' Isn't it a lovely day, All the children laugh and play'. Then the paper is folded forward, just enough to conceal the rhyme, and passed to the player on the left.

A further couplet is written, guided by the next phrase of the chosen song. The folding and passing of the paper continues until two or three verses are completed. Finally, the paper is passed to the person chosen to sing the final composition.

Mime relay

An adult is appointed game-master in advance and draws up a list of 20 familiar activities e.g. playing tennis, riding a motor-bike, tossing pancakes, eating spaghetti, conducting an orchestra, skiing etc.

The teams are placed out of earshot of each other and the game-master sits at an equal distance from each team. A member from one team is made referee for the other team and vice versa (or two adults fill this role). Each referee is given a copy of the secret list. Each team sends a player to the game-master who whispers the name of the first activity. The player returns and mimes the activity to the team.

At the correct guess a second player goes immediately to hear the second activity from the game-master. The first team to complete the list wins. If the actor speaks, then the referee must count steadily to thirty before play can resume.

Artists' relay

Played in a similar way to Mime Relay above but the game-master makes a list of 20 items e.g. cream tea, pizza, violin music, sweet dreams, car wash, supermarket, rubbish etc. The team member must make a drawing of the item instead of miming it, but no words may be written or spoken. Modelling clay could also be used instead of paper and pencils.

Telegrams

Someone repeatedly pushes a pin into the page of a newspaper to obtain several letters, e.g. MATBMS.

All the players have to compose an old-fashioned telegram using each letter to begin a word, e.g. 'Mother Arrives Tuesday Brings Manuscript Stop' The telegrams are read out and a prize goes to the most original.

(This game could be played a second time, attempting a reply to the winning entry of the previous game.)

Fill the sandwich

Choose a long word e.g. 'deliberately' and write it *vertically* once forwards (on the left of the paper) and once backwards (on the right of the paper) so that the horizontal lines will read:

d _____	y
e _____	l
l _____	e
i _____	t
b _____	a
e _____	r
r _____	e
a _____	b
t _____	i
e _____	l
l _____	e
y _____	d

The task for the players is to fill the gap with letters to make a word e.g. dairy, eternal, lie etc. When the first player fills all the gaps or when a time limit is reached, the words are read out. A point is awarded for every word completed plus an extra point if that word was not used by another player.

Alphabet hunt

(an outdoor game)
The guests form teams of two or three. Each team has a carrier bag, a pencil and a list of the letters of the alphabet. The task is to gather objects in the bag and write each down against the appropriate letter of the alphabet, e.g. 'leaf' against 'L'.

Set a time limit (say, five minutes for a frenzied game, longer for a more thoughtful one). When time is up, the teams gather and one reads out what they have for A.

If other teams have the same object they all score one. If a team has an object that no one else has they score two. The first team then moves to B, and so on. The objects must be shown each time.

The team that has gathered the most letters may have two extra points. The team with the most points wins.

Forty winks

If there are fifteen players, invite seven to sit in a circle of eight chairs. The other eight players stand as 'guards' behind each chair.

The guard behind the empty chair winks secretly at one of the seated players who then runs for the empty chair, unless she is held back by her guard. The guard must try to prevent the escape by placing both hands on the shoulders of her charge. If a guard allows an escape, then she must take up the winking.

Allow up to five minutes play before everyone changes places. (One guard must volunteer to stay on.)

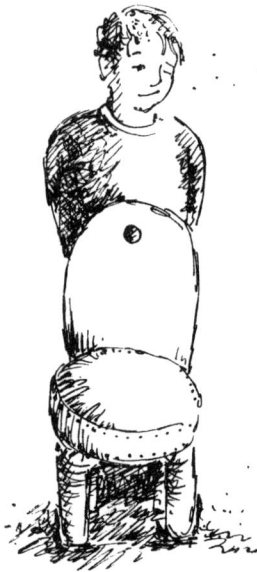

Games for adults and family parties

Any party which includes adult guests needs to be planned with certain things in mind:

- One cannot assume that adults enjoy playing games.
- Those adults who can enjoy playing games may draw the line at rolling around on the floor making animal noises, or running around the park trying to catch someone.
- Include a hint of the entertainment you have planned with the party invitation. That will give adequate warning to a 'game-phobic' who might wish to take evasive action.
- Some games are more suitable for gatherings of family and intimate friends than for company which includes people who are not so well known to each other. Choose the games with care and tact.
- Adults usually like to look their best for a social occasion. Make sure that the games respect this.
- When announcing a game, ask for volunteers to play. If the game is then repeated, open it up to include those who may wish to join.

An older person can often enjoy a walk down memory lane to revisit the games of her youth.

Guessing games, word games and memory games are also popular:

Who am I?

For a comfortable after-dinner version of this game (see page 85), use a self-adhesive label positioned on the forehead where it can be read by the whole company. Turn all mirrors to the wall.

Remember, remember

Place fifteen objects on a tray. Cover the tray with a cloth. Remove the cloth and allow the players to view the items for thirty seconds. Replace the cloth and ask players to write down the objects they remember. The longest correct list wins.

Lists

Allow the players three minutes to write as many e.g. flowers, famous people, film or book titles, things in the room, as they can beginning with a certain letter. Read out the names. For ten players, if ten have the word, score zero; if nine have the word, score one; if eight have the word, score two, and so on.

Spoon tap quiz

There are two teams, each with a captain who has a spoon and one player who keeps score. A player calls out the name of a town, (or flower, animal, bird etc.) beginning with A. The captain of that team begins to tap the spoon while counting to ten. The other team must name another town beginning with A before the count of ten. If two players call a name together, the opposing team may take the second name for themselves.
When a team cannot answer then they give one of their players to the other team, and play moves on to B.

General knowledge quiz

Arrange teams with 2–4 players. Present a question to team A. If they cannot answer, open it up to team B and then team C, and so on. Present the next question to team B and (if there are three teams), if B cannot answer then open it to team C and team A. The correct answer gains a point for the team.

After each round, present a series of three questions open to all players; the first correct answer gains a point but all wrong answers lose a point.

Desert island holiday

One player leaves the room. The others decide together who is to go on holiday. (This could be a very famous person, it could also be one of the players.) Each player thinks of an item which she would put in the boat *for that particular person.*

The absent player is called back to ask the others, one by one, to name the item they have chosen. The task for the questioner is to discover the name of the holidaymaker using the fewest possible clues.

Even adults can let their hair down sometimes and play silly games:

Spoon the spud

Place a potato and a dessert spoon on a coffee table. Allow each player a steady count of twenty to spoon up the potato without pushing it against anything or letting it fall off the edge of the table.

The gift mug

(for mature people only)
This game offers a chance to cultivate the Buddhist ethic of non-attachment. It is best played with a minimum of twelve people: it cannot be rushed but it offers a lot of fun to the uninhibited. It is not recommended for children or excessively well-mannered people.

You will need:
Small pieces of paper, one for each guest, numbered 1,2,3, etc. and folded twice
A hat out of which to draw the papers
One gift (enticingly wrapped) for each guest. (We suggest that every guest is asked to bring a wrapped gift with them: anything from a brooch to a banana. It helps the game if there are at least two really desirable gifts.)
Second set of paper slips, each bearing one written instruction and each folded twice. Examples of such instruction slips are given below at the relevant place in the game.

Display all the gifts on a table and ask each player to draw a number from the hat.
Whoever draws no.1 unwraps one parcel from the table.
The player who has drawn no.2 now has a choice: either to unwrap another gift or, if she likes the look of no.1's gift, she may take that item from no.1 player.
No.1 now has no gift, so he may choose another parcel and unwrap it.
Now it is the turn of player no.3 to select a parcel or relieve no.1 or no.2 of their gifts.

The player who has lost their gift can take a new present from the table, or from any other player *except* the player who has just 'robbed' them.
At least one transaction must take place before a robbed player can claim back her original gift.
No one may possess two gifts at the same time. So, as the game progresses, the players with the higher numbers have a wider selection of known gifts to choose from.
When the last gift is unwrapped then that player must draw an instruction slip from the hat and read it out loud.

Examples of possible instruction slips:

All pass a gift one place to the right
Everyone passes a gift three places to the left
If you are player number 6, exchange your gift with player number 3
Exchange gifts with a person of your choice
Exchange with someone who really needs your gift, making sure you give a faultless reason for this. Other players may not accept your reason and if after three attempts you fail to convince a majority then you must keep your gift
You are out of the game with your gift
Stay as you are
Exchange your gift with the person on your right or sing *Twinkle, twinkle little star* to the tune of *Happy birthday to you*

The instruction having been fulfilled, play continues clockwise and the next instruction is drawn and read out. In this way, all the instructions are followed one by one. The game is now at an end and some players at least, may be pleased with their prizes.

Invite some friends and play it – *it will soon become clear!*

Chapter 8

PARTY ACTIVITIES

Some of the pleasantest children's parties are these at which only a few guests are present and at such entertainments there may be a treasure hunt, a lucky tub, the entrance of a pony or very large dog drawing a little cart filled with presents which are distributed by some person appropriately garbed in fancy dress, or the entertainment provided may consist solely of games.

Certainly no one need fail to give their children the pleasure of entertaining because they cannot afford to give an elaborate party, for a gathering of about eight children of suitable age for tea, and progressive games for inexpensive prizes, seldom fails to be a success.

Lady Troubridge, *The Book of Etiquette*, 1931

A birthday party which includes a creative activity can be a rewarding and memorable event for a child; the whole party could even be arranged around such an activity.

Making things together breaks the ice at the beginning of a party, is a balance to exciting games and will give restful and concentrated moments before collection time. There is nothing so satisfying and so confidence-building as to hold up an object and say 'I made this!'

As with most things, the quality of the experience depends on the preparation that goes before, therefore we strongly recommend that maximum preparation is done in advance.

Preparation

- Prepare all patterns and cut them out for children who are too young to do this without supervision. Prepare one or two extra, in case some are spoiled accidentally.
- When gathering the necessary materials allow extra to cover breakage or spoiling.
- If there are more than three children under five years then prepare such things as threaded needles and knotted yarn.
- Check that there is enough equipment to go round (e.g. at least one pair of scissors for every two children) and enough table space.
- Have plenty of newspapers or cloths ready to protect work surfaces and floor.
- If the activity is messy, make a request on the invitation for old clothes to be worn or overalls to be brought.
- Whatever you plan for the children to make, always make it yourself first to check the instructions and grasp the whole process. Encourage your helpers to do likewise.

Engage one helper for every four children.

Bear in mind that the party could be an opportunity for a seasonal activity (see page 113).

Some items from the Gifts section (see pages 153–162) would also be suitable for a party activity.

On the day

- Gather all necessary materials and, if possible, lay them out on the work surface (cover them with a cloth) before the party begins.
- Demonstrate each step of the process slowly and clearly, making sure that each child has seen and understood.
- Give praise and encouragement at every stage.

- Label each piece of finished work with the maker's initials.
- One-to-one adult supervision is needed if a sharp blade or drill of any kind is used.
- The age range we have indicated is only a guide. Younger children may enjoy the activity if they are given extra help. Small groups (i.e. four or five children) may like the challenge of cutting and sanding wood e.g. the dowelling for the windflower (see page 100).

Activities for ages one to two

There is no need to plan a special activity for toddlers, a few toys, cushions and rugs to sit on will be adequate. Outdoor activities could include sand and water play, but make sure a paddling pool is well supervised.

Activities for ages three to four

Imitation is important for this age group and they will appreciate an adult joining in the activity with them. The four-year-old will engage purposefully in a task and will be delighted to take home the finished piece of work.

Watercolour painting

Prepare screw-top jars containing a teacupful of diluted artists' watercolour (test for strength). Choose two colours only: red and yellow, red and blue, or blue and yellow, (the three colours together will make brown).

Protect work surface if necessary.

Supply fairly large, soft brushes and a large sheet of damp painting paper, (run cold water over the paper, hold it vertically to drain, then lay it – without creasing – on a painting board, water resistant table or newspaper).

Chapter 8 Party activities

Have sponges or cloths at hand for mopping up, and allocate jars of paint for sharing between two or three children.

The end result of this activity is not important, the children will enjoy being free to experience the movement of flowing colour. Offer a new sheet when the paper is covered with colour.

Bread rolls

Prepare a standard bread dough using a mixture (1:3) of wholemeal and strong, white unbleached flour.

Place the dough to rise for the second time in a refrigerator about three hours prior to the activity. Bring dough to room temperature before giving it to children.

Protect children's clothing and see that they wash their hands. Allow each child a small handful of dough at a time to fashion into any shape.

Brush finished roll with egg beaten in a little milk and supply a choice of decoration e.g. sunflower, sesame or poppy seeds; currants, raisins or other chopped dried fruit; Demerara sugar or strips of marzipan.

Place on a baking sheet in the top of a hot oven (Gas mark 6, 200°C/400°F) for 15–20 minutes. The roll should be golden on top and sound hollow when tapped smartly on the base.

Coronets

Prepare a rectangle of plain, thin card, (approx. 55cm x 4cm) for each child.

Supply wax crayons and encourage them to cover the whole surface with colour.

Offer glitter glue or self-adhesive stars for further decoration.

Fit the crown around each child's head and use a stapler to connect the ends.

Alternatively, double the width of card, fold in two along its length, apply glue along one inside surface and insert pressed autumn leaves or fresh evergreen so that they project from the card. Maintain pressure until glue is dry.

Activities for ages five to six

This age group are busy developing their inner creativity and can be given every opportunity to use imagination and fantasy. Their coordination is advancing and they enjoy exercising their skills with scissors, sewing and construction.

Suitable activities from previous pages:
Watercolour painting, page 92
Bread rolls
Coronets

Dressing-up

Plan an activity around a dressing-up box. The contents need not be sophisticated costumes, for a motley collection of pieces of cloth, cast-off clothing, jewellery and scarves will allow children's imagination more scope. Try to include some shoes, hats, evening bags and interesting fabrics e.g. velvet, lace, brocade, feathers. Have safety pins, hair clips, ribbons and some face paints to hand.

Cake decorating

Buy or make cup cakes. Stir together sifted powdered sugar and a small amount of lemon juice and water to make a smooth but not-too-freely-flowing icing. Supply nuts, coloured sprinkles, chocolate chips, little jellybeans and other small things for decoration. Have aprons and damp cloths available.

Magic stew treasure hunt

Place a fairly large bowl or basin in an adequately large drawstring cloth bag.

Prepare a small cloth bag containing treasure e.g. chocolate sovereigns, polished stones, to be shared among the children. (This bag could be a circular piece of dark cloth gathered up around the treasure-trove and tied firmly with ribbon in a double-knotted bow. Slip one loop of this bow over the handle of the wooden spoon as illustrated.)

Insert the treasure bag with spoon into the basin within the large bag. Position the opening of the large bag directly above the basin and almost close the drawstring around the handle of the spoon.

The following words are an indication of what could be spoken by an adult or by a glove puppet:

> 'Hullo children, today it's John's birthday and so I have decided to make a Magic Stew – but I shall need special things to go in it. Will you find them for me? First I shall need a pretty shell... oh, thank you very much! Next I would like a little coloured ball... and now a small feather... Now a clothes peg.... And now I have to ask the girls to look for a safety pin... now the boys can bring me a petal from a white flower. Who hasn't found anything for me yet? Ah, Mariko, please would you bring me a very small stone?'

The items are dropped through the opening of the drawstring bag, or handed to the puppet who will drop them in. Every so often the spoon is ceremoniously stirred. When the last item is added the stirring grows to a climax as the spoon (with bag attached) is lifted through the drawstring, the magic is declared to have done its work and the treasure is shared out.

This treasure hunt can be played indoors or outdoors and the adult either places items in readiness or improvises with the small things they can see around them.

Pat-a-pom-pom

You will need:
Ten circles of tissue paper in different colours, 7.5cm diam. (see page 210)
Needle threaded with 35cm of sewing cotton, ends knotted together
Small bell, max. 1.5cm diam. with hanging loop
Length of elastic shirring thread, approx. 50cm

Note: Bells and small items are not suitable for children under three

Fold each circle of paper in quarters. Thread needle through each of five folded circles at approx. 2mm from the point.
Thread on the bell before taking needle through the other five folded circles.
Separate threads by the knot and pass needle between. Knot one end of elastic. Thread

94

needle through this knot to draw it tightly towards papers.

Secure thread with a few stitches. Make a loop at other end of elastic to slip over a child's right hand.

Open up folded papers to create pom-pom.

How many times in succession can the child pat the pom-pom with the right hand? For left-handed children, hang the pom-pom from the left hand.

Party hat

You will need:

Circle of stiff, coloured paper, 24cm radius

Eight streamers of crêpe paper, approx. 45cm x 2cm in two or more colours

Length of narrow elastic, approx. 40cm

Scissors, stapler, glue and large darning needle

Cut a quarter out of paper circle and discard. Overlap cut edges generously to create cone to fit child's head. Staple the two layers together near rim.

Insert end of one streamer between the two layers of paper, as close to point of hat as possible, and glue in place.

Glue next streamer immediately below or overlapping it. Continue until all streamers are attached to hat. Glue seam together firmly.

Pierce hat on opposite sides 1.5cm from the rim. Thread elastic through the holes from inside, knotting each end on outside of hat.

The hat could also be decorated with lengths of silk or dress net, or three tissue-paper pom-poms (see above) hanging from the point.

Bell-catcher

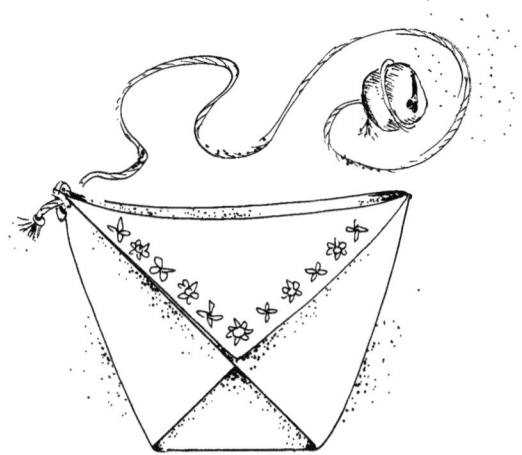

You will need:

Strong paper 25cm x 25cm

Length of string or fine cord approx. 60cm

Bell, approx. 2cm diam, with loop

Large darning needle

Optional: crayons, glitter glue

Fold paper in half diagonally.

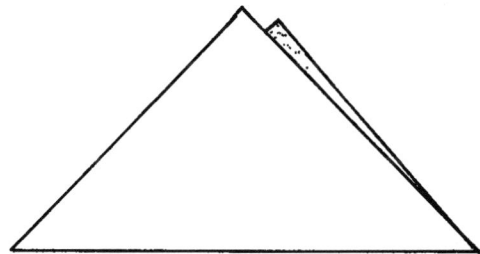

Fold each corner across as shown:

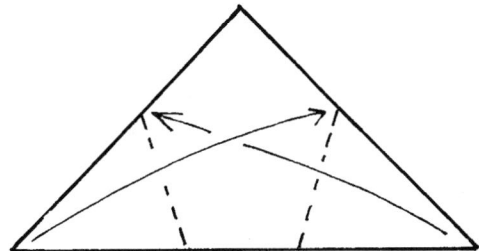

Fold down each triangle at the top as indicated, to create cup. Decorate cup as desired.

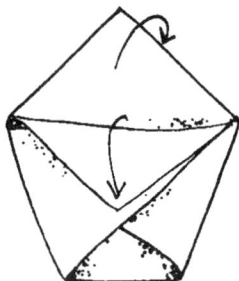

Thread needle with string (knotted at one end) and draw it through one corner of cup. Tie other end of string to bell.

The challenge is to swing the bell into the air and catch it with the cup.

Activities for ages seven to eight

Children at this stage can still enjoy dressing up and are capable of 'acting the part'. Their skills are ready for a challenge and they enjoy discovering how things work.

Suitable activities from previous pages:
Bread rolls, page 93
Coronets, page 93
Cake decorating, page 93
Pat-a-pom-pom, page 94
Party hat, page 95
Bell-catcher, page 95

Royal tea party

Begin with each guest making a crown (see page 26) or coronet (see page 93) in gold or silver card. Supply a variety of dressing-up clothes (including some rich fabrics), costume jewellery and safety pins.

Hide one toy ring for each child in a not-too-difficult place and organise a search after they have dressed up. When a ring is found, that child is out of the game, (the last child to find one may need some help). Scatter gold (chocolate) coins over the tea table and take tea in royal fashion…

Fairy tale play

Read the children a fairy tale that is not too long. Hide a bundle of dressing-up clothes (or even a single item e.g. a hat, shawl or coronet) for each child and organise a search. The clothes will indicate the character in a particular fairy tale e.g. Grimm's *The golden goose*. Then read the fairy tale again allowing the different characters to mime the action required.

A shorter story could be Tolstoy's retelling of one of the Russian tales *The bean seedling* or *The little house*. Use simple wraps or cloaks in appropriate colours for the animals and an adult's fur-fabric jacket for the bear.

Jet plane

You will need:
A 4 sheet of paper (21.1cm x 29.7cm)
Ruler and scissors
Materials to decorate

Fold sheet of paper in half lengthways to obtain a central crease.

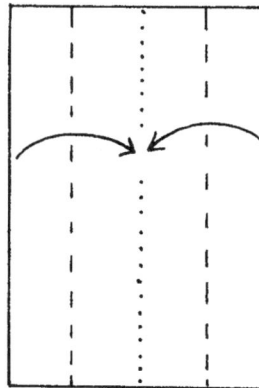

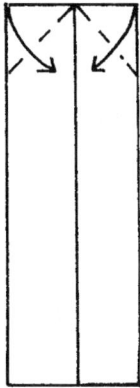

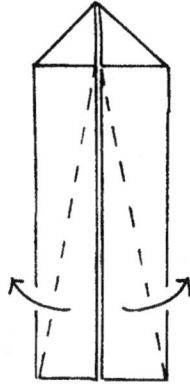

Colour the planes individually, and hold a
  sporting event to measure the furthest of
  five flights for each plane.

Flying butterfly

This butterfly is easy to make out of a cheap
paper napkin. It will flap its wings as the
cane is moved up and down.

You will need:
Paper napkin, single ply, in plain colour
Scraps of different coloured tissue paper
Glue and strong craft knife
Bamboo cane (available at a garden centre)
  approx. 35cm x 8mm diam.
Optional: 2 'stamens' for artificial flowers,
  to use as antennae (available in craft
  shops, some florists, and suppliers of cake
  decorations)

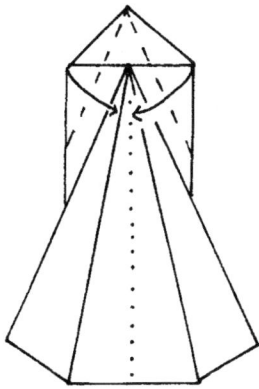

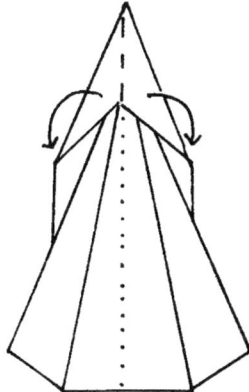

Unfold paper napkin and follow instructions
  for Butterfly (see pages 133–134) from ♦♦
  to ★★.
Cut circles of tissue paper (1cm diam.) in
  contrasting colours and glue to topside of
  wings.
Dip lower half of each stamen in glue and
  insert between 'nose' end of butterfly's
  body and underside of each wing.
Bend stamens outwards to right and left.
Your butterfly will now look like this:

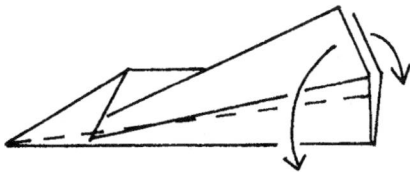

Lift wings into the horizontal and the jet
  plane is ready to fly.

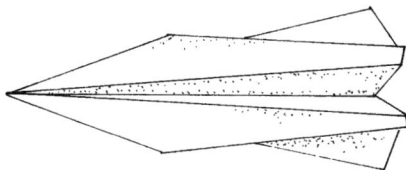

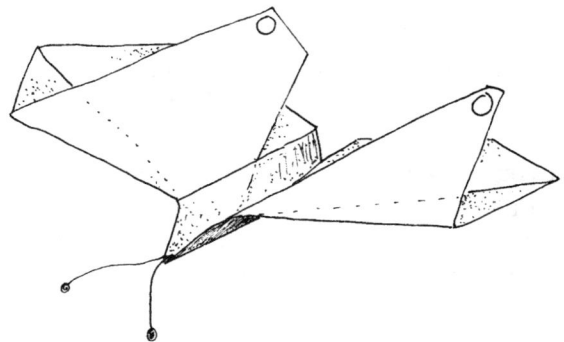

97

Cut a slit (approx. 1.5cm) in one end of cane and insert butterfly's body as shown:

Paper basket or box

Turn to page 170 (Seven gift boxes) and follow instructions to make a simple open box. Convert it to a basket by gluing on a strip of paper as a handle.

Alternatively, make a lidded box. Pre-fold and cut papers if a large number of children will be involved and remember to pencil the child's initials on the box base.

(Ensure that the box or basket contains a few goodies by the end of the party.)

If you think the children will appreciate a touch of mystery, line the baskets with dry moss, carded sheep's wool or tissue paper and place in a 'special' area of the house/garden for the house/garden fairy to fill them before take-home time.

Earth candle

You will need:
Wick for candle of large diameter
Twig approx. 30cm long
Small metal weight
Quantity of melted wax (see page 209)
Small trowel

Make hole in damp earth (in ground outside or in earth-filled clay flower pot). Judge size of hole carefully for there must be enough wax available to fill it, allowing for some wax to sink a little way into the walls. Press sides of hole to firm earth.

Cut length of wick at least 12cm longer than depth of hole. Tie an end of wick to metal weight and other end to middle of twig.

Position twig across hole so that weight lies centrally at bottom and wick is vertical. If necessary, turn twig to take up slack.

Pour melted wax carefully into hole. When surface of wax has set, cut wick to 1cm and remove twig.

Snappy dragon

This fearsome dragon is made from stiff paper and can be used for the party game below. If each child has a different coloured paper it will make their dragon easier to identify.

You will need:
Sheet of paper 20cm x 20cm
Scissors
Crayon, felt-tip or pencil in dark colour

Fold paper to create fold **a-b**. Open out.

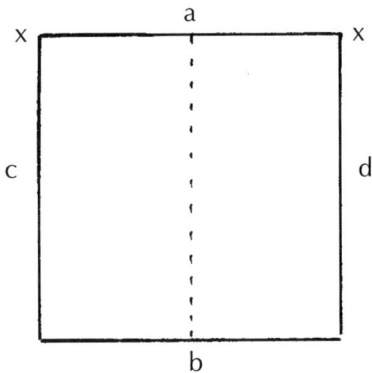

Fold in half, creating fold **c-d**.

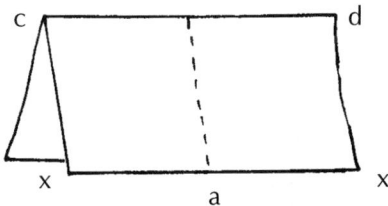

Fold top half of paper only, so that corners **x** lie on **c** and **d**.

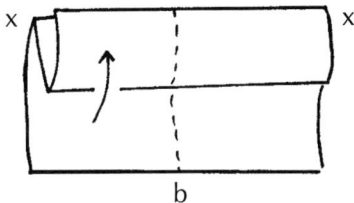

Turn paper over.
Fold bottom corners as indicated below. Fold top corners (3 layers of paper).

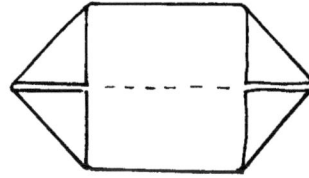

Fold bottom edge to top as shown:

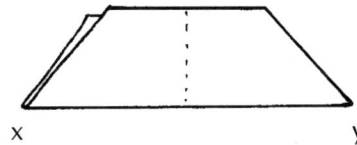

Make a 1cm cut into centre crease and cut out dragon's teeth as shown.
Draw a fearsome eye on both sides of head.

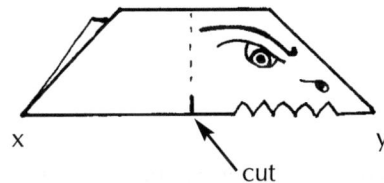

Fold paper back from cut on either side as shown:

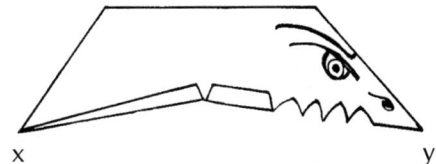

Open up inside of form bringing **x** and **y** together.

99

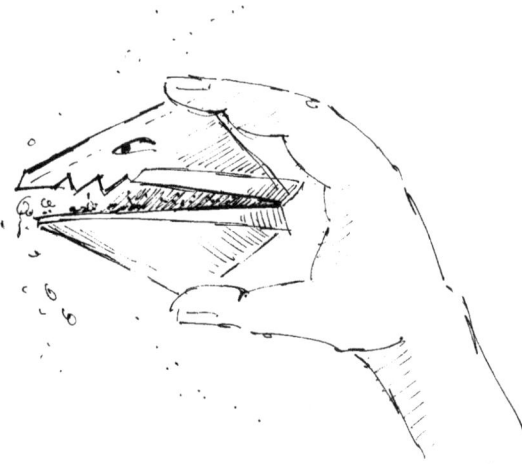

Snappy dragon's supper

Each child holds his dragon in one hand and keeps the other hand well behind his back. They are then allowed to roam outside to look for items for the dragon's supper. The dragon must pick up and hold in his mouth as many different objects e.g. a stone, a twig, a feather, a leaf, as possible within a limited time period, say five minutes.

At the end of the game each object in the dragon's mouth is exchanged for something sweet (duplicates don't count, but one white feather and one black feather might be accepted...). The child with the highest total wins a prize.

Variation: A room is prepared with a large number of small pieces of candy, e.g. Smarties or sugared almonds, scattered around or semi-hidden. Then it is a race to see how many the dragon can snap up – and hold in his mouth – before the time runs out.

Activities for ages nine to ten

It is natural for a child of this age to go through a phase of feeling vulnerable or insecure. Testing skills in one way or another can bring the reassurance he seeks. For this reason it is important that children succeed in whatever activity is chosen for the party, and they may need tactful help, encouragement and praise. The activities below will develop a variety of skills and give new insights into the way that different things work.

Suitable activities from previous pages:
Jet plane, page 96
Snappy dragon, page 99

Windflower

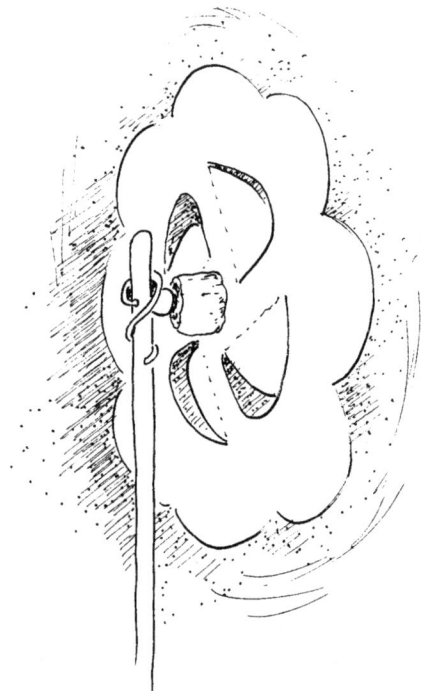

You will need:
Windflower pattern, page 215
Medium weight card 16cm x 16cm
Craft knife, scissors and glue
2 round wooden beads, approx. 8mm diam.
Wine bottle cork cut to 2cm length
Thin metal knitting needle for piercing cork
Length of wire approx. 12cm x 1mm diam.
Dowelling approx. 50cm x 8mm diam.
Electric or hand drill with 1mm drill bit
Coloured crayons, paint, felt-tip pens or
    scraps of coloured paper for decoration

Transfer (see page 210) pattern to card.
Cut outer shape of flower with scissors. Cut
    other solid lines with craft knife and score
    dotted lines (folding lines) with back of
    scissor blade.
Decorate flower and make small hole in
    centre.
Bore hole lengthwise through centre of cork.
    Glue cork to back of flower carefully
    matching both holes.

Make small loop at one end of wire (using
    pliers if necessary) and thread on one bead.
Push wire through flower and cork and finally
    through second bead.

Drill (on low speed) through dowelling stick
    approximately 15mm from one end.
Push wire through hole and secure by
    winding end of wire tightly around stick.
    It is most important that the bead between
    cork and stick has room for easy movement
    allowing windflower to turn freely.
Open up petals of flower by bending flaps
    forward along dotted lines.

Friendship bracelet

This activity is ideal for a limited party
space. Have more than six colours of thread
available to allow for individual preferences.

You will need:
6 different coloured lengths (80cm) of
    embroidery cotton
Scissors and adhesive tape

Tie threads together in a knot about 12 cm
    from one end.
Sit at a worktable and place adhesive tape
    just behind knot to fix threads to work
    surface.

Separate strands and arrange a colour
    sequence.

Start to knot as follows:
- take Strand One on the left and cross it over Strand Two
- loop it round and back through itself as seen below:

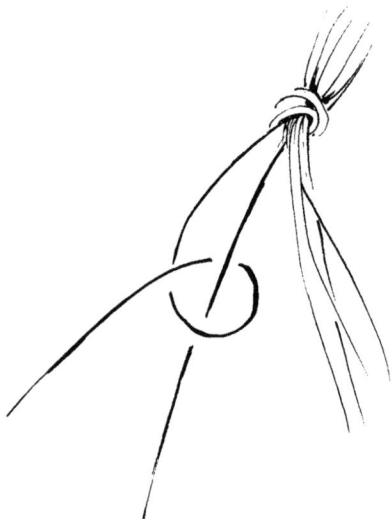

Pull knot tight and repeat process once more with the same two threads.

Then knot Strand One twice over Strand Three. Continue in this way until first strand has reached the right side, and created a slanted line of knots.

Start next row by taking new left-hand thread and repeat process across the other five colours.

Continue knotting until bracelet is long enough to fit the wrist.

To finish off:

Divide threads into three groups of two and make a simple plait about 3cm long.

Tie a knot and trim ends.

Untie large knot at beginning of bracelet and finish off in the same way.

Floating candleboat

These candleboats burn for an hour or more and look delightful sailing outdoors at dusk. If each child made more than one boat, and if the host provided a suitable area of water, then a grand sailing of boats could take place at the close of the party.

Adults must accompany children at the waterside.

For inside, a large washing-up bowl or baby bath will give enough space for at least six boats. Cover the bed of the 'sea' with pebbles, stones or shells, and drape the outside of the bath with a coloured cloth (see page 211).

Warning: Do not leave lighted candles unattended. Bear in mind that these boats are made of paper and could catch fire.

You will need:
Square of drawing paper 14cm x 14cm, well-covered on one side with wax crayon
Birthday cake candles
Molten wax (see page 209)

With coloured side up, crease square diagonally from corner to corner to find centre point.
Fold corners to centre.

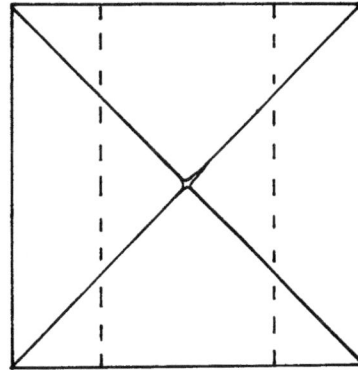

Fold two sides to centre along fold lines.

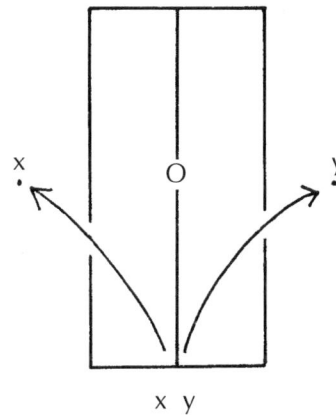

Hold firmly at **O** and move corner **x** to point **x**, and corner **y** to point **y**. Your form will look like this:

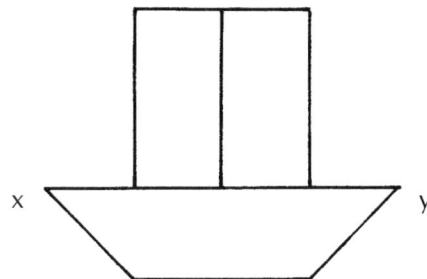

Repeat at other end.

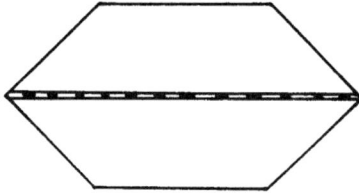

Fold top half of form backwards and
downwards to meet bottom half.

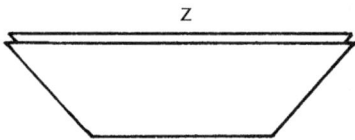

Reach inside front 'pocket' at **z** and carefully
pull out inner flap, so that front of form
looks like this:

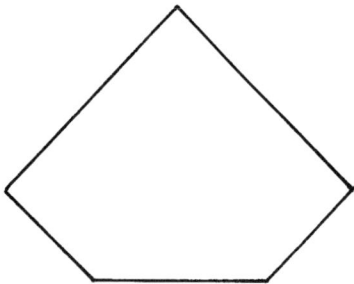

Turn form over and repeat last process on
other pocket. Fold corners forward along
fold lines shown below:

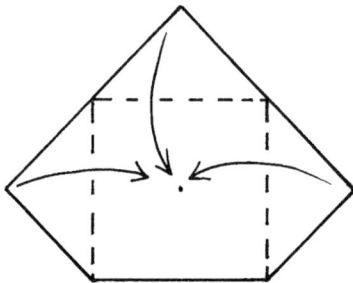

Turn over and repeat last process.

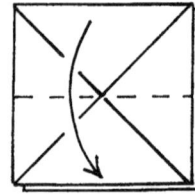

Fold down top edge only. Turn over and
repeat. (You may discover that this form,
if opened out, becomes a useful little box.)

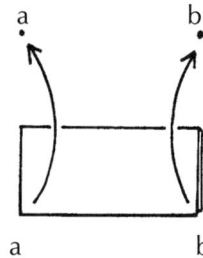

Take top two layers only and move the
corners **a** and the corners **b** to points **a**
and **b**. Now a flat, plain, square surface is
uppermost.

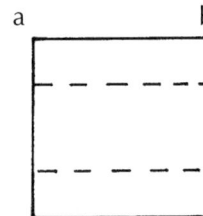

Fold edge **ab**, of top layer only, to centre
crease along fold line. Repeat with
opposite edge of square.

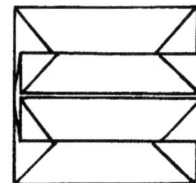

Turn over. Lift back centre edges – you will see two points meeting at **z**.

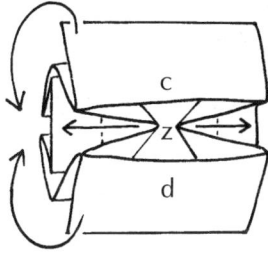

Take these points outwards in direction of arrow, allowing paper to fold flat along the dotted line indicated. At same time, lead flaps **c** and **d** round and back to meet on underside of form.

Press all down firmly. The form now looks like this with coloured side up at **d** and **c**:

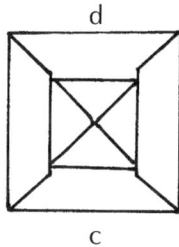

Fold right half of form backwards so that the two halves come together. Quarter-turn, so that long side **cd** is horizontal.

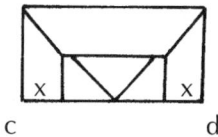

Grip with finger and thumb at **x** on each side and pull gently but firmly outward and upward. The boat is taking shape:

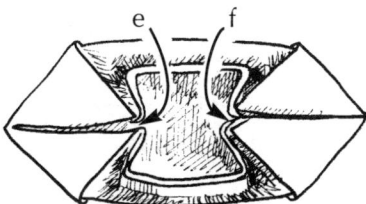

Insert finger under points **e** and **f** and raise a 'sail' at each end of boat.

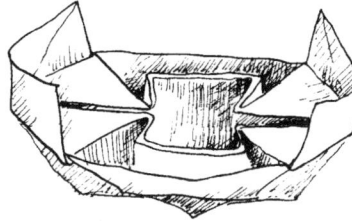

Float boat in bowl of water and pour molten wax into square cavity of boat.

Make sure wax is not too hot and hold boat with one hand to keep it horizontal for this process.

(Younger children need close supervision at this stage and extra adult help is needed. Make sure hot wax is kept well out of the way of small children's curiosity and older children's boisterousness!)

As skin forms on the wax, insert candle and support it until wax hardens. When wax has set, candle should be vertical.

Remove boat from water and place somewhere cool to dry until needed.

Humspinner

You will need:
Pattern for humspinner, page 216
Flexible card (or colourful used greetings card)
Length of fine cord or string approx. 1m
Hole punch and thick needle
Optional: crayons, felt-tip pens or coloured paper and glue for decorating

Transfer (see page 210) pattern to card. Cut around form and fold on dotted line.
Position hole punch carefully over one small circle and punch a hole through both layers of card. Repeat for each small circle.

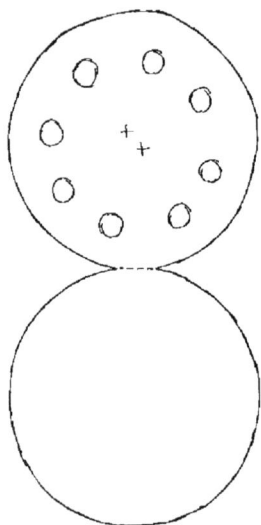

Kazoo

You will need:
Pattern for kazoo, page 217
Flexible card
Tracing paper or greaseproof paper (baking
    paper)
Scissors and glue
Optional: crayons or felt-tip pens to decorate

Thread needle with cord and pierce the two
    layers of card at a point **x**.
Draw cord halfway through card and return
    through two layers of card at other point **x**.
    Knot ends of cord together.
Decorate humspinner if desired.
Loop cord around two fingers of each hand
    and flip humspinner round and round
    until cord is well twisted.
Keeping humspinner upright, move hands
    steadily apart and back, making cord first
    tight and then relaxed and allowing
    humspinner to turn alternately one way
    and the other.
This needs practice but the rhythm is soon
    mastered and the humspinner will begin
    to hummm…

Transfer (see page 210) pattern to card. Cut
    along outer solid lines and those on inside
    of shaded area. Score (with back of scissor
    blade) and crease all dotted lines
Cut tracing paper to cover hole and extend
    over shaded area. Glue in place.
Fold edge **a–b** over edge **c–d** and glue in
    place. Hold firmly until dry.

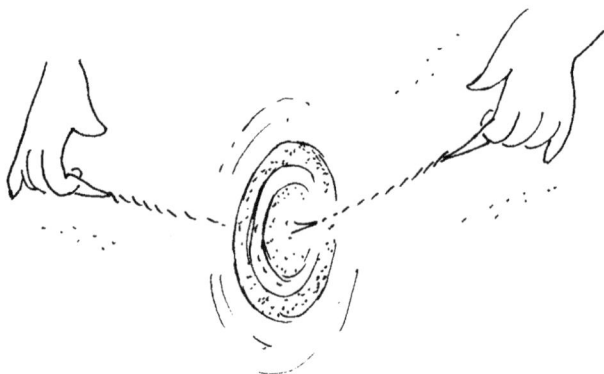

Place end m of kazoo gently between the lips
and call whoooo loudly and with breath. Feel
the lips tingle! Use this technique to hum
and sing your favourite tunes.

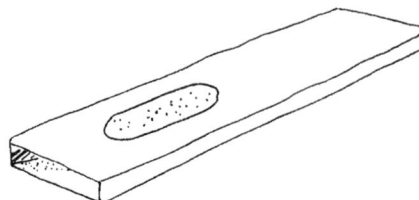

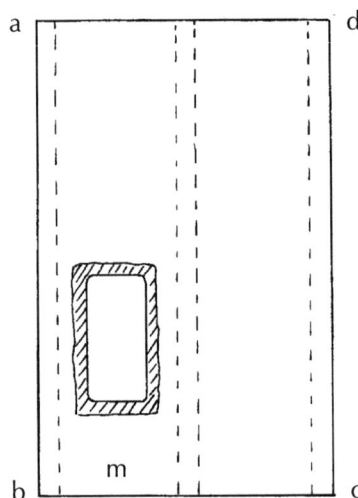

Shocking shark

You will need:
Flexible card in plain colour 15cm x15cm
Strong brown parcel paper 17cm x17cm
Ruler and pencil
Scissors and glue
Wax crayons or felt-tip pens

Crease card on one diagonal.
Place brown paper shiny side down and cut
   the shape below.
Crease along dotted lines:

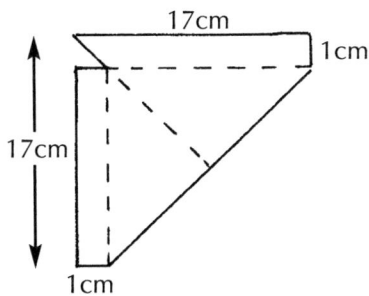

Place square of card on top of brown paper
   so:

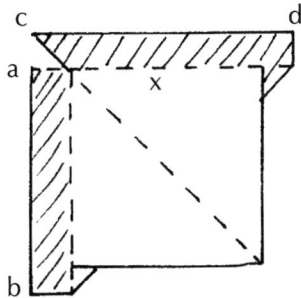

Spread glue on shaded area **a-b** and fold
   over to stick to edge of card. Repeat
   procedure for edge **c-d**. The form will
   now look like this:

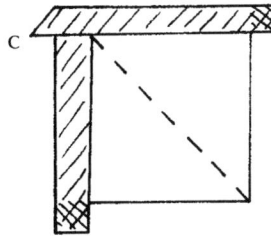

Fold point c back and under the form, glue
   in place. Trim excess brown paper (cross-
   shaded).
Fold form in half along dotted diagonal:

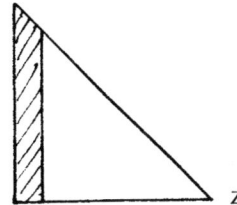

Hold card at **z** between finger and thumb
   and jerk sharply downwards to discover
   the shock.
To discover the shark – use crayons to draw
   an eye on each side of the brown paper.
   Cut sharp teeth and colour the body.

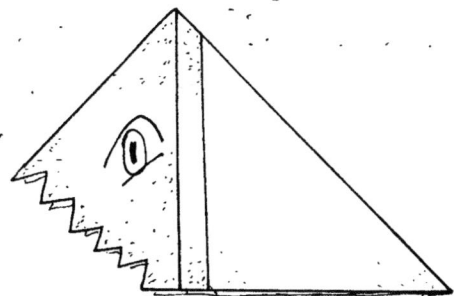

Croaker

You will need:

Pattern for croaker, page 218
Flexible card, not too thin
Ruler and scissors
Large needle or thumbtack
Metal washer approx. 12mm diam.
Two elastic bands 2.5cm diam.

Transfer (see page 210) pattern to card and
   cut round form.
Score along dotted line with back of scissor
   blade and crease.
Pierce card with needle to make four holes at
   x. Make four small cuts from **y** to **x**.
Attach elastic bands to washer as shown:

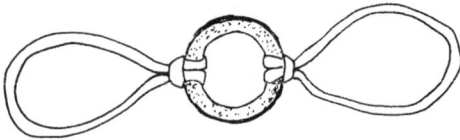

Slip loops of elastic into slots **xy**, so that the
   washer is held between them:

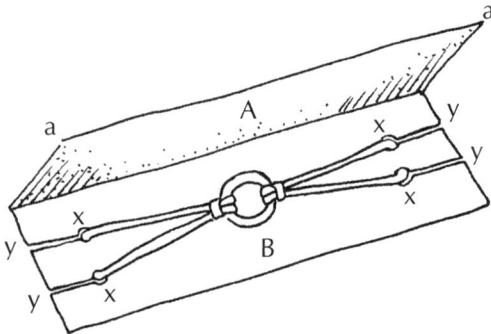

On back of face **A** , and with edge **a-a** below,
   draw and colour picture of a frog among
   stones and plants.
Turn washer forty times to wind up elastic.
Holding washer in place, fold card together
   and hold upright on a flat surface with
   picture of frog facing the audience. Ask
   'Shall I make my frog croak?'

Then draw back face **B** separating it from
face **A**, at the same time squeezing the
sides of face **B** together slightly to release
washer and surprise the company.

Activities for ages eleven to twelve

Take care not to offer this age group any
activity which they might consider babyish.
Look to the birthday child for guidance in
this respect as peer pressure is very strong
and what may have been acceptable to
friends last month has probably become
unthinkable now.

Nevertheless, children of this age can still
enjoy being creative together in a festive
atmosphere as long as the activity is carefully
chosen. Be ready for the preferred activity to
become a visit to a sport's centre, theatre or
wildlife park etc.

Preparing and eating food is a very social
occupation and barbecues have almost
universal appeal, so a picnic barbecue or a
make-your-own-pizza-supper (see below)
could, on their own, be the substance of a
party.

Suitable activities from previous pages:
Friendship bracelets, page 101
Humspinner, page 105
Kazoo, page 106
The shocking shark, page 107
Croaker

Dream catcher

This comes from a North American Indian tradition. It is said that a dream catcher hanging in the window will catch and hold the good dreams but allow the bad dreams to slip through the holes and be burnt by the rising sun.

You will need:
Metal or wooden ring (8–18cm diam.)
Length of yarn (2–3m)
Embroidery cotton (approx. 1.5m)
Darning needle
Glass beads and/or sequins
3 or more small feathers
Or, make a ring by winding a 60cm length of fresh willow (current year's growth), or well-soaked craft cane, into a circle as below:

Conceal ring by winding wool as shown. Sew in ends.

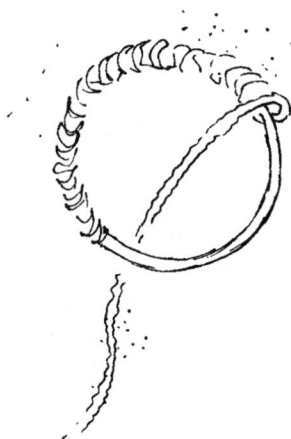

Secure one end of embroidery cotton to the ring and thread other end through needle. Loop thread around ring at seven or more regular intervals:

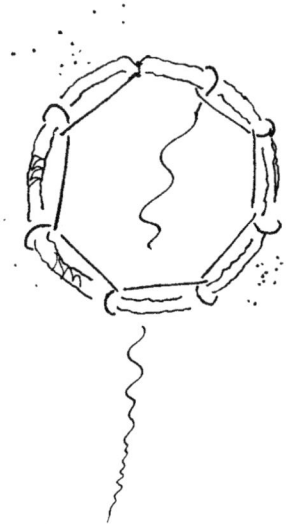

Continue round, connecting each loop to a thread from previous round. Keep tension in the work by pulling slightly on each loop. Thread in a bead or sequin occasionally.

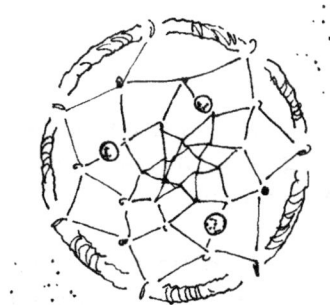

Continue until gap in centre is of an appropriate size. Tie end of thread securely.
Beads and feathers may be hung on threads from ring as shown.
Attach a loop for hanging. Sweet dreams!

You will need:
Portion of dough or ready-made pizza base
  for each guest
Thick tomato-based pasta sauce
Selection of pizza toppings: e.g. slices of
  tomato, pepper, courgette (zucchini),
  mushroom, spring onions, olives,
  pineapple, anchovies, ham, sausage
Variety of grated or sliced cheeses
Baking sheets for each guest

Prepare all ingredients in advance and
  display them on a table. Ask the cooks to
  wash their hands!
Set each pizza base on a baking sheet where
  it may be covered with a layer of tomato
  sauce and topped with other ingredients.
Pencil initials of each guest on baking
  parchment to slip under pizza before
  cooking.

Decorated T-shirts

Supply white, pure cotton T-shirts for each
  member of the party.
Cut strong card into discs the size of a large
  dinner plate. Place card centrally inside
  chest area.
Gather cloth firmly behind card and secure
  with string, checking that material
  covering the card is wrinkle-free but not
  over-stretched.
This area is now ready to receive an original
  work of art! Distribute textile crayons and
  follow manufacturer's instructions.

Activities for teenagers

Young people of this age are very individual in
their tastes and generalisation is inappropriate.
Peter's idea of a perfect birthday celebration
may be to enjoy a concert with a friend,
whereas Jack's idea would be to invite the
whole class to a hired hall. We shall concern

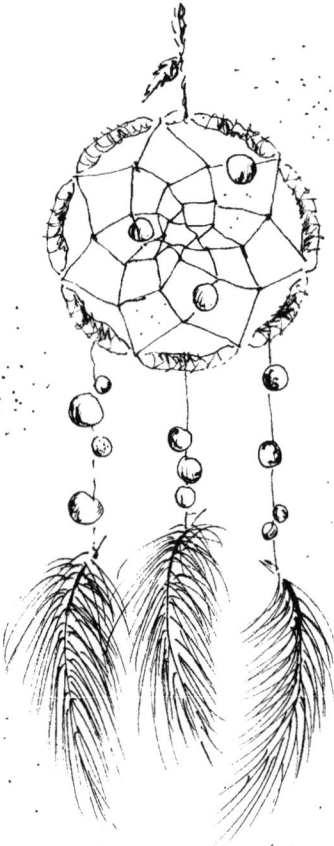

Personal pizzas

Arranging a personal pizza topping is a
creative and gastronomically satisfying
exercise for many children.

Pizza bases can be bought or baked
beforehand; alternatively, a portion of dough
could be given to each guest to shape for
themselves.

Careful thought must be given to the
number of guests: young children usually
prefer to work together around a table, older
children and adolescents are not easy to
organise in large groups. Ask the guests to
bring their own aprons.

ourselves here with teenagers who wish to celebrate at home with the family. Parties of this kind seem to fall into four groups:

1. Parties where 'silly games' are played.
2. Parties where the guests relax in each other's company while listening to music.
3. Parties which are all about communal cooking and the eating of food.
4. Parties which involve a surprise.

Suitable activity from previous pages:
Personal pizzas, page 110

Surprise trail for teenagers

This trail takes place in the locality. It could be fairly low-key or more flamboyantly eventful but its success depends on preparation and organisation. It would be most suitable for an extrovert character.

Arrange a birthday meal for invited friends in the evening and tell the birthday child to expect a surprise event before the meal. Ask him not to make any appointments that day/afternoon, but to be available in case extra help with the preparations is needed.

The trail could be long or short (in both time and space) depending on the extent of your imagination and effort and the possibilities available to you. Below are some ideas which might be helpful ('John' is the birthday child):

A possible surprise trail

✧ Give John some money 'just in case', and ask him to deliver an urgent letter or item to a shop assistant you know well or to a friend or acquaintance. They will give him a pre-arranged 'phone-message' from you to send him on the next task – to buy two bananas.

✧ Arrange for John's best friend to 'accidentally' meet up with him and accompany him on task No. 2. When the bananas have been bought, John's friend gives him a sealed envelope containing a note declaring that John and friend are now on a surprise trail and must go to a particular place, eat the bananas and wait for something to happen.

✧ Arrange for another friend to meet them there with instructions for the next task sealed in an envelope. This clue directs them to a shop window or a road sign etc where they will find some numbers, (e.g. the price of a particular jacket or the number of the road to…) and asks that they make certain calculations with that number: e.g. subtract x, multiply by y, divide by z and add 2. The clue explains that the answer is a telephone number, unfamiliar to John but actually of a friend or relative living some way off, which they must now dial to receive the next clue.

✧ This clue directs them to a particular café where they must look out for something unusual. In the café will be two more of John's friends perhaps with a helium balloon at the table. They will have been given enough money to buy everyone a soft drink (but strict instruction not to eat anything) and the usual sealed envelope bearing the instruction 'Do not open until … o'clock'. Inside is written 'prepare to receive a call on your mobile phone'.

✧ (Allow John and his friends about forty minutes at the café.) The phone call will tell them to go straight to the house of a friend or relative. There they will find a feast of cake or pancakes etc. and maybe one or two more friends to join the trail. The host will give them a number-and-word riddle to lead them to the next address e.g. 'a centenary number where the three digits add up to 1' (100), and 'TRESENHOTRT' – a cold road?' (North Street); or 'Go to 13, 9, 20, 1, 12, 9's house' (MITALI's house, numbers relate to position in the alphabet).

✧ Some entertainment has been planned for them there e.g. a comedy video or a trip to a bowling alley. (It is also possible that a parent or older sibling might meet them to host such an outing.) The next instruction is handed to John at the end of the entertainment.

✧ The instruction is for John alone to be delivered to the house of another friend or relative where he can be greeted with a drink and kept in conversation for a while. Then he is invited to take a shower and dress in clean clothes (left for him beforehand). Meanwhile, his friends will prepare for the party at John's house or other convenient venue, where they have previously delivered their clothes. John receives a call to return home when his friends are ready to greet him and the birthday meal will then follow.

Tips for preparing the trail:

Detailed advance preparation is most necessary.

The trail could be followed by bicycle if desirable; bus or train journeys could also be included (fare money or tickets would have to be supplied with the clue).

The trail could be a house-to-house collection of a few or all of John's invited friends. At each place the company would receive a treat of some kind and/or play a party game (see pages 85–88).

If appropriate, siblings would naturally be included on at least part of the trail.

Enlist as much help as possible from family and friends but give plenty of notice.

Do not expect to accomplish too many things during the time of the trail (e.g. food preparation) – there may be many distractions.

Ensure that John or his best friend have a mobile phone with them.

If some distances are too long to walk or are not on a bus or train route, design a clue which instructs the group to be at a convenient pick-up place at a certain time. They can then be driven to their next destination.

It is important to get the timing right. Most teenagers enjoy 'wasting' time in good company, but not by themselves. Make sure that the arrangements for meeting are foolproof and do not try to fit too many stages into the trail in case one task (e.g. a bus ride in rush hour) takes twice as long as planned. Allow 'buffer zones' in the timing (e.g. lingering time at a café or friend's house).

Instruct the best friend to telephone John's home occasionally, or if they get stuck or feel they are on the wrong track.

A surprise-trail for a girl might include a foot massage before she collects any friends, or a facial as the last 'task' before the meal.

The various helpers on the trail may appreciate a note of thanks after the event.

Activities for adults

The question of what to do on one's birthday as an adult arises most acutely for the single person. This may be someone in a demanding career or a single parent of young children, someone just starting a new job in a new city or someone retired from work. It could also be someone born on Valentine's Day who is partner-less and finds that all his friends are dining out in couples that evening…

Whatever the circumstances, how does one do justice to the occasion when there are no friends or relations at hand to make one feel celebrated?

The obvious answer is to give oneself a treat but the need for this is often only realised late in the day. Such an event needs advance planning and even, perhaps, the creation of a special fund.

Answering the question 'What would I most enjoy doing on my own?' can begin quite a profound excursion in self-knowledge and is almost a birthday present in itself.

If no friends are near, then make a friend! Buy some flowers and present them to the extra helpful librarian or the cheery shop assistant....

If friends are at hand, endeavour to make the day different from other birthdays: take a luxury picnic or a hike; make music together; have tea in a very exclusive hotel; take a boat trip... or take a lead from a busy lady that we know who cooked a really good meal and invited her friends round to share it – after they had done a makeover on her back yard!

Seasonal activities

Spring

Flying butterfly, page 97
Butterfly, pages 133–135
Earth candle, page 98
Garland, page 27

Other ideas:
Candle dipping
Sowing mustard and cress or other seeds
Making shortbread Valentine hearts

Summer

Floating candleboat, page 103
Windflower, page 100
Kazoo, page 106
Paper flowers, pages 135–136

Other ideas:
House building outdoors
Skipping
Maypole dancing
Kite flying
Making outdoor fairy gardens
Soap bubble blowing

Autumn

Pressed leaf coronet, page 93
Earth candle, page 98
Tiny elf, pages 157–158

Other ideas:
Lantern making
Bonfire party
Kite flying
Bread baking
Corn dolly making
Making indoor gnome garden
Making conker animals

Winter

Dream catcher, page 109
Earth candle, page 98
Evergreen coronet, page 93
Star wand, page 138
Pom-poms, page 94, in red, green or white

Other ideas:
Decorating gingerbread/ gingerbread houses
Candle making
Decorating candles with coloured beeswax
Making candleholders with air-drying
    modelling material

Chapter 9

ENTERTAINMENT

The Birthday of Guru Nanak (1469–1538 CE), founder of the Sikh religion is generally celebrated in November with a grand procession and a twenty-hour long religious meeting where the holy book is read from beginning to end. The meeting ends about 1.20 am, said to be the time of the Guru's birth.

Magician's corner

Children over four years will respond with delight to the mystery and wonder of some simple 'magic' tricks.

Children over nine years may suspend their belief while trying to discover 'how it's done'.

A good magician will practise the tricks beforehand, resist repeating them too often in case the secrets are spotted, and will never, *never* tell…

The amazing paperclips

Take a strip of writing paper approx. 21cm x 3cm, and place two paperclips as shown:

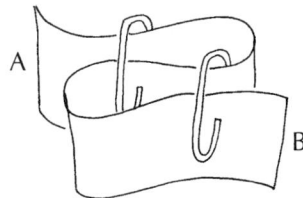

Take hold of end **A** with one hand and **B** with the other; pull firmly, and the paperclips will join themselves together.

Magic number cards

Print each of the six tables below on a piece of card. Offer the cards to a member of the audience. Ask that person to think of a number without speaking it. Then ask her to return only the cards on which that number appears.

The magician will discover the answer by adding up the numbers in the top left-hand corner of the cards received.

1	3	5	7	9	11	13	15
17	19	21	23	25	27	29	31
33	35	37	39	41	43	45	47
49	51	53	55	57	59	61	63

4	5	6	7	12	13	14	15
20	21	22	23	28	29	30	31
36	37	38	39	44	45	46	47
52	53	54	55	60	61	62	63

32	33	34	35	36	37	38	39
40	41	42	43	44	45	46	47
48	49	50	51	52	53	54	55
56	57	58	59	60	61	62	63

16	17	18	19	20	21	22	23
24	25	26	27	28	29	30	31
48	49	50	51	52	53	54	55
56	57	58	59	60	61	62	63

2	3	6	7	10	11	14	15
18	19	22	23	26	27	30	31
34	35	38	39	42	43	46	47
50	51	54	55	58	59	62	63

8	9	10	11	12	13	14	15
24	25	26	27	28	29	30	31
40	41	42	43	44	45	46	47
56	57	58	59	60	61	62	63

Flying arms

Invite volunteers to stand in a doorframe and push out against the frame with their wrists for the count of forty. When they step away from the frame they will feel as if their arms wish to fly.

The five pound trick

Take five coins of the same type, but not too large. Hide one of the coins inside the spine binding of a hardback book. Place the book on a table and open it in front of the audience. Ask someone to place the other four coins on the open book.

Wave a magic wand over the coins, pour them into the cupped hands of the volunteer and, hey presto, the four coins have become five.

The walnut shell mystery

Place three walnut shell halves and a coin on the table. In front of the audience, cover the coin with one of the shells. Turn your back to the table and ask a volunteer to move the shells around so that you will have to guess which shell the coin is now under.

You will manage to guess because you will be able to detect the fine hair that you have previously fixed to the coin with an appropriate glue.

Dozy dice

Hold three dice firmly in a line between finger and thumb of one hand, as shown. Say to a volunteer 'Touch the middle dice with the magic wand and say 'Abracadabra, go to sleep'. As she does that, release the pressure on the dice and the middle one will 'drop off' straight away!

The secret is to moisten finger and thumb before gripping the line of dice.

The unbreakable cocktail stick

Take a man's classic cotton handkerchief with a broad hem all round the edges. Ask a member of the audience to place a cocktail stick on the handkerchief.

Fold the handkerchief loosely around the stick and ask the volunteer to feel for the stick through the material and then break it in half. The handkerchief is shaken out revealing an unbroken cocktail stick.

The secret is that a second stick has been concealed beforehand within the hem (as shown below) and the magician makes sure that this is the stick that is felt and broken.

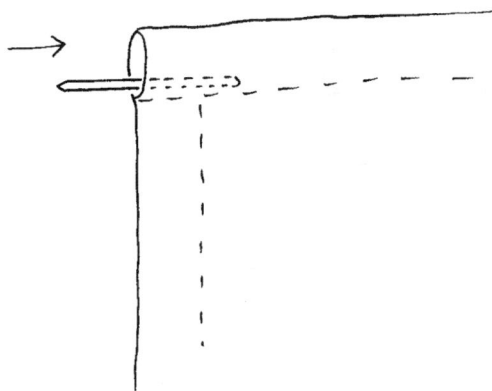

Tricks with an assistant

Forky camera

Explain to the audience that the fork you have is really a camera. Ask your assistant to take a photo of someone while you leave the room. When you have left, the assistant 'takes a photo' with the fork. On returning, you study the audience by squinting through the tines of the fork. Then you announce which guest had her photo taken.

(After your return to the room, the assistant has copied the exact pose of the subject of the 'photo'. A quick glance at the assistant should help to detect the child in question.)

Mind reader

The magician leaves the room. The guests silently select an object in their surroundings. The magician returns and the assistant points at different objects asking if this is 'the one'. When the assistant points to something black, the magician will know that the very next object to be pointed out will be 'the one'.

(If this is to be repeated with older children, arrange with the assistant a series of colours, say, first black, then blue, next time green etc. to point to before the chosen object.)

Puppet show for a birthday party

(For children aged 4 to 8 years)

One way to ensure a peaceful and happy end to the festivities is to close with a story or, better still for the younger age group, a puppet show. The puppet show that we have included here is a quiet and gentle story, suitable for both boys and girls, which involves the children without over-stimulating them.

The puppet 'theatre' is the top of a low table or chest, or a board stretched between two chairs; the scenery is minimal; the puppets are easy-to-make little figures which are moved by hand.

Many details of scenery and plot are deliberately omitted from the presentation to allow room for the children's own imagination. The story itself becomes a celebration, not only of the birthday child but also of all the invited friends.

To set the scene

You will need:
Low rectangular or oval surface (coffee table, chest or other stable construction)
Plain cloth or bed sheet in a dark colour to cover this surface to the floor
Cloths, preferably muslin, in green, yellow and blue (see page 211)
Pieces of wood or building bricks to form a house
Birthday Child puppet
Mother and Father puppets
Wise Gnome puppet
'Guest' puppet for each guest
Candle in a candleholder
Optional: small pot plant, a crystal or rock, two or three pebbles and fir cones

Set up the puppet show in advance, if possible in a separate room from other party activities.
Arrange everything along the lines of the picture below. The mountain can be built up with almost anything – a bundled piece of clothing works very well. Cover it with a green or blue/green cloth.
The house is simply constructed with two sidewalls and a lintel. A green cloth covers and softens the line of the building.
Arrange a circular yellow area in front of the house to serve as a birthday party arena.

Blue cloth runs along the side of the table nearest the puppeteer, to suggest a stream.

Stand the candle to the far left of the table and away from the front edge.

The father and mother figures are placed on the right-hand side of the house, and the Wise Gnome is perched, half-visible to the audience, toward the rear of the mountain.

The building of the Rainbow Bridge we leave to the superior capacities of the imagination.

To make the puppets

You will need (for the Birthday Child):
Dowelling 3.5cm x 1.5cm diam.
Skin-coloured cotton stockinette 5cm x 5cm
Small handful of fleece or cotton wool
(Alternatively, some craft shops sell small wooden 'doll' figures which could be used as a base)
Felt in pastel colour 3.5cm x 7cm
Scrap of yellow felt for collar
Scrap of dyed fleece or mohair yarn for hair
Glue, needle and thread

To make head:
Stuff fleece or cotton wool into stockinette to make a ball the size of a small marble. Tie securely with thread.

Dab glue around one end of dowelling and attach head by pulling 'neck' cloth firmly downwards over dowelling. Secure head further by tying thread around body.

To dress puppet:
Fold felt in half and sew 3.5cm edges together. Turn garment inside out. Run gathering thread around one edge.
Pull garment over dowelling and draw in gathering thread tightly around neck.
Secure with a few stitches.

Make a birthday-collar from yellow felt as seen below and secure it around the puppet's neck.

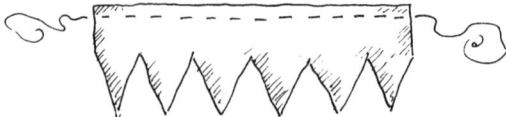

Stitch or glue dyed fleece on head as hair.
All the other puppets are made in the same way as the Birthday Child but choose another pastel colour for garments of Guests and omit collar.
Dowelling for Mother and Father puppets should be 4.5cm long. Adjust length of garments accordingly and add features of style or colour as appropriate.

Wise Gnome has a long, white fleece beard and hat made from a triangle of red felt folded in half and stitched as below:

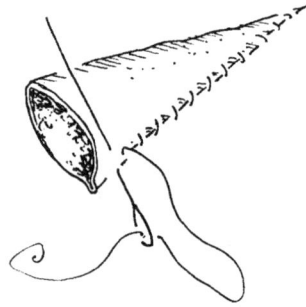

Once you have made a set of puppets they can be re-used year after year.

The story

Ideally, the story would be memorised by the puppeteer, but a story-teller could sit on one side, close to the centre of action but taking care not to distract the audience.

The numbered notes should help with practical details. Blanks have been left for names, and the story is written as if for a girl and three female guests.

More guests can be added as needed, and the sexes adjusted as appropriate. Allow twenty minutes for the show.

The story of ....'s birthday

Once upon a time (1) there were two little angels who were great friends. They spent all their time together and told each other all their secrets. One day, the first little angel had rather special news to tell:

'Today is the day when I must go over the Rainbow Bridge to make my way in the world.' she said. 'Will you come a little way with me, and will you keep watch for me until I return?'

'Yes, I shall come some of the way with you,' said her friend, 'and then I shall keep watch faithfully, for you may be gone a long time.'

So the two friends set out over the Rainbow Bridge (2). Halfway over, the first little angel took off her wings and gave them to the second little angel to look after; the second angel received the wings and handed over a small bag, saying:

'Here are some treasures to remind you of the beauties of the heavens where we have spent such happy times together.'

'Oh, thank you, my friend,' cried the little girl – (for I must call her a little girl now that she has no wings) – and she looked into the bag. To her delight she saw (3) a sunbeam and a moonbeam, a piece of rainbow and a radiant shining star.

'These are precious things,' she whispered 'and they will remind me of you.'

So they said goodbye and parted. The angel kept watch* as the little girl walked on (4) over the Rainbow Bridge, carrying her treasure bag.

At the end of the bridge she came to a stream running through a green meadow. A gnome suddenly appeared beside her (5).

'Welcome to our land' he said.

The girl looked around her and exclaimed, 'What a very beautiful land it is! May I paddle in that sparkling stream?'

'That's what it's there for,' replied the gnome.

The little girl put down her treasure bag (6) and jumped into the water. She paddled and splashed. Seeing a path leading away on the other side of the stream she stepped out of the water and started off down the path (7) forgetting all about her treasure bag. But the gnome had not forgotten it (8) and he carried it carefully away.

The girl followed the path for quite a long way (9) until she came to a house. A kindly man and woman were waiting there (10).

'Welcome, at last!' they said. 'We are your Mother and Father; we knew you were coming and have everything prepared for you.'

They gave the little girl a name .... (11), and all lived happily for many years.

One day, ...'s mother said:

'Today is your birthday. You are .... years old. This afternoon we shall have a party and you may invite your friends.'

So .... invited her friends to a party, and at ... o'clock there was a knock on the door. In walked .... (12) and gave .... a present. Then there was another knock on the door. In walked .... and she also gave .... a present. Finally, there was a last knock at the door and in came .... and gave .... another present! Now the party was complete (13).

They played games and had nice things to eat and they all sang a birthday song (14). Then it was time to go home, but .... was perplexed.

'All my friends have given me such wonderful presents, and I have nothing to give them. Oh dear!'

The Birthday Fairy was not very far away and she whispered in ....'s ear (15). She reminded her of the little treasure bag which was left by the stream, and told her that the Wise Gnome had hidden it safely until such time that it was needed.

'Shall I go and ask him for it?' whispered the Birthday Fairy.

'What a good idea!' cried .... 'Yes, please do.'

And so the Birthday Fairy went to the Wise Gnome of the mountain and he climbed deep into his treasure cave (16) and brought out a sunbeam. He called .... (17) and said:

'This is for you, be sure to keep it safe.'
And .... said:

'Thank you, Wise Gnome,' and put it around her neck. Then Wise Gnome climbed into his treasure cave again and brought out a moonbeam. He called .... and said:

'This is for you. Be sure to keep it safe.'
And .... said:

'Thank you, Wise Gnome,' and put it around her neck. Then Wise Gnome went to his cave another time and brought out a piece of rainbow. He called .... and said:

'This is for you. Be sure to keep it safe.'
And .... said:

'Thank you, Wise Gnome,' and put it around her neck (18).

Wise Gnome then climbed into his treasure cave for the last time and brought out a radiant shining star. He called the Birthday Girl and said:

'This is for you. Be sure to keep it safe, for this is your own special star which will light up life's path as you make your way in the world.'
And .... said:

'Thank you, Wise Gnome', and put it around her neck. As she did so, she thought of her angel friend standing faithfully beyond the Rainbow Bridge keeping watch for her (19).

And far away, across the Rainbow Bridge, her angel friend looked down and smiled; then the whole world began to sing (20).

(1) If the candle is alight before children enter the room, it sets a peaceful and expectant mood. This mood can be deepened with a little improvised music before the action begins – xylophone, lyre, flute or recorder would be appropriate. Rather than use recorded music if no instruments are available, ring a little bell to signal the beginning of the story. The opening section until * is played out in the imagination.

(2) Whoever is telling or reading the story could use a hand gesture here to indicate the Rainbow Bridge, which arches down to end at the stream.

(3) There needs to be a treasure for each guest (not forgetting siblings of the Birthday Child) and a star for the Birthday Child herself. (If the number of guests exceeds four then this sentence should finish with '...and many other beautiful things'.) If possible, hang the treasures on gold thread to make the necklets that are indicated in the text. The local craft shop should be a rich store of 'heavenly treasures', either as sequins or beads or other components of jewellery etc. Here are some suggestions for things to use:

- *sunbeam:* round/oval gold sequin
- *moonbeam:* round/oval silver sequin, or mother of pearl disc
- *piece of rainbow:* fragment of abalone shell or iridescent bead
- *radiant star:* sequin or other star shape in a 'precious' material
- *golden bird:* sequin or other gilded bird shape
- *butterfly:* sequin, gilt or glass
- *heavenly dewdrop:* clear or faceted glass 'drop'-shaped bead
- *star-flower:* mother of pearl star
- *heavenly rose:* something from the craft shop jewellery counter may do, or look for tiny roses made from ribbon

– *moonlight/rainbow wrapped up in crystal:*
  some quartz crystals can give this effect
– *angel bell:* very small coloured bell

Note: small items are not suitable for
children under three.

(4) At this point, using R.H. (right hand),
walk the Birthday Child puppet at earth level
towards stream.

(5) With L.H. (left hand), move Wise Gnome
from back of mountain towards the Child.

(6) With R.H. walk Child a few paces away
from Gnome and mime the placing of
treasure bag. Return Child to Gnome's side
before she jumps into stream.

(7) Follow a winding route to give an
impression of distance.

(8) Release Child and use L.H. to walk
Gnome to where treasure bag was left. Mime
the picking up, and move Gnome to resume
his original position behind mountain.

(9) Again, with Child in R.H., follow a
winding course.

(10) Single parent families may wish to adjust
this sentence and parts of the following text.

(11) The name of the birthday child.

(12) The name of first guest to arrive. Try to
keep sequence of guests accurate as far as
memory allows; such details are important to
children.

(13) If the birthday child has siblings, this
sentence could read: 'When .... had
called her brother .... and her sister
.... to come, then the party was complete.'

(14) Use a birthday song (see pages 174–180)
that everyone knows or else the traditional
Happy birthday to you. The audience is
encouraged to join the singing.

(15) The Birthday Fairy is best left as an
invisible being, but the reader or puppeteer
could cup an ear as the Fairy is whispering.

(16) The necklets can be pinned separately
(to avoid tangling) on the tablecloth behind
the mountain, hidden from the audience.
The finger and thumb with which Wise
Gnome is held become his arms and he is
able to carry the necklets to the front of the
stage to present to the children.

(17) Name of first guest. Keep right sequence
of guests for the presentations. The children
are invited to come to the stage to receive
their gift.

(18) Repeat this sequence for any siblings
who are present.

(19) Puppeteer gestures towards invisible
watching angel.

(20) Audience joins in the final rendering of
a birthday song.

Chapter 10

EATING AT A PARTY

...the tea-room, where the table should be radiant with bright colours, preferably pink for the shades, candles and sweetmeats. Homely things (notwithstanding the doctor's warnings) must for this occasion be eschewed, and all that can tempt the eye as well as the appetite be exhibited in profusion. Care must be taken that there is enough for everybody, for children 'love a good feed'. The children's tea-table is presided over by the eldest daughter of the house, or the governess or some lady who acts as lieutenant for the mistress. The 'up-growns' are simultaneously at tea in another room...
Advice on 'Juvenile Parties' from *Jack's Reference Book*, 1915

As there are many books available specialising in party food, we will restrict this section to some important but general considerations (more especially those relevant to children's parties), along with our favourite and most useful recipes.

Tips:
- Always check for food allergies and special diets among the guests. For children's parties avoid artificial colouring and flavouring, and food that is very salty, very sweet or very rich.
- Make extra food for unexpected visitors and have plenty of water or diluted fruit juice available.
- Remember to cater for helpers and for parents who may stay with their young children.
- If children arrive at a party straight from school offer them a drink and a snack before the party programme begins.

- Allow about half an hour for a children's meal.
- The sharing of a child's birthday tea is often easier to arrange indoors; a more social atmosphere is created by seating the children together around one table.
- Protect a polished table with a waterproof cloth and cover with a disposable cloth.
- Arrange the seating of guests with the birthday child beforehand. Write name-cards or make name-flags on cocktail sticks and set them in bread rolls or pineapple cubes.
- If the birthday meal is a picnic, seat young children in a circle and give them each a prepared selection of food on a plate. Offer second helpings and serve the birthday cake last. If the day is breezy, use cake candles that re-light themselves.
- Many children prefer to take their portion of birthday cake home, so be prepared with sandwich bags or boxes.
- There is no real need for novelty-cut sandwiches and decorated biscuits unless you have the time and inclination to do it. (Remember that what you do one year will most likely be expected by your children for years to come). Food looks festive enough when laid out carefully on a plate or board and decorated with edible flowers, pretty leaves or an arrangement of vegetable sticks.

Party food for one to three years

Suggestions

Bite-sized, plain finger-food: bread with a simple cheese or dairy-free spread; cheese or herb-flavoured pastry sticks; buttered toast; mini rice crackers; lightly cooked vegetable sticks; small portions of birthday cake; plenty of well-diluted organic fruit juice, water and milk to drink.

Cater for adults separately: sandwiches, slices of quiche or pizza, vegetable sticks with a choice of dips, cake. A selection of teas or coffee to drink.

Tips:
- Make a choice of fruit available and ask parents to prepare it for their own children if and when required.
- Avoid rich sugary toppings for the birthday cake. Use a thin covering of whipped cream or try sifting icing sugar on a paper doyley pressed on to the top of the cake. Lift doyley off *very* carefully.
- Ask parents to bring feeding cups for the toddlers.
- Ask a helper to serve the adults.
- Respect children's individual need for food and avoid pressing them to eat.

Party food for three to six years

Suggestions

Small servings of finger food: open sandwiches; mini cheese pastries; mini pretzels; vegetable sticks with unsophisticated dips; small squares of pizza; pieces of fresh fruit; fruit fool; individual yoghurts; birthday cake. Diluted fruit juices or bottled spring water to drink (with straws).

Tips:
- Make enough for adult guests/helpers or cater for adults separately (see above).
- Children above five years often like the birthday cake to be a surprise.
- Serve the birthday cake at the end of the meal but leave other food on the table for the benefit of slow eaters.

Party food for seven to twelve years

Suggestions

This age group can really appreciate, for example, decoratively cut vegetables and fruit, interesting garnishes, novelty cakes, etc., so if you have the talent and the time why not use them? If you do not wish to be tied to making a novelty cake every year then establish a tradition of 'special' birthdays, perhaps at age seven, nine or ten and /or twelve.

Party food for teenagers and adults

Suggestions

Plan the whole menu in consultation with the teenager (fashions change in food as in everything else). Older teenagers may enjoy cooking a meal for, or with, their friends (see page 110). In this case the adult may demonstrate helpful concern which is, of course, not to be confused with interference!

For an adult birthday, it should only be necessary to check the menu for dietary preferences. Apart from having a birthday cake of some kind, there are no general rules for adult party food except that one provides enough of it.

Recipes

Swan lake children's dessert

For the swans: (make them at least two days in advance)
Modelling icing (to make):
1 scant tbsp of egg white
5ml (1tsp) liquid glucose
150g (approx.) sifted icing sugar

(To store): Wrap icing in cling-film and a plastic bag. Keep in refrigerator for up to 6 weeks.

Mix egg white and glucose in a bowl. Add spoonfuls of sugar to form a stiff paste.
Knead until smooth (add more sugar if sticky). This will make enough for approx. 5–10 swans.
For individual 'lakes' use 25g of icing for the swan. Double that quantity for one lake in a serving bowl.

To model the swan:
Take a ball of icing about 2cm diam. (25g), gently squeeze out a sausage (approx. 2.7cm) at one end for the neck.
Hollow the back and bring up wings on either side, pinching them together at a point for a tail.
Make a crease with a knife between bill and head, pinch sides of bill inwards and flatten top slightly. Arrange neck and head as illustrated.
Leave in dry atmosphere to harden.

For the lake: (prepare at least one day in advance)
1/2 litre natural fruit juice
15ml (3 slightly rounded tsps) powdered gelatine (**vegetarian option:** 2 slightly rounded tbsps agar flakes)
Crystallised green angelica

Make up fruit jelly following manufacturer's directions for use of gelatine/agar flakes.

Cool for two minutes, pour into warm glass bowl or individual serving dishes. Chill until set.

Take 3cm stick of angelica and slice lengthwise to make 'reeds' for the lake. Insert reeds (say, in three groups of three) into jelly so that they are stable.

Place swans on jelly immediately before serving.

Personal candle cakes

Pipe each guest's name in icing on an individual chocolate-covered Swiss roll, and add a candle. After the birthday child has blown the birthday cake candles out, each guest also has a chance to blow – and also, perhaps, to wish…

Exotic rhubarb purée

Wash a small, thin-skinned organic orange, remove the rosette core and cut the whole fruit, with peel, into chunks. Feed these into a blender at high speed.

When puréed, lower speed and fill blender with stewed rhubarb sweetened with brown sugar. Blend well. Pour into small dessert bowls and top with a whorl of whipped cream.

Deliciously easy chocolate dessert

Place 150g dark chocolate chips in a blender and add 300ml single cream heated to just *below* boiling point. Blend until smooth.

Add one egg, a few drops of natural vanilla essence and a small pinch of salt. Blend briefly.

Pour into small, warmed dessert dishes and chill overnight. Add a garnish of whipped cream with a crystallised violet or a few shavings of dark chocolate.

Seedy crackers

Smear plain crackers, water biscuits or tea matzos with a very thin layer of cream cheese or honey.

Brush on melted butter seasoned with a little salt. Sprinkle well with sesame or poppy seeds.

Place on a baking sheet in a hot oven for 5 mins or until the crackers are lightly toasted.

Avocado dip

Press an avocado pear through a sieve and add a similar amount of crème fraiche, the juice of a small lemon and a pinch of salt.

Stir well and flavour with one of the following as required: chopped chives, garlic, cayenne pepper, chilli powder, curry powder.

Serve with vegetable sticks.

Dragon loaf

Pierce through the centre of a French loaf, lengthwise, with a pointed stick to within 3cm of one end (this end will be the dragon's head).

With a sharp knife, cut the bread in a spiral around the stick, beginning at a point about 5cm back from the dragon's nose.

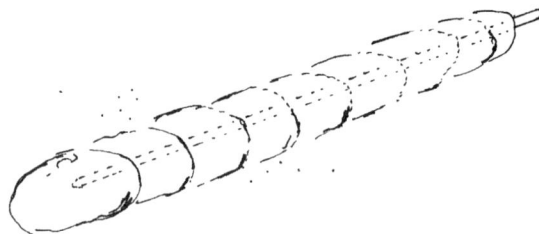

Make sure the knife always meets the stick as it cuts. (The knife might have to be shifted as the loaf is turned over to keep the spiral cut moving downwards.)

Make a knife-cut for the mouth of the dragon and insert a forked tongue cut from a red pepper.

Halve an olive stuffed with pimento. Remove small discs from the crust to make eye sockets, insert half a cocktail stick (blunt end down) and press the half olive securely on to the stick so that the 'eye' protrudes from the socket.

Prepare a suitable board or cloth on which to place the dragon, withdraw the stick and settle the loaf there (perhaps on a bed of watercress).

Make 'markings' on the dragon's back with crossed strips of anchovy or thinly-sliced red or green pepper.

Savoury loaf

(for approx. 15 servings)

Make a standard bread dough using 400g strong white flour and 100g wholemeal flour.

After the first rising, knead briefly and roll out to a rectangle approx. 36cm x 28cm.

Crush a clove of garlic and spread it over the dough.

Lay on slices of salami, sliced olives, lightly cooked mushrooms and sun-dried tomatoes.

Add a good sprinkling of dried oregano.

Roll up the dough starting with a long side.

Make the seam of the dough the base of the loaf, bring dough down over ends and tuck under base to finish off.

Brush with beaten egg and make 7 light, diagonal knife-cuts across the top length of the loaf.

Bake in a hot oven for approx. 35–40 mins. Serve warm or cold.

Real lemonade

You will need:
6 large, organic lemons
150g sugar
1.5 litres water

Wash lemons and finely peel zest from three of them. Place zest into a fairly large bowl. Squeeze juice from all six lemons and add to bowl.

Boil water and pour over zest and juice. Add sugar and stir. Leave overnight. Check for sweetness, strain and serve.

Rosy apple punch

You will need:
1 peppermint teabag
2 rosehip and hibiscus teabags
150 ml organic apple juice concentrate
1.5 litres water
Optional: 3 cloves; fruit slices for garnish

Boil 350 ml water and pour over teabags (with cloves if preferred). Leave for five minutes.

Squeeze out and remove teabags (and cloves). Add apple concentrate and rest of water.

Optional: Add fruit slices.

Chapter 11

DECORATION

'Balloon?' said Eeyore. You did say balloon? One of those big coloured things you blow up? Gaiety, song-and-dance, here we are and there we are?'

A.A. Milne: *Winnie the Pooh*

Decorations are fun and can utterly transform a room from the mundane to the 'special', just as a birthday should transform life for at least one day.

If you have no **birthday ring** (see below), suspend a small leafless branch horizontally above the table and hang decorations from it. Use the decoration ideas for the ring below or try some pom-poms (see page 94).

Consider decorations well in advance of a themed party.

Crêpe paper streamers in contrasting colours twisted together give instant effect. The **paper chain** on page 146 is simple enough for a child to make, but looks quite sophisticated.

Keep paper decorations away from a naked flame and bear in mind that damp crêpe and tissue paper can stain.

Hanging birthday ring

This ring makes a central decorative feature for the birthday without taking up valuable table space. It can be transformed with ease to suit many different birthday events. The colour mood is altered by selecting different ribbons and appropriate decorations which are quickly pinned in place (see page 133).

You will need:
Strong wire ring, (approx. 25 x 30cm diam.): available at craft shops, or cut one from an old lampshade of the right size. Florists and garden centres sell double rings which can be separated with wire cutters
A few sheets of old tissue paper for padding
Strong invisible thread
Large darning needle
For raffia ring: straw-coloured raffia
For ring of summer grasses: quantity of long

131

grass, best cut when it is straw-coloured

Tip: Cut much more grass than you think you need.

Raffia ring

Fold tissue paper into strips and wind round wire base until ring is padded thickly and evenly (approx. 3cm diam.). Use some glue if necessary and secure with thread.

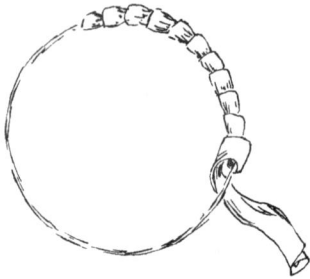

Wind raffia firmly and evenly to conceal padding. Sew in ends with needle.

Ring of summer grasses

Fold tissue paper into strips and wind one layer around wire base. Secure with thread.

Take a small handful of grass and begin covering the paper. Work on a 12cm section at a time, winding invisible thread around grass to hold it fast.

Add more grass if necessary to cover all paper on one section of ring before moving on with thread. Overlap sections of grass to maintain constant thickness of covering.

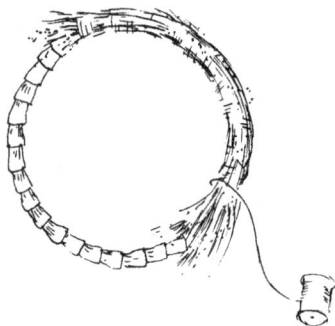

When all tissue paper is concealed by grass and ring is of even thickness, finish by winding one strand of raffia around ring as seen below:

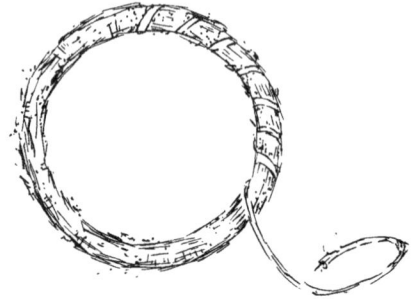

Suspend ring from three points at required height, using plaited raffia (at least nine strands per plait).

Tip: This ring has the advantage of allowing pins to slide into it easily.

Decorations for birthday ring

Here are some suggestions for dressing the ring to accompany birthdays in each season:

Acquire ribbons in various colours: 4.5m of each colour (2.1m to wind around the ring and 2.4m to make four individual bows – three to pin on the ring at regular intervals and one to attach to hanging point.)

Tip: Use dressmakers' pins to fix the ribbon to the ring.

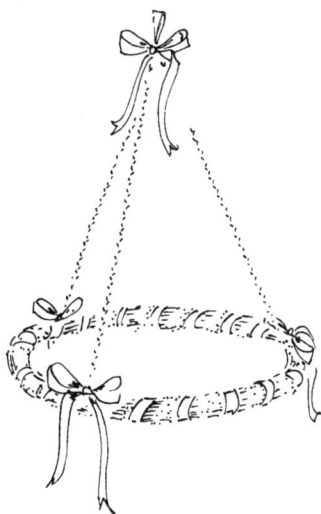

Bunches of narrow ribbon or crêpe paper strips in various matching colours make effective additional decorations.

A crêpe streamer (cut across grain of paper) is made more decorative by stretching the edges into a frill using thumb and forefinger.

Spring birthday ring

Wind primrose yellow and pale green ribbons around the ring and suspend butterflies at varying heights. Add yellow paper flowers (see pages 135–136)

You will need: (for a butterfly)
White or coloured tissue paper 15cm x 15cm
Small piece of tissue paper in contrasting colour
Small piece plasticine
2 stamens (available at craft shops for making artificial flowers)
Black thread, glue

♦♦ To fold butterfly's wings, follow diagrams below:

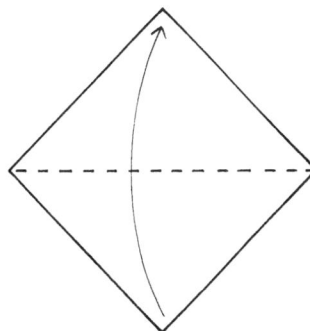

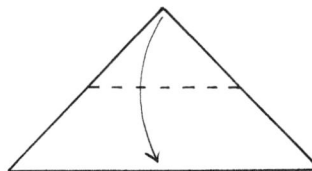

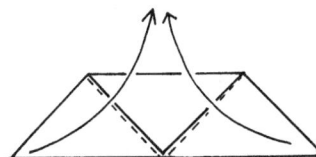

133

fold over to
the back

turn over

'nose'

To make body

Roll a small 'sausage' of plasticine approx.
2.5cm long and the diameter of a
matchstick.

Tie black thread around plasticine and trim
sausage to 2cm, keeping thread central.

Thinly coat plasticine with glue and place
within V-channel of butterfly.

Lay one stamen on each side of plasticine to
create antennae:

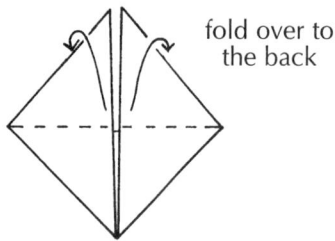

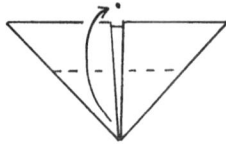

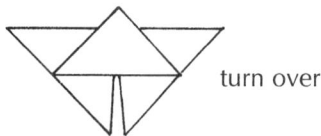

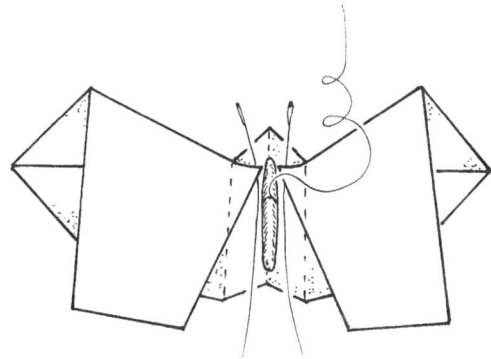

Turn form over and slip finger between top
layers of right wing as indicated:

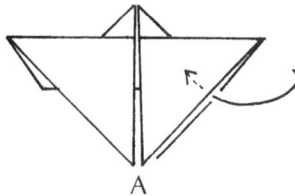

A

Push wing up slightly to create new folding
line:

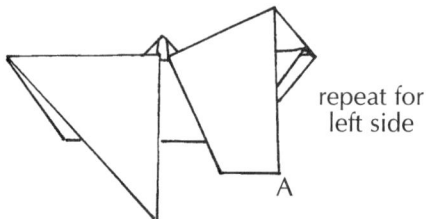

repeat for
left side

A

Fold sides of V up around plasticine and
antennae, concealing and securing plasticine
while keeping hanging thread free.

Test balance of butterfly immediately and
adjust by moving antennae forwards or
backwards, or by inserting another small
plug of plasticine.

Cut two small circles of tissue paper in a
contrasting colour and fix them to upper
side of each wing with a dab of glue.

Repeat process for left wing. Fold left and
right wings up vertically so that they meet:

Fold each wing outwards along dotted line
creating a V-shaped channel which will
become the butterfly's body.   ★★

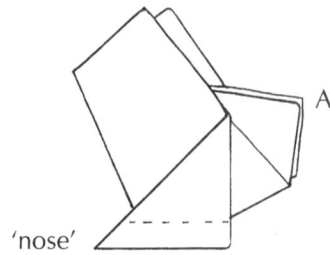

1/2

fold

fold

1/4

fold

fold

1/8

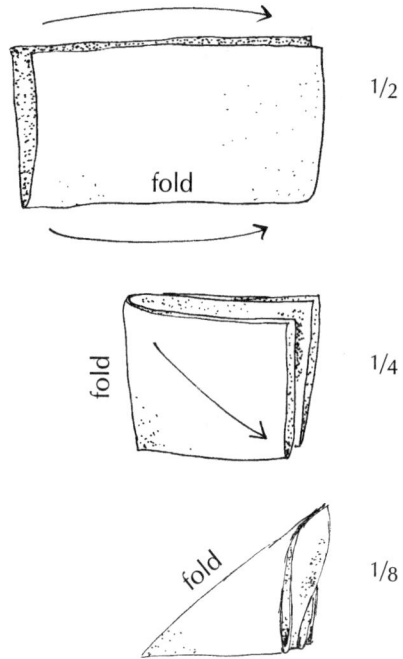

Summer birthday ring

Wind the ring with golden yellow ribbon and attach colourful crêpe or tissue-paper flowers and streamers.

You will need: (for a paper flower)
Crêpe or tissue paper,
- green 13cm x 13cm
- colour of choice 11cm x 11cm
- yellow paper 10cm x 2cm
Thread, thin wire, scissors

Fold green paper into one-eighth of its size
  as follows:

Cut into leaf shape as seen below and unfold.

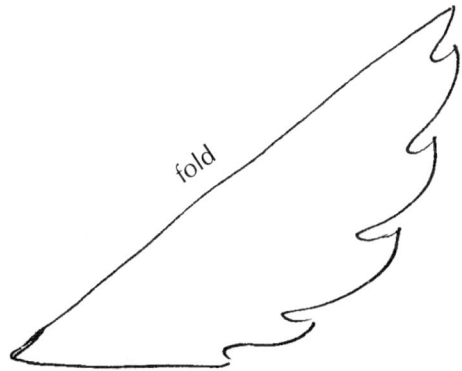

fold

Fold coloured paper in same way and cut petal shape as illustrated. Unfold paper.

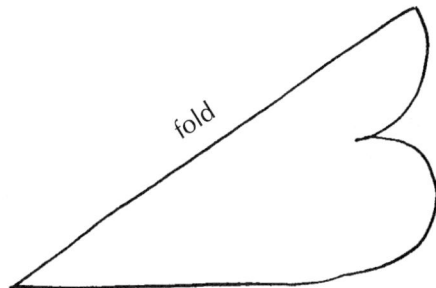

fold

Loosely roll strip of yellow paper and gather
    tightly at base to form 'stamens'.

Arrange petal-shaped paper around this by
    squeezing base of petals carefully towards
    the centre. Tie with thread.

Trim or fringe stamen ends as required.

same time. (Streamers are quickly made
by flattening a rolled sheet of paper and
cutting narrow lengths from one end.)

Crêpe streamers can be frilled (see page 133)

**Do not expose streamers
to a naked flame.**

Tip: Try hanging pom-poms (see page 94)
approx. 10cm below this ring

Autumn birthday ring

Place flower in centre of leaf-paper. Gather
    leaves around flower and tie with thread
    to secure.

Bind stalk with wire, twisting ends tightly
    together. Leave 3–4cm wire free to attach
    to birthday ring.

To decorate ring

Attach each flower to ring, adding ribbons or
    streamers of tissue or crêpe paper at the

Red ribbon, wired fir cones and pressed autumn leaves decorate this ring. Prepare the leaves in advance and string them with invisible thread.

You will need: (to wire pine cones)
Various pine cones
Medium-gauge florist's wire and pliers
Dry pine cones in a warm place until scales open.
Cut a 10cm length of wire and weave it around scales at base of cone.
Leave one 3cm end to twist around longer end to secure.
To attach cone: slide wire into ring.

To press leaves:
Place clean, dry, autumn leaves between pieces of paper towel and then between sections of a large book.
Place the book under a pile of books and leave for two weeks or longer.

Winter birthday ring

Use a deep blue ribbon – the colour of a night sky in winter – to wind around the ring.
Hang stars to correspond with the age of the child. (Stars can be strung together with gold thread to make hanging chains.)

You will need: (for gold star)
Star pattern A, page 219
Thin gold card 12cm x 24cm
Scissors, ruler and pencil
Sewing needle and gold thread
Paper clips and glue

Transfer (see page 210) pattern to reverse-side of card and mark all lines as shown on pattern.

137

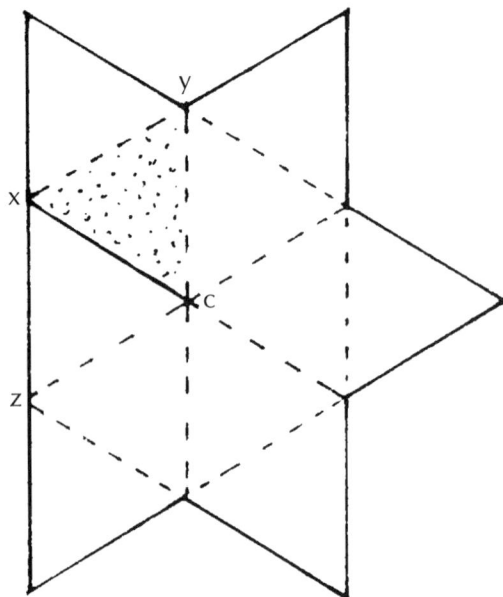

You will need:
The items listed on page 137 for large star
Dowelling or bamboo stick 45cm x 6–10mm
    diam.
Small quantity of cotton wool or tissue paper
5 paperclips

Follow instructions on pages 137–138 for
    making star, but pause before gluing two
    halves of star together.
Fill concave hollow of each half-star with
    cotton wool or crumpled tissue paper.

Score along dotted (folding) lines with back
    of scissor blade. Cut along solid lines.
Fold star along scored lines (back of card
    facing), opening out flat after each fold.
Cut from point x to centre c.
Glue triangle **y – x – c** on triangle **z – x – c**
    (**x** lies beneath point **y**).
Hold in place with paper clip while glue
    dries. Repeat for second star and glue the
    two stars back to back.
With needle, draw gold thread through star
    point to make hanging loop.
Follow same process for smaller star, using
    pattern B.

Smear glue around tip of stick. Place tip
    between the two filled stars and glue them
    together, securing points with paperclips
    while glue dries.

Star wand

This idea comes from a mother who always
includes such a wand among the flowers on
the birthday table. One can elaborate the
theme by spraying the stick gold, winding it
with narrow ribbon or attaching ribbon
streamers to each point of the star.

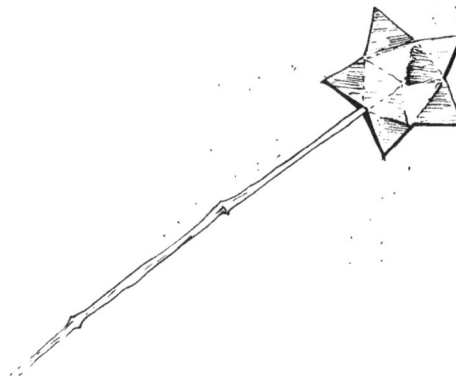

Decorative paper ball

An intriguing decoration to hang from the birthday ring. Select colours to harmonise with the ribbons on the ring.

Sew through tissue paper and card along crease in a figure-of-eight as shown below. End by passing needle through knot and back to pierce card at point **A**:

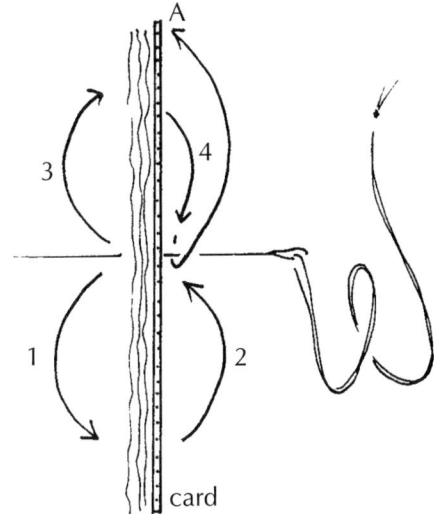

You will need:
Circle of thin, coloured card 7.5cm diam.
34 circles (see page 210) of coloured tissue
    paper
Needle and black sewing cotton
Several sheets clean scrap paper
Glue stick (fairly new), small bead

Fold card in half to crease.
Similarly, fold one circle of tissue paper.
    Unfold both.
Pile 30 circles of tissue paper neatly on the
    card, with creased tissue circle uppermost.
Match creases at top and bottom of pile.
Take 40cm length of black cotton and knot
    ends together. Thread needle.

Release needle to leave a loop for hanging the finished ball.

Place circles, card uppermost, on work surface.

➤➤Fold back half of card circle, place clean paper beneath top layer of exposed tissue paper and glue shaded area:

Close card to stick firmly to top sheet of tissue.

Now glue other sheets alternately at points **A** and then points **B** as on diagram below, each time placing *clean* paper beneath tissue to be glued, to avoid unplanned sticking.

Always close flap down over glue rather than bending glued paper upwards.

To ensure that paper lies correctly when project is finished, turn pile over and stick last five sheets in this position, closing the whole construction into a semicircle each time a sheet is glued.

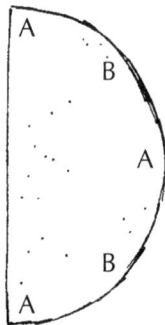

When 30 semicircles are glued, turn pile over, card uppermost, and repeat process from ➤➤.

Now make a tassel (see page 143)

Knot bead on end of 24cm length of black cotton.

Use needle to draw thread through centre of tassel from below until bead is hidden and holds thread firmly in place.

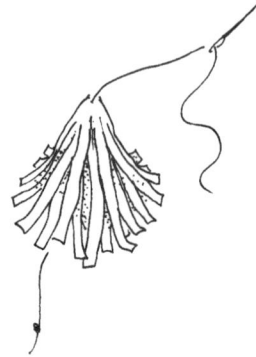

Pass needle through crease at bottom edge of card on the ball and secure with a knot, allowing tassel to hang approx. 1.5cm below the ball.

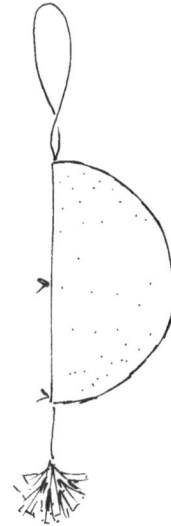

Fold two sections of card back-to-back and pin carefully together with small paperclip.

Gently tease apart tissue paper inadvertently stuck together, using blunt end of needle.

The ball is now ready for hanging.

To store: Remove paperclip and fold ball into semicircle, hold closed with paperclip.

Paper lantern decoration

These lanterns are easy to make but care and patience are needed. They can be made in plain colours, but combinations of two or three colours are also effective: pink, lavender and purple; or red, yellow and orange; or three shades of blue or green. Harmonise the choice of colours with the napkins or tablecloth.

Small lanterns are an attractive decoration for the birthday ring (see pages 131–138). Make 4 or 7 and hang one a little higher or lower than the rest in the centre of the ring.

You will need:
A4 sheet of plain white paper
Pair of compasses and pencil
36 circles (see page 210) of coloured tissue paper 13cm diam. or 7cm diam. for small lantern
Glue stick (fairly new)
Sharp scissors, craft knife and newspaper
2 circles of fairly stiff card to tone with chosen colour range, 13cm diam. *or* 7cm diam.
Darning needle
Embroidery cotton to tone with chosen colour range

Using compasses, draw circle radius 6.5cm (3.5cm for small lantern) on white paper. Mark equally spaced sections as below:

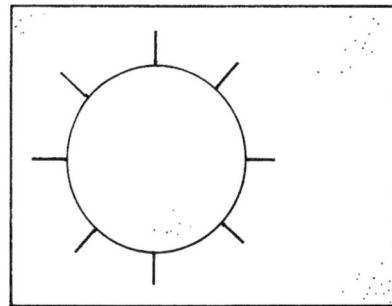

This will be your gluing guide.
Arrange a pile of 32 tissue paper circles in chosen colour sequence. (A lively effect is achieved by layering colours irregularly.)
Place first circle from pile (circle one) on gluing guide. Make a pencil mark on tissue circle between each guide-line as shown:

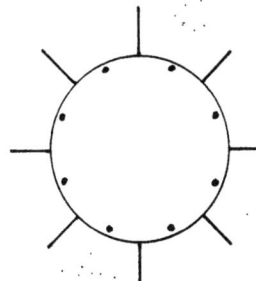

141

Turn circle over, keeping pencil marks in position between guide-lines. (These marks will be used later.)

Hold circle steady while placing dab of glue at each guide-line near, but not on, very edge of circle. Dab gently to avoid tearing paper.

This is gluing pattern A:

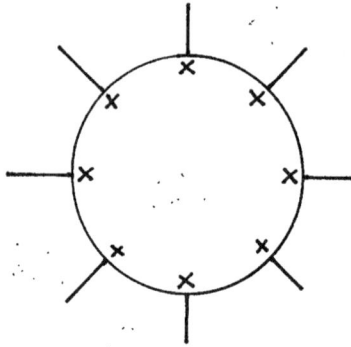

Place next circle of tissue on top and press firmly. Keep papers aligned with gluing guide.

Now place dab of glue *between* each guide-line.

This is gluing pattern B:

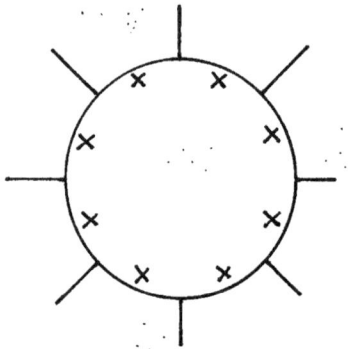

Press down next circle and dab glue as in gluing pattern A.

Continue to glue circles together, alternating patterns A and B, taking care to keep growing pile of circles neatly aligned with gluing guide.

Finally, make pencil mark at each glue point (Pattern A) on top circle of pile.

Place pile of glued circles on folded newspaper and use craft knife to cut a circle (5cm diam.) from centre (not necessary for smaller lantern).

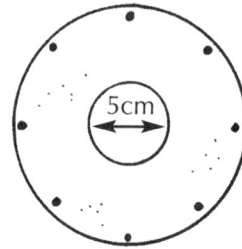

Dab glue on pencil marks around edge of top circle and press down one circle of coloured card.

Make tassel (see page 143) with remaining tissue circles.

Take 15cm length of embroidery cotton and knot end.

Using darning needle, pull thread through centre of tassel until knot is hidden and holds firmly:

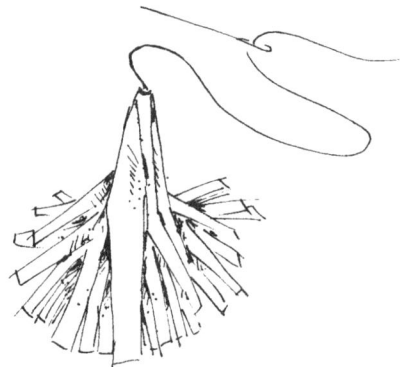

Thread cotton through centre of second circle of card and secure with knot, allowing tassel to hang by 2–3cm of thread.

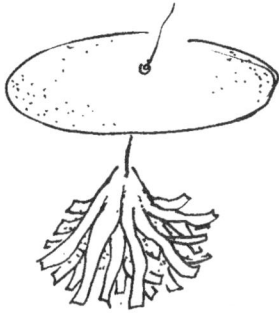

To make paper tassel

Place 4 circles (see page 210) of tissue paper in a pile. Fold pile as shown below:

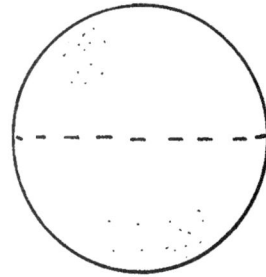

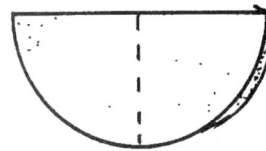

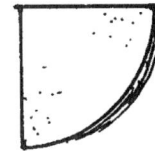

Complete lantern by placing dab of glue at each pencil mark on tissue paper circle one. Press circle of card, with tassel uppermost, down on glue.

Turn lantern over. Using needle and embroidery cotton, make hanger as shown:

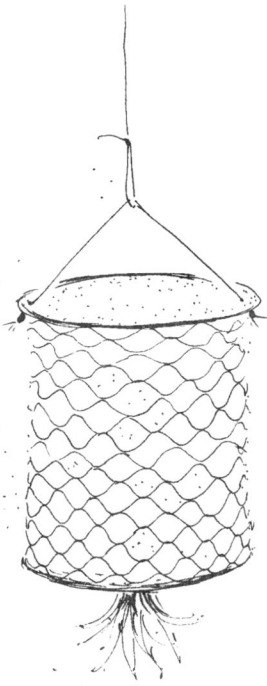

Make cuts with scissors, as shown, glue at **X** and fold one more time.

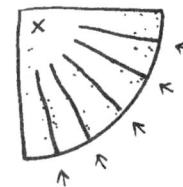

Shake out lantern, teasing apart any leaves of paper inadvertently stuck together, with blunt end of needle.

Bounce tassel on flat surface to fluff it up.

Festoon

This chain looks very complicated but the method is simple and the effect is stunning. Patience and a gentle touch will be rewarded. Make it in a single colour or a variety of harmonising colours such as yellows and greens, blues and purples, reds and oranges. A rainbow effect can be achieved by using two or three circles each of crimson, orange, yellow, green, blue, purple and mauve, and repeating the sequence.

You will need: (for a chain approx. 4.5m long)
48 circles (see page 210) coloured tissue paper 10.5cm diam.
Household iron
Sharp scissors, glue stick (fairly new), ruler
2 circles fairly stiff coloured card (gold, silver or toning with chosen colour range) 10.5 diam.
Darning needle

Embroidery cotton (to tone with chosen colour range) 30cm
Optional: Invisible thread (4.7m), 1 small bead

Method:
Arrange a pile of 48 circles of tissue paper in colour sequence of your choice. (A lively effect is achieved by layering the colours irregularly.)

➥➥Take first 12 circles, fold pile in half as shown below and cut with scissors along dotted lines leaving gap of approx. 1.5cm between **w** and **x**.

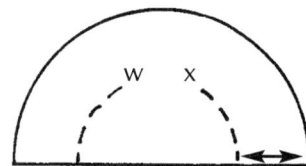

approx. 1·5cm

Unfold pile carefully and refold as below. Cut along dotted lines leaving gap between **y** and **z**.

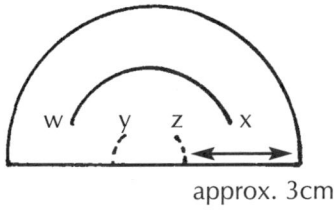

approx. 3cm

Unfold and press pile flat with medium hot iron. Repeat process from ❧ until all 48 circles have been folded, cut and pressed. Take care to retain chosen colour sequence. Place one circle of coloured card on work surface and dab glue in centre. This is gluing pattern **A**:

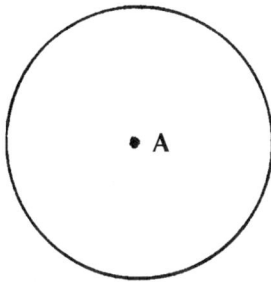

• A

Press down first circle of tissue paper on the card. Use glue stick gently to avoid tearing paper, and place two dabs of glue at x as shown in gluing pattern **B**:

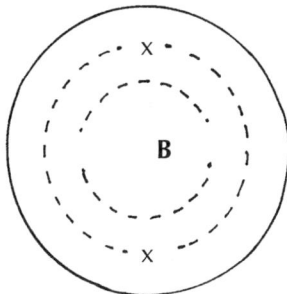

Repeat patterns **A** and **B** until all circles of tissue *and* second circle of card are glued together. If necessary, trim tissue paper to edge of card.

With needle and embroidery thread, sew a loop through centre of each end card for hanging.

Optional: use invisible thread to strengthen chain and avoid stretching.

Method:
Attach bead to end of thread as shown:

Thread needle and lead right through centre of chain.
Choose a new point of entry to return needle back through card **B** only, and secure inside with a firm knot.

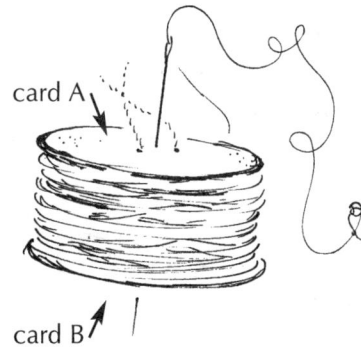

card A

card B

Make 5mm slanted slit in the edge of card **A**.

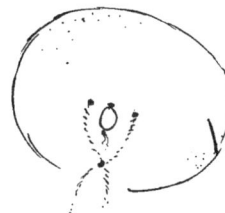

145

To hang: Hang chain by the loops of embroidery cotton. Tease apart circles inadvertently glued together using blunt end of needle.

To shorten: Pull bead to take up slack thread and draw thread deep into slit at edge of card.

To store: Fold by placing card B on floor and feeding rest of chain on to it from above, ensuring tissue paper is never crumpled. Take up slack invisible thread and wind it around closed chain, securing thread in slit at edge of card.

Paper chain

Cut piece of crêpe paper approx. 50cm x 14cm. Fold in half lengthways and then in half again lengthways. There are now four layers of paper.

Make cuts with scissors (approx. 1.5cm apart) according to diagram. Open out paper.

Make several of these sections and glue **together** to reach required length. Use **blu-tack** to hang the chain.

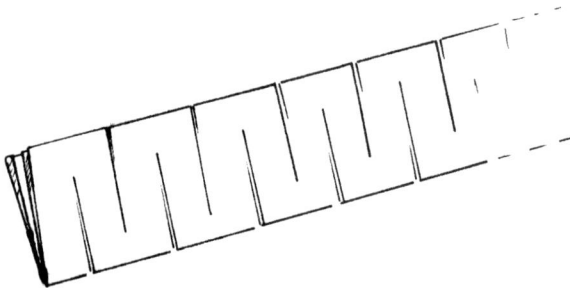

Windflower decoration

This brings colour and movement to an outdoor party.

You will need:
Windflower pattern (see page 215)
Pieces of medium card 16cm x 16cm each
Round wooden beads approx. 8mm diam.
Craft knife and scissors
Thin string or embroidery cotton

Make windflowers with pieces of card (see pages 100–101).

Tie bead at one end of string. Pass string through flower from front to back and through a second bead.

To add more flowers, make a knot around each supporting bead at the required distance:

Hang up the flowers and let the wind do the rest....

146

Napkin decorations

Simple napkin fold for formal birthday meal

This fold works well for plain square linen or cotton napkins. It creates a useful pocket for name card, chocolate, or a flower.

You will need:
Square napkin folded in quarters, or paper napkin straight from the packet

Place napkin on table with four free corners at top. Fold down two corners as shown:

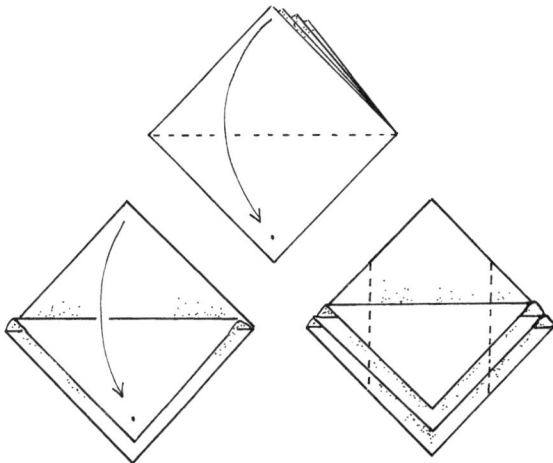

Fold back side corners to overlap beneath napkin:

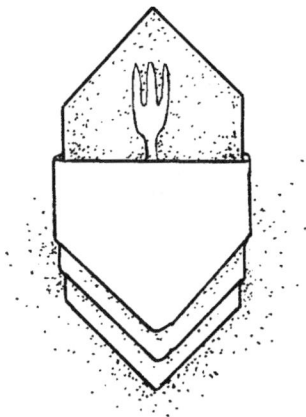

Water lily

These soft petal folds will grace the table of a summer party. Use a white starched linen napkin or a golden yellow paper napkin approx. 32cm square and place an orange or shiny red apple within each finished 'lily'.

Method:
Open napkin and fold corners to centre. Press to crease (using iron on linen napkin).
Repeat process as indicated:

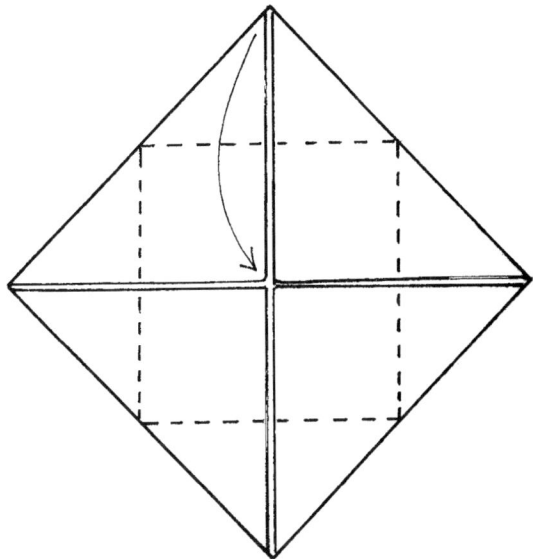

Turn napkin over. Repeat process and press. The napkin should now look like this:

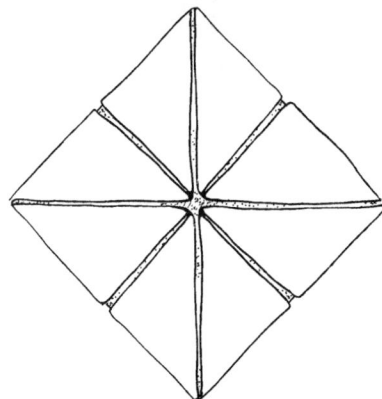

Hold centre points down firmly with one
hand.

With other hand pull up points which lie
underneath, in two stages – first the ones
of double-thickness:

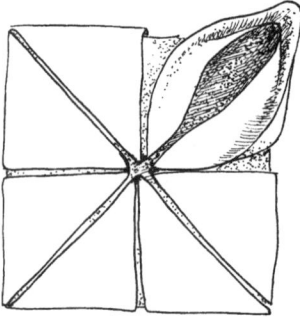

Continue to hold centre firmly, pull out
single-thickness points from underneath,
gently tugging upwards until 'water lily' takes
shape:

Sugar stick

Here is a crisp and colourful addition to the
party table. The fold is simple enough for a
six-year-old to manage.

You will need:
Paper napkins in two contrasting or
harmonising colours, at least 32cm square
(cheap one-ply napkins work well).
Tumblers or wine glasses

Open up napkins and place one over another
of a different colour, creating an overlap
of 2.5cm. Roll up from below.

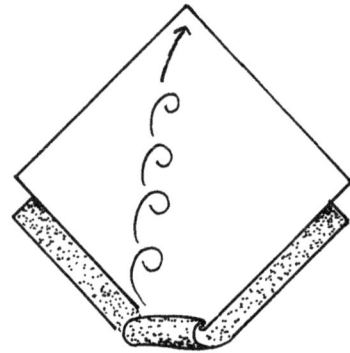

Bend 'sugar stick' in half, allowing ends to
meet at top.

Insert folded end in the glass.

St. Nicholas day party table napkin

On the Eve of St. Nicholas (5 December) many children across Europe leave a clean shoe at the window, on the doorstep or by the hearth, hoping that St. Nicholas will pass by and reward their good behaviour with something sweet.

Here is a charming little red boot to decorate each place at the birthday table – tucked inside is the child's name and a wrapped favour.

You will need:
Red paper napkin, at least 32cm square
Small gold or silver self-adhesive star

Fold napkin in half, twice, to make rectangle approx. 8cm x 32cm. Follow folds indicated below:

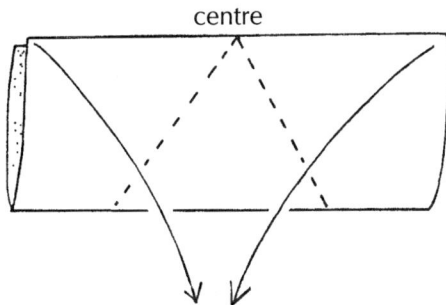

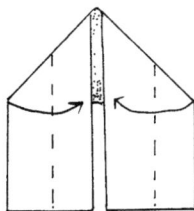

Now fold long sides together and turn sideways, so:

Fold top layer only:

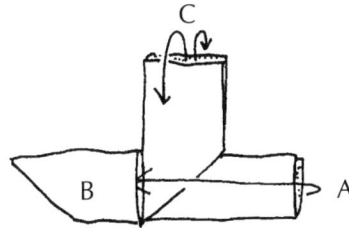

Ease end **A** under **B** and secure with a dab of glue. Roll down top edge **C**.

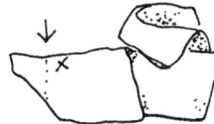

Press down to crease toe of boot. Place star at **X**.

Napkins should be folded neatly. The French method, which is very easy, of folding the napkin like a fan, placing it in a glass, and spreading out the upper part, is very pleasing. But the English method of folding is like a slipper, and placing the bread inside of it, is convenient as well as neat.

Enquire Within upon Everything ca. 1881

Table tips

✧ The festive atmosphere of a children's party table will depend largely on the choice of colour for the tablecloth, napkins, straws, name cards etc. When choosing these keep in mind the colours of other decorations e.g. paper chains, the hanging birthday ring, balloons etc. Harmonising or complementary colours are most effective.

✧ For a centre piece, try the Dragon loaf (see pages 128–129) or make a plain flag for each child using crêpe paper of different colours. (12cm x 14cm); glue one short side to a cane or plant-stick approximately 30cm in length. Set them in a colourful container half-filled with pebbles for stability. The flags can be distributed at going-home time.

✧ Coloured bed sheets can make good tablecloths.

✧ Sprinkle the table with fresh rose petals or metallic confetti.

✧ Pin or sew large bows of ribbon to the tablecloth so that they sit at each corner of the table.

✧ For an adult dinner party, consider having tea lights in matching holders, one at each place setting.

✧ Set a seasonal 'favour' (see pages 164–165) at each place.

✧ Lay a 'maypole' table: position a large, 18–25cm high church candle in a stable container at centre of table. Wire paper flower(s) to the wick. Attach crêpe streamers (2–3cm wide) to top of candle with blu-tack and lead a different colour to each place setting.
Warning: some crêpe paper stains when damp.

The whiteness of the tablecloth, the clearness of glass, the polish of plate, and the judicious distribution of ornamental groups of fruits and flowers, are matters deserving the utmost attention.

Enquire Within upon Everything ca. 1881

Chapter 12

GIFTS

In 1946, on the sixtieth birthday of the Aga Khan, he received his weight (110 kilos) in diamonds from his prosperous followers. He was weighed on a huge scale at a public ceremony where the diamonds were heaped until they balanced his portly frame. The diamonds (on loan from England) were returned and the equivalent in cash distributed to charity.

In times long past it was customary for the gods to receive offerings on their 'birthdays' from those who sought their divine protection. As kings and emperors came to be revered as gods they too would receive birthday offerings, possibly from similar motives. Perhaps the giving of birthday presents to men of lower rank, and now to women and children, is not only an indication of the modern ethic of equal rights, but also a growing acknowledgement of the personal 'genius' of the other who bears the godlike power to grasp and fashion his own destiny, and influence the destiny of others.

For centuries gifts have also been considered necessary on this vulnerable (see page 4) anniversary of birth because, as 'good deeds', they had the power to ward off negative influences.

> The only gift is a portion of thyself. Thou must bleed for me. Therefore the poet brings his poem; the shepherd, his lamb; the farmer, corn; the miner, a gem; the sailor, coral and shells; the painter, his picture; the girl, a handkerchief of her own sewing.'
>
> Ralph Waldo Emerson,
> *Gifts*, Second series of essays

Gift ideas

For newborn babies

- Muslin cloths (see page 211)
- A very simple doll (see pages 153–154)
- Measuring post (see page 154)
- Large woven basket for toy-tidy
- Sheepskin to lie on
- An attractively bound blank notebook to record the progress of the child and all the funny things he will say one day
- A very large 'life candle' to be lit at future birthdays
- For a girl, a bead of the birthstone. One to be given every year until, at eighteen, they are strung as a necklace
- A tree seedling in a pot

For toddlers

- Wooden pull-along toy; Jumping Jack (see pages 158–159)
- Small chair; sandbox; doll's bed / cradle
- Picture books of animals, preferably art-work in colour (which stimulates the imagination) rather than cartoons or photos
- Apron/overall; tubes of watercolour in red, blue and yellow; beeswax crayon blocks
- Bucket and spade
- An assortment of cut and sanded wooden shapes for creative building

For pre-school child

- Soft doll to dress (with long hair to plait)
- Doll's pram or buggy; doll's clothes
- Wooden cars/dumper trucks/train without tracks
- Large wooden beads
- Wooden iron and ironing board
- Small broom; brush and dustpan
- Toy saucepans etc. (A 'cooker' can be made from a large, sturdy, cardboard box. Four circles of card indicate cooking rings and an 'oven door' is cut in the front.)

For 5–7 years

- Small wheelbarrow; garden tools; bulbs to plant
- Special box for 'treasures'; large shell, crystal
- Small rucksack; dressing-up clothes; ankle bells
- Snakes and ladders board-game; large, light ball
- Simple doll's house with furniture; small clothes pegs
- Hardback book of fairy tales (see pages 181–182); book of children's classic verse
- Box of wax crayons; modelling wax
- Small beanbag with 45cm polyester ribbons attached – for throwing high

Tip: When giving a box, purse, bag, rucksack or garment with pockets always slip in a little surprise gift.

For 7–10 years

- Simple glove puppets (undefined characters e.g. man, woman etc. will allow the imagination more scope)
- Glitter glue, sellotape, hole punch; pack of coloured paper
- Small hammer, saw, variety of nails, sandpaper; offcuts of wood
- Skipping rope; simple kite; stilts
- Origami paper; sewing kit; knitting needles and wool; squares of felt
- Ludo board game; airtight container of real clay
- Some coins buried in a pot of sprouting cress
- An apple bearing the child's initial: Choose a type of apple which reddens when ripe. Some weeks before harvest when apple is green, stick paper, cut into shape of initial, securely on sun side of apple using blu-tack. Protect with loose plastic bag with corners cut off for air flow. Wait and watch.

Gifts to make

Most people, even quite young children, experience enormous satisfaction in making something, especially a gift for a loved one.

When engaging a youngster in a creative process, the secret is to maintain their enthusiasm by keeping the process moving. Children do not like sitting around waiting for materials to be found, things to be measured, patterns to be drawn, etc. Good preparation will avoid this.

Add lots of encouragement and try hard not to notice the imperfections. Be tactful in offering help and avoid 'taking over' unless the child is about to cause damage or injury. Well-supervised practice in handling tools builds confidence and develops co-ordination and expertise.

Dolls for babies

Knotted doll

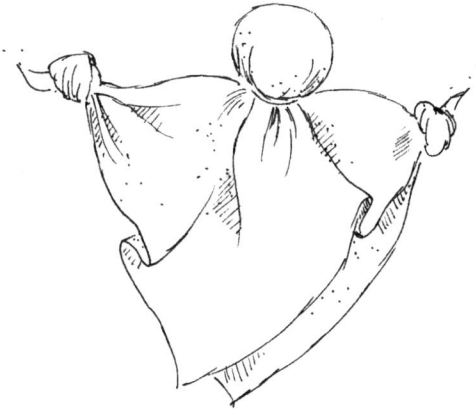

You will need:
Silk or brushed cotton square 30cm x 30cm in pastel colour
Thread in same colour; sewing needle
Length of embroidery thread in same colour
Washed and carded fleece (or substitute) to stuff head

Sew narrow hem around square.
Place enough fleece in centre of square to make a round, fairly firm 'head' of approx. 4.5cm in diameter.
Tie a 'neck' firmly with embroidery thread, distributing folds in the fabric neatly and evenly.
Arrange fabric to lie in a triangle below head and knot the corners of fabric to right and left of head as seen above.

Small doll

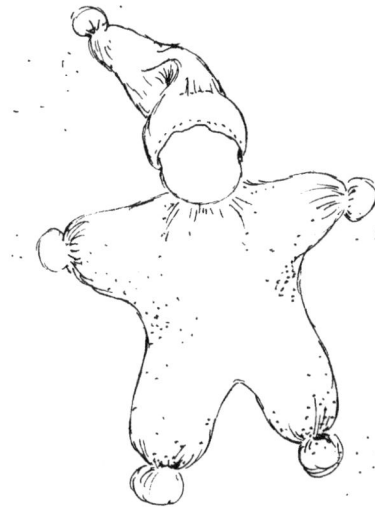

You will need:
Doll pattern, page 220
Cotton fabric (medium weight) 32cm x 22cm
Washed and carded fleece for stuffing
Needle, sewing thread and scissors
Strong thread matching colour of fabric
Stockinette 13cm x 13cm in skin colour

Transfer (see page 210) patterns to paper and cut out.
Fold fabric in half, right sides inside. Pin patterns to fabric and cut out.
Sew body pieces together along sewing line, reverse-side facing, leave opening to insert neck.

Clip fabric under arms and in crotch as indicated on pattern.

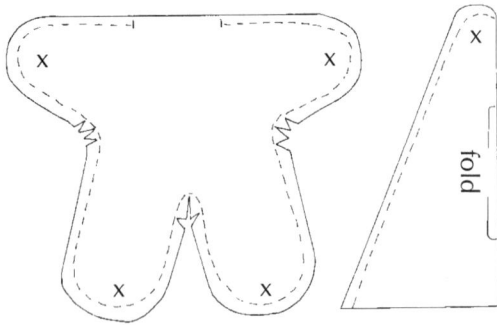

Turn body inside out.

Sew hat seam.

Push small quantities of fleece into extremities only (**x**) and tie off with strong thread to make firm, small hands, feet and bobble on cap, of approx. 1.5cm diameter.

Stuff body so that it remains soft and flexible.

Place enough fleece in centre of stockinette to make a round, fairly firm 'head' approx. 4.5cm in diameter.

Tie a neck tightly with strong thread, keeping a 'face' area as free of folds as possible.

Insert neck and secure with stitches.

Fold rim of hat under and attach it to head with small stitches.

Measuring post

A very personal gift for a new baby or for a first birthday. On each birthday, the post is marked with the date and the child's height.

You will need:
Wooden pole approx. 2m x 5cm diam.
Or wooden slat 8cm x 2cm x 2m

Sand wood. Carve, paint or use pokerwork to write child's name and date of birth at top of post.

If post is round, drill hole for threading hanging-cord. For a square post, drill hole near top and near base to screw to wall.

Complete package with two suitable screws and rawlplugs (expansion bolts).

Walking star boy and jester

These little puppets could be made by a child of nine years or older as a birthday gift for a younger sibling. The jester will walk, skip, jump and amuse any toddler, and the star boy has sometimes appeared tiptoeing over the duvet to give a last kiss at bedtime...

You will need:
(basic requirements for each doll)
Stockinette, skin-coloured, 15cm x 15cm (a good skin colour is obtained by dyeing white T-shirt cotton in ordinary, black Indian tea)
Fleece for stuffing
Length of thin yellow or brown wool for hair
Optional: Scraps of blue and pink embroidery cotton for face.

Star boy

You will need: (in addition to the above)
Star boy patterns, page 221
Dark blue felt for hat and body 12cm x 28cm
Light blue felt for waistcoat 14cm x 6.5cm
Yellow felt for collar 10cm x 10cm
Embroidery cotton to match felt colours

Transfer (see page 210) star boy patterns to
paper and cut out. Pin patterns on
appropriate colour of felt (see above). Cut
out felt pieces.
Cut square of stockinette 10cm x 10cm for
head. Place enough fleece in square to
make round, firm ball, about 3cm across,
when tied as indicated below:

Similarly, cut two squares 4cm x 4cm from
stockinette to make two small hands, each
'hand-ball' no larger than 1cm diam.

Insert 'neck' into neck opening of felt body-
piece and secure with a few stitches. Avoid
fabric wrinkles appearing at front of face.
With blue embroidery cotton, sew together
front and back of body on each side,
starting from sleeve as seen below.
Sew inside trouser legs as illustrated. *Do not
sew across bottom openings of trouser legs.*

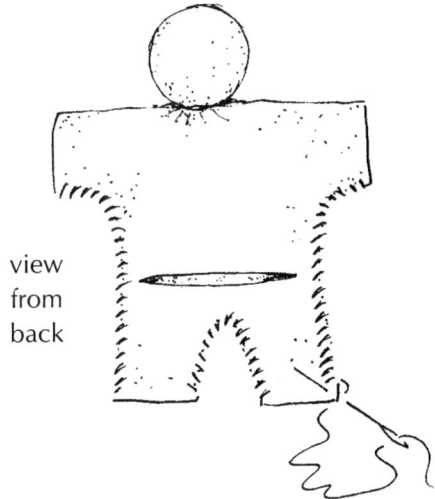

view
from
back

Sew each hand into a sleeve. Stuff small
amounts of fleece into arms and top half
of body via back opening.
Sew loops of woollen thread on top of head
(not too near face) and secure each loop
with small backstitch. Cut loops to make
individual hair strands for a fringe.

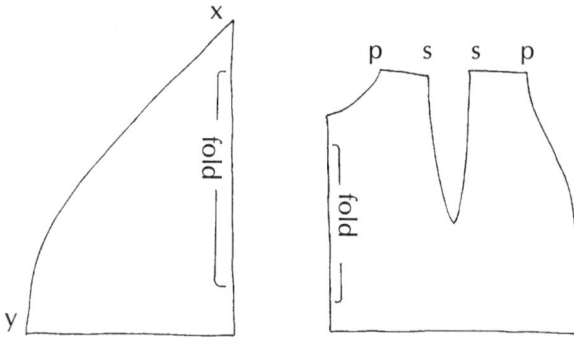

Sew up hat from **x** to **y**, using same stitching technique as for body.

Fix hat to head with small stitches around base of hat. Trim hair fringe if necessary.

To make waistcoat, stitch across shoulder seams matching **s** to **s** and **p** to **p**.

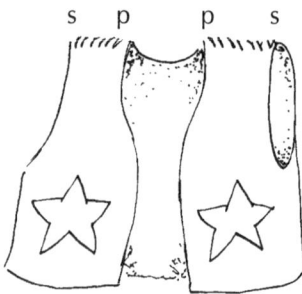

Cut four stars from yellow felt and sew two to waistcoat as seen above.

Sew other two stars together around tip of hat, using yellow embroidery thread.

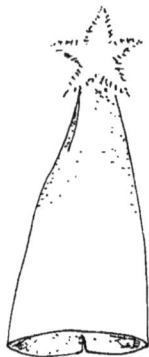

Dress star boy in waistcoat and secure star collar around neck with a few stitches.

Optional: Use a very few small stitches to indicate eyes and mouth.

Jester

You will need (in addition to basic requirements):

Jester patterns, page 222

Felt in three bright colours:

- Colour one – 30cm x 6cm
- Contrasting colour – 30cm x 6cm
- Felt in third colour for collar – 10cm x 10cm

Optional: 2 tiny bells for hat (not suitable for children under three)

Embroidery cotton to match felt colours

Transfer (see page 210) jester patterns to paper and cut them out.

Begin by making the hat.

To make up hat:

Cut out one **front piece** and one **back piece** in first colour choice and cut out second front and back pieces from second colour.

Starting with first colour, sew front and back together matching letters (**a** to **a**, **b** to **b**, **c** to **c**). Place finished half of hat, front uppermost, on work surface.

Place two cut-out pieces in second colour alongside finished first half so that the two points (**b**) of the hat, point in opposite directions.

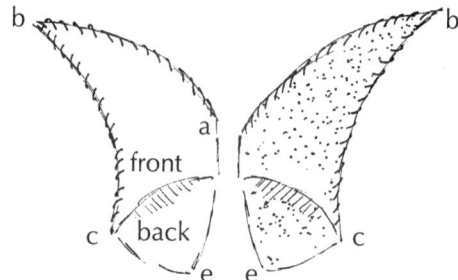

Sew second half of hat together matching letters as before. Now sew two halves together from **d** to **a** and from **a** to **e**.
Cut body pattern in half along dotted line. Cut out each half in a different colour.
Arrange body pieces to be joined in reverse colour order to hat. Sew together as shown:

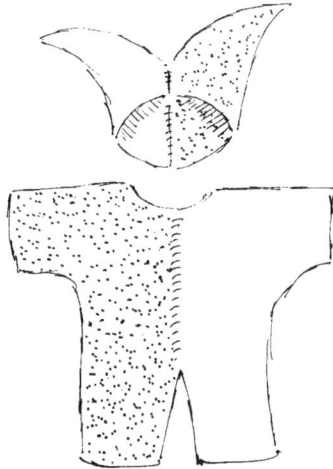

Make up head, hands and collar of jester as described above for star boy.
Optional: Sew one bell to each point of hat.

Tiny elf

Dress each elf in a different colour of the rainbow and offer them as a set or make sure that a new one is sitting on the birthday table each year. (Elves love to have a house made for them, with a garden in which they can play and discover new tricks....)

You will need:
2 pipe cleaners
Wooden bead 1cm diam.
Scraps of felt for dress and hat
Needle and thread
Scissors and glue

Cut 8cm length of pipe cleaner and fold in half. Push folded end into bead.
Cut 4cm length of pipe cleaner for arms and twist body around them as shown.
Bend back 2–3mm at each end of pipe cleaner to indicate hands and feet.

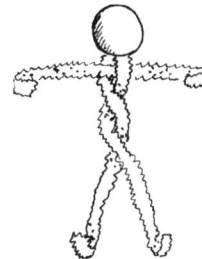

Cut out dress and hat from felt according to pattern below. Make small hole in dress for neck opening as shown:

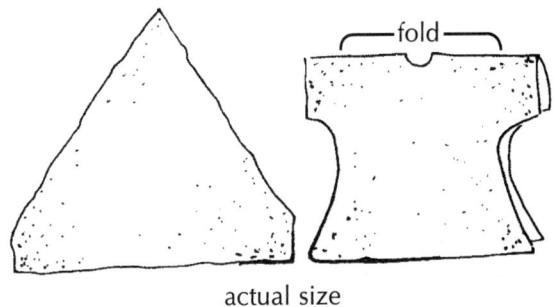

fold

actual size

Remove bead and slip dress over body.

Dab glue on 'neck' and replace bead. Sew up
side seams of dress.
Fold triangular piece in half for hat and sew
together as shown. Glue hat on head bead.

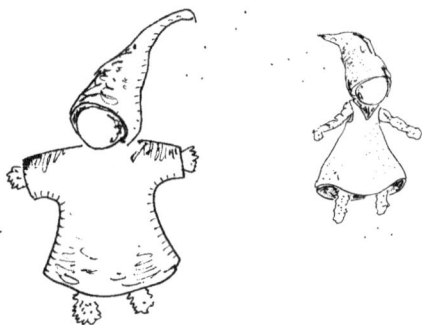

Jumping Jack

This is an ideal present for ages 3–5 years or
for a gentle two-year-old. An older child
could easily make this for a younger sibling.
It may also be constructed from plywood,
with strong cord knotted on both sides to act
as joints.

You will need:
Jumping Jack pattern, page 223
Piece of strong card 21cm x 21cm in pale
colour
4 metal paper fasteners
Metal meat skewer or pointed scissor blade
Fairly large wooden bead
Thin string and wax crayons

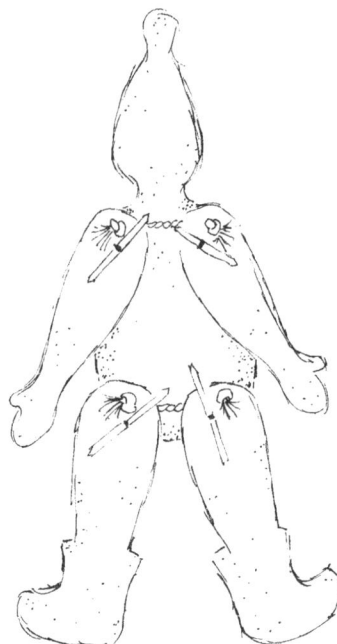

Transfer (see page 210) pattern to card.

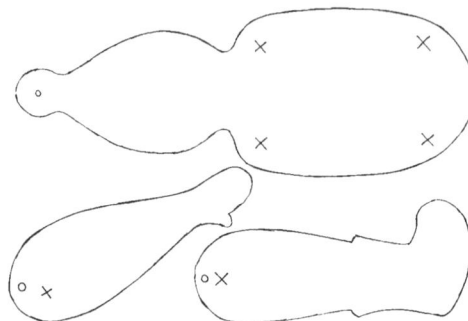

Cut out body, two arms and two legs, and
colour them in plain, bright colours
(make sure you create both a left and
right arm and leg).
Pierce points marked X and O with skewer.
Connect limbs to body at points X using
paper fasteners, opening out fasteners at
the back.
Working on the back, hold limbs down and
thread short length of string through each
hole O on arms, and knot at both ends.
Repeat this with legs to form two 'crossbars'.
(Strings should not be slack when limbs
are at rest.)

Thread bead on 40cm of string. Attach one end of string to centre of arms' string and other end to centre of legs' string.

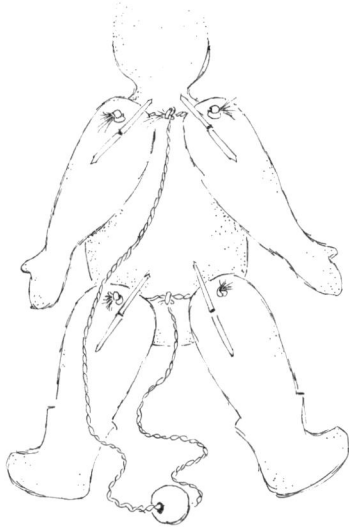

Loop string through hole in hat to hang Jack up, and tug gently at the bead to make him jump!

Ball of surprises

Here is an unusual present for anyone who likes to knit or crochet, and a helpful encouragement for a hesitant beginner. As the knitting grows, tiny surprises fall out of the ball of wool one by one. Do not include chocolates as they may melt.

You will need:
Ball of double-knitting wool
Numerous small gifts, individually wrapped e.g. hairclip, pencil sharpener, eraser, jewellery, small bell, coin, charm, ribbon, tiny wood or china animal, sticker, bath pearl, flower seeds, pretty stone or shell, small yo-yo or spinning top, beads etc.

Begin with the most exciting present and wind enough wool around it to almost conceal it, then add the next present and wind more wool, and so on.
If a tiny box containing a polished stone or bell is included, then the ball will rattle or ring mysteriously when shaken…

Note: Bells and small items are not suitable for children under three.

Paper jewellery

Older children and teenagers can experiment and be more adventurous with colours and size of bead.

Necklace

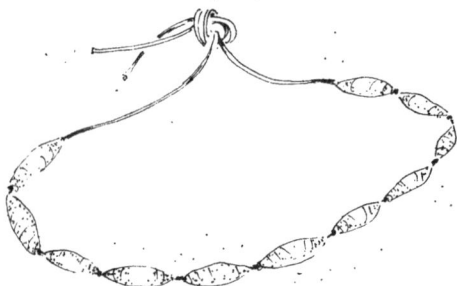

You will need: (for 11 beads)
Patterned paper of a favoured colour scheme, 30cm x 18cm
Glue, scissors, ruler and pencil
Thin leather cord or shoelace for stringing beads
Thin knitting needle
Optional: Polyurethane varnish, gloss or matt

Use reverse-side of paper to draw elongated triangles measuring 3cm at the base, as shown:

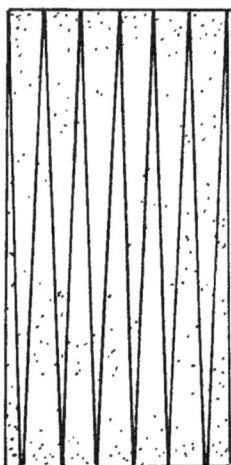

Cut out eleven triangles.
Begin at base of triangle and roll it evenly around knitting needle, securing the end with a dab of glue.

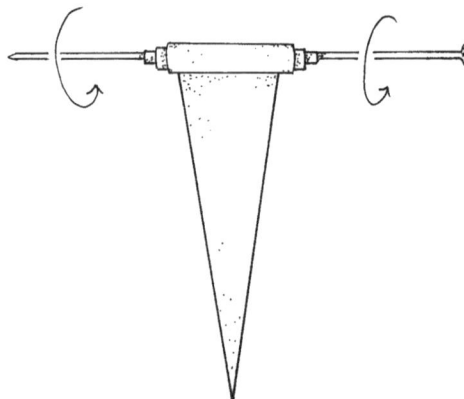

Slip bead off knitting needle and thread on leather cord. Repeat process until all beads are made and threaded.
The cord can be fastened with a simple knot; alternatively, suitable clasps are available at craft shops.

(For a more durable finish, apply varnish to beads before assembling necklace. Thread beads on string stretched tightly between two chair backs. Protect floor and furniture from drips. Apply coat of varnish to each bead. Space beads with clothes pegs. Allow adequate time to dry.)

Earrings
Buy fittings at a craft shop.
Thread paper bead on silver wire and add a small glass bead in a matching colour.
Twist end of wire as shown:

String tidy

An attractive and truly useful present that can be made by a young child with adult help.

You will need:
Tin with removable lid (plastic or metal) large enough to hold a roll or ball of string
Roll or ball of string
Drawing paper
Crayons or coloured pencils
Tape measure, glue, scissors
Metal meat skewer or large nail

Measure height and circumference of tin.
Cut out drawing paper according to these measurements and add 1cm to width for overlap as shown:

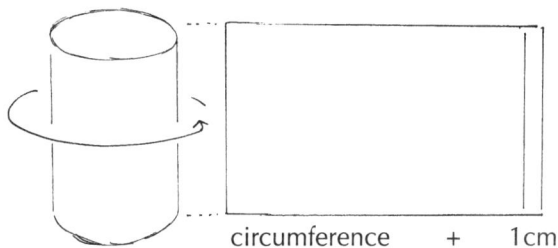

circumference   +   1cm

Cut a circle of paper large enough to cover top of lid, using lid as pattern.
Invite child to decorate both pieces of paper on one side only, covering the whole side with colour.
Glue circle of paper to top of lid. Glue other paper around tin.
Use skewer from above downwards to pierce a hole in centre of lid. (Flatten sharp metal edges with a hammer.)
Place ball of string inside tin and lead end of string through hole in lid before closing tin.

Calendar of birthdays

The dimensions of this useful birthday calendar allow for a postcard-sized picture for each month. Select 12 cards or draw, paint or print your own pictures. These could relate to the seasons, family events or festivals. Photographs or children's drawings could also be used. A great present for an aunt, uncle or godparent from an older child.

You will need:
12 sheets of (thin) coloured card 21cm x 29.7cm (A 4 size)
Ruler, coloured pencil or pen, eraser
Pictures of your choice
Hole punch, glue
Length of thick wool or pretty string approx. 50cm

On each sheet, measure and draw faint pencil lines according to diagram below:
Write name of each month lightly in pencil above squares as seen below, spacing letters evenly.
Draw over letters in coloured pencil or ink. Erase pencil marks if necessary.
Centre hole punch at top end of calendar and make holes.

Glue pictures in space available.
When all twelve pages are ready, thread
25cm length of string or wool through
each hole and knot them as seen below:

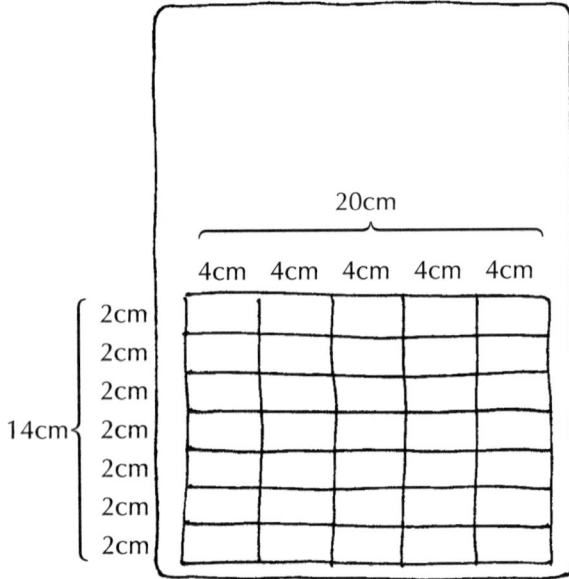

To a Lady, with a Present

My dear Catherine,
I have taken the liberty to present you with the enclosed
souvenir. The acceptance will confer a greater amount of
satisfaction on the donor than the receiver can possibly derive
from it. As a mere straw may tell how the wind blows, so such
a trifle as this may indicate how the current of my friendship
flows towards you. Accept it then as a token of how much and
how sincerely your friendship is esteemed by
           Your devoted humble Servant

        Constans Walton

The Gentleman's Letter Writer (19th century)

Chapter 13

GIFT-WRAP

Bounty always receives part of its value from the manner in which it is bestowed.

Samuel Johnson

Wrapping paper

Create your own gift-wrap with a roll of thin wall-lining paper decorated with a simple motif. Print matching gift tags on small pieces of card.

You will need:
Wall lining paper
Potato, medium size
Sharp kitchen knife
Poster paint (or water colour) and
    paintbrush

Cut potato in half and carve a simple raised shape, about 1cm high as shown:

Apply paint to top surface only of potato
    stamp, making sure paint is not too thin.
Print all over paper, renewing paint as
    necessary.

Sun-bleached paper

Take a sheet of tissue paper in a strong colour.
Fold it 'untidily' a few times, i.e. so that
edges cross, rather than meet each other.

Attach it to the glass of a window where it
will receive strong sunlight and wait for
light to bleach patterns on the paper.

Place e.g. maple leaves, bits of string or lace-
work between paper and glass for other
interesting effects.

Other ideas

- Use fine-textured Japanese paper napkins
  for wrapping. Try hessian or dress net.
- Crumple tissue paper into a ball and
  spray briefly with gold paint. Allow to dry
  before opening.
- Experiment with layers: e.g. white tissue
  paper over a strong-coloured paper,
  cellophane paper over a patterned paper.

Gift-wrap accessories

What transforms a modest gift into something
quite special? It is, of course, the care and
thought that has gone into its presentation.
Once the parcel is wrapped, there are many
ways of adding a touch of artistry to delight
both the giver and the recipient.

A simple enhancement can be achieved by
tucking a small 'favour' under the ribbon and
gift tag on the parcel. The character of these
favours could be chosen according to the
season. Here are some examples:

Note: Bells and small items are not suitable
for children under three.

Spring

Fresh spring flowers with stalk ends wrapped
in damp kitchen paper and covered neatly
with foil; a pale yellow or green candle; twigs
from a tree or shrub that is coming into leaf;
origami frogs, or the butterfly on page 133.

Summer

Fresh, paper or silk flowers; threaded shells
or pebbles with holes; fresh herbs; bells; a
lavender bag; a beeswax candle; a string of
glass beads or sequins sewn on a ribbon.

Autumn

Pressed and dried autumn leaves; stalks of
dried grass, wheat, oats or other grain; a
simple corn 'dolly'; a bunch of the winged
seeds or 'pigeons' of the sycamore or maple;
dried seed heads from nigella, aquilegia or
common poppy; a 'posy' of dried apple rings
tied together with thread.

Winter

A sprig of evergreen and a red, white or gold
candle; a twist of dried orange peel; a sprig
of winter berries; cinnamon sticks; tinsel, a
gold star (see page 137).

All seasons

Choose colours appropriate to the season for both gift-wrap and favours. Add pom-poms (see page 94), tassels (see page 143) or a bunch of narrow gift-ribbons tied tightly together in the middle and each end curled with a knife.

Bird favour

This little bird could be made in different seasonal colours. For the warmer, russet tones of autumn, a grey or brown feather should be used. The paper tail is tucked under the parcel ribbon, while the feather tail lies on top.

You will need:
Coloured paper 10cm x 7cm (e.g. good quality notepaper or lightweight drawing paper)
Pointed scissors
Glue and a fine needle
Goose feather or similar in white or brown as appropriate, approx. 4–5cm long (feathers that are slightly curved, with some soft down at the root of the quill are most suitable).

Transfer (see page 210) pattern to a piece of scrap paper. Cut away and discard all paper below fold line.
Fold coloured paper so short ends come together and position pattern on paper and against fold. Cut round pattern through all layers of paper.

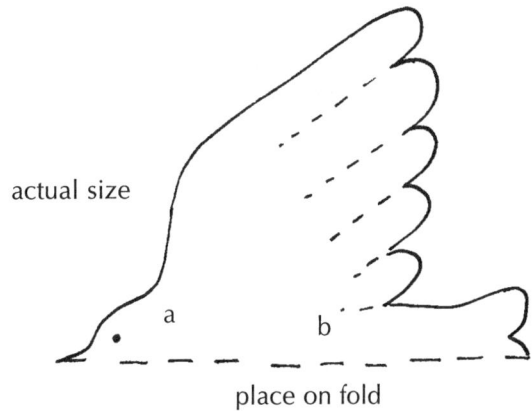

actual size

place on fold

Cut along dotted lines on wing to create feathers. Use needle to pierce an eye.
Curl wing feathers using a scissor blade as shown:

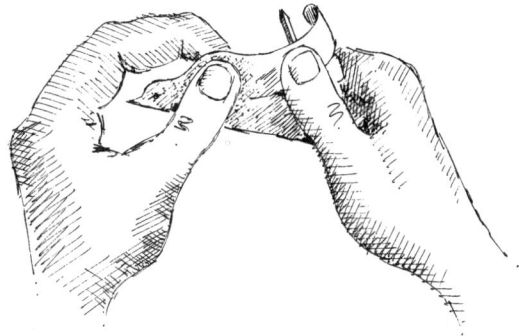

Fold each wing outwards along a line from **a** to **b** as indicated on pattern. Crease well.
Place dab of glue on fold line at **x** as shown below:

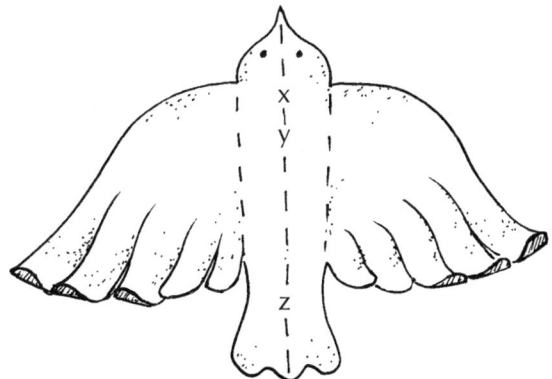

165

Pinch the two sides of bird's body together at **x** and hold in place until glue is dry.
Dip quill end of feather into glue and insert into body at **y**.
Bend tail downwards at **z** so that it flattens.

Gift tags

Experiment with one of the many craft punches available. Cut card for tag so that design can be punched centrally. The hole can be left or lined with contrasting paper, tissue paper or silk.

Retain perforations spilling from the punch and glue one, two or three of them close together on paper of a complementary colour 5 x 10cm folded in half as a gift tag.

Ribbon (of cloth)

These can be stiffened by saturating with a sugar solution (3tsps to half a cup of water). Allow to dry, then iron with moderate heat between clean scrap paper.

Money gifts

Teenagers or young adults are usually very happy to receive money on their birthday. Here are some ideas for presenting banknotes in a creative way.

You will need:
3, 5 or 7 banknotes
Glass clip frame – approx. A4 or larger
Sheet of white paper to fit frame
Coloured crayons, paints or pencils
Blu-tack

Fold each banknote into a flower head as shown:

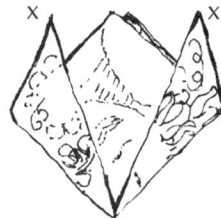

Draw or paint stems and leaves on paper as illustrated and hold money flowers in place at end of stems with blu-tack.

Enhance picture with sunshine and touch of
    colour around flowers.
Assemble picture and frame.

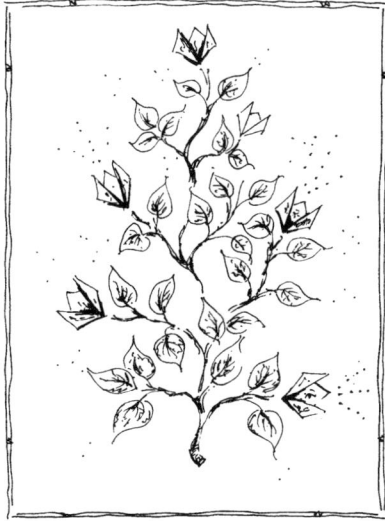

When one of our sons reached eighteen he
wanted his first proper suit. The idea
described above was extended, using a 15cm
x 21cm clip frame, to make a suit from
folded banknotes with cut-out photograph as
head, and coins for hands and feet.

Decorative frame for a banknote

You will need:
Square of coloured paper or gift-wrap paper
    Size: 15cm for £5; 16cm for £10;
            16.5cm for £20; 17cm for £50.
Glue stick

Begin with reverse-side of paper facing.
    Follow instructions for decorative open
    box (see below) until fifth diagram only,
    omitting instructions for second diagram.
Secure flaps at back of frame with glue. This
    makes a flat pouch with decorative frame.
Insert a once-folded banknote of appropriate
    size, with one of the portraits uppermost.

Tip: This frame could become a gift tag. Slip
in coloured card bearing name and message.

Money tree

Prepare a budding, flowering or leafy branch
    in a stable vase.
Punch a hole in one corner of several small,
    decorated envelopes.
Place a coin or banknote inside each
    envelope and seal.
Attach them to branch with ribbon.

Gift boxes

Decorative open box

This is more effective when paper with
different coloured faces is used.

You will need:
Square of coloured paper (a 9cm square will
    make a box approx. 2.3cm square)

Crease paper twice diagonally to find centre.
Fold all corners to centre. Turn over and fold
    all corners as shown:

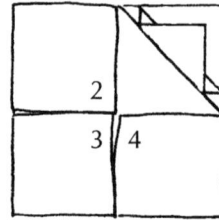

reverse face

Fold centre corners back to the edge:

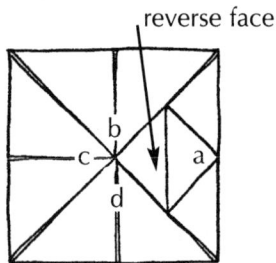

reverse face

Turn over and fold centre corner to outer corner and back towards centre as shown, creasing well each time. This begins a 'concertina' fold.

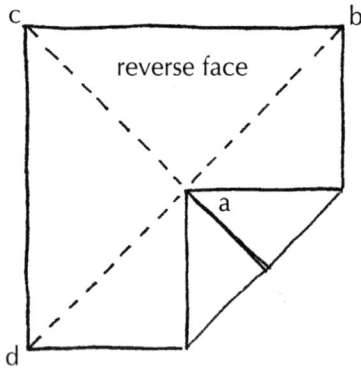

top face

crease very well

Continue concertina fold as shown below, for all four corners:

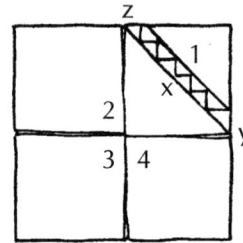

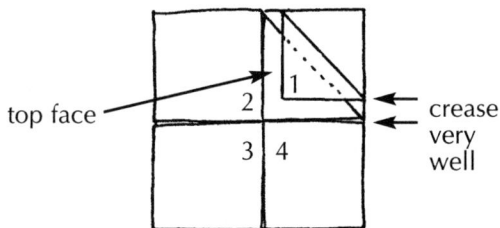

Slide finger of one hand under concertina fold and into corner 'pocket'.

With finger and thumb of other hand, squeeze sides of pocket together so that concertina fold peaks.

Repeat for all corners until form takes shape of an open box as shown:

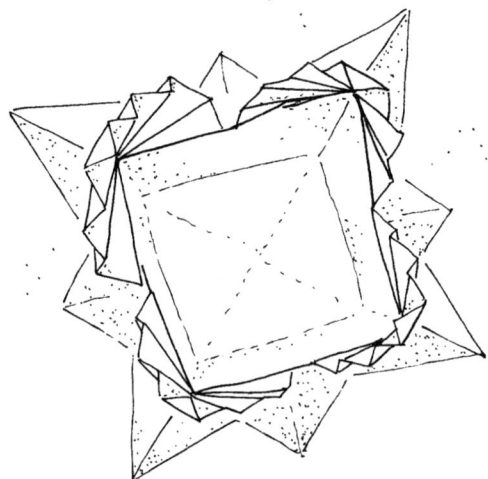

Gift pouch

Gold or silver card will give this box the
sheen of luxury.

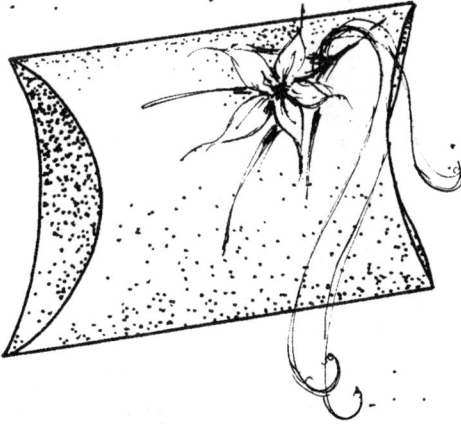

You will need:
Gift pouch pattern, page 224
Medium card or stiff paper 19cm x 23cm
Pointed scissors and glue

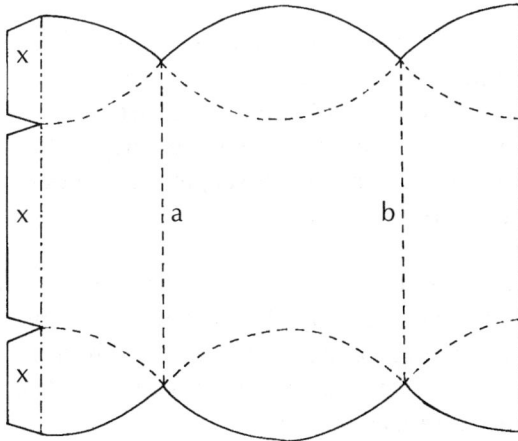

Transfer (see page 210) pattern to card
    enlarging or reducing it as necessary.
Cut along solid lines and score along dotted
    (folding) lines with back of scissor blade.

With right side down, fold lines **a** and **b**,
    bringing tabs towards straight edge of card.
Apply glue to topside of tabs (**x**) and press
    straight edge of card down firmly on the
    glue.

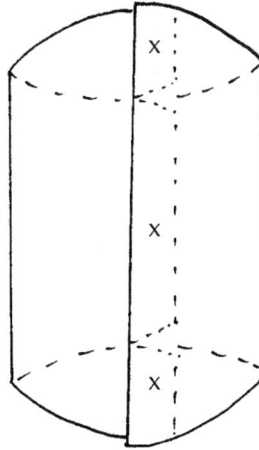

When glue has dried, press down each end
flap, encouraging folds along the scored
lines by applying slight pressure to each
side of pouch.

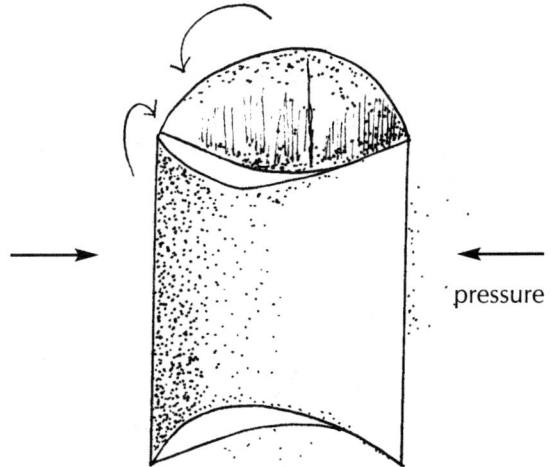

pressure

Decorate pouch with glitter glue, pressed
    flowers or leaves, or a collage of magazine
    cuttings.

Flap lid box

You will need:
Flap lid box pattern, page 225
Piece of card 19cm x 19cm
Ruler, scissors and glue

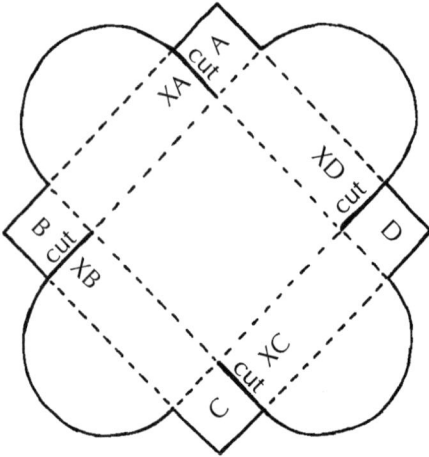

Transfer (see page 210) pattern to card. Cut along solid lines. Score along dotted lines with back of scissor blade.

Fold card along all scored lines, opening and laying it flat again after each fold.

Glue flap **A** on **XA** (on the inside of box). Repeat with flap **B** on **XV**, **C** on **XC** and **D** on **XD**

To close box, arrange the four rounded flaps as seen below:

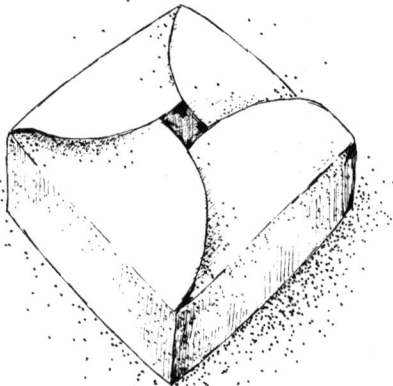

Seven gift boxes

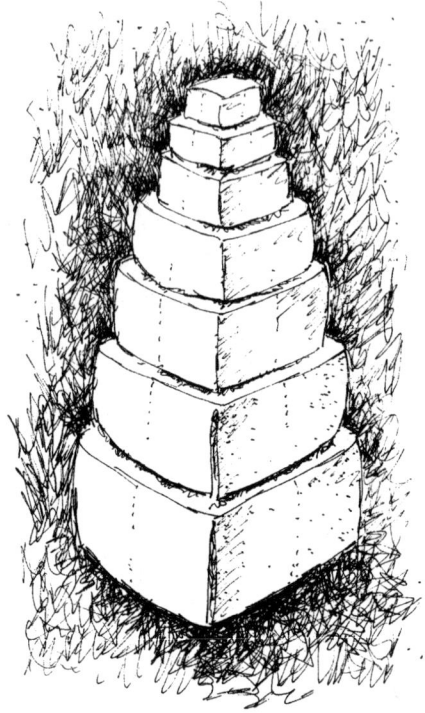

A set of boxes, one nestling inside the other like Russian dolls, looks wonderful in gold, silver or other exotic paper and is a delightful present in itself. They are useful containers and ideal gift boxes. Below are instructions for making a set of seven, but there is no need to stop there – a teenager may well appreciate a stack of boxes, one to mark each year of her life.

A child who opens an empty box will not fail to be disappointed; when offering a set of boxes therefore, keep in mind the child in each of us and make sure that the smallest box contains a surprise...

You will need:
3.5 sheets of cartridge paper (A2 size) or thin card
Layout plan, page 226
Ruler, pencil and scissors

Each box is made from a square piece of paper, and its lid is another square just 1cm larger.

Cut 14 squares in the following sizes:

For box:	*For lid:*
10cm x 10cm	11cm x 11cm
13.5 cm x 13.5cm	14.5cm x 14.5cm
17cm x 17cm	18cm x 18cm
20.5cm x 20.5cm	21.5cm x 21.5cm
24cm x 24cm	25cm x 25cm
27.5cm x 27.5cm	28.5cm x 28.5cm
31cm x 31cm	32cm x 32cm

To make both box and lid

Fold appropriate square twice diagonally to find centre. Fold corners of square to centre (**x**). Open all folds.

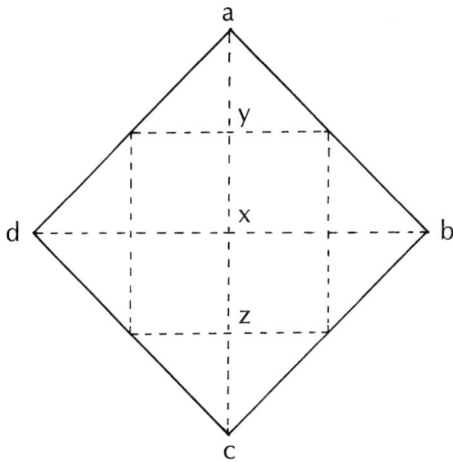

Fold **c** to **y** and crease. Open fold. Fold **c** to **z** and crease. Open out.

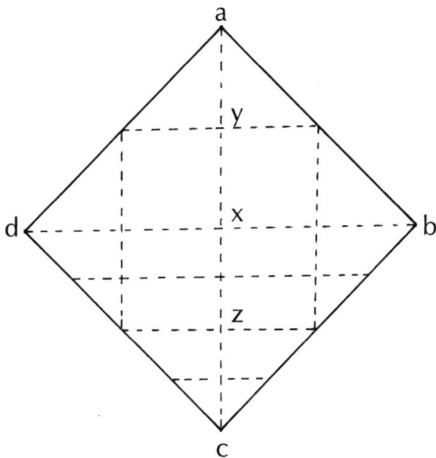

Repeat last procedure with corners **a**, **b** and **d**. Cut along solid lines indicated below:

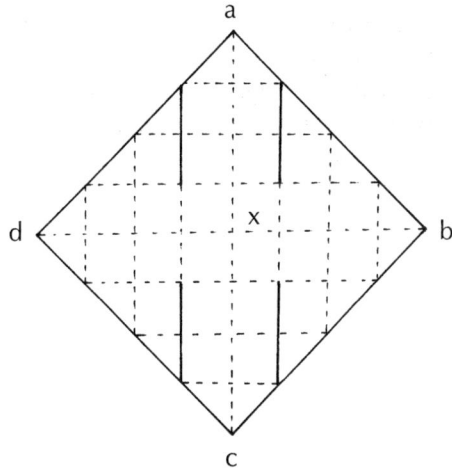

Fold corners D and B to meet at X and make sides of box as shown:

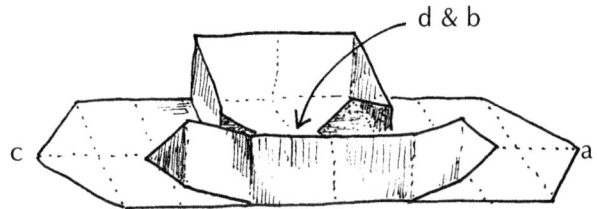

Fold corners A and C over the two sides so that they also meet at X.

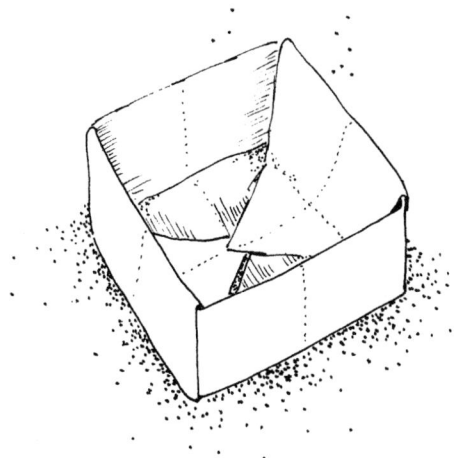

Tips:
- Attach Flower with a message (see page 63) to lid of box as gift tag.
- If used as single gift boxes the lids could be trimmed with a decorative square cut from a used greetings card. Cut square 1–2cm smaller than lid dimension and glue with care.

Chapter 14

POEMS AND SONGS

Someone born between midnight on Friday and cock-crow on Saturday is known as a 'chime child' and, traditionally, is endowed with second sight.

Birthday wisdom

Monday's bairn* is fair of face,
Tuesday's bairn is full of grace,
Wednesday's bairn is child of woe,
Thursday's bairn has far to go,
Friday's bairn is loving and giving,
Saturday's bairn works hard for its living,
But the bairn that is born on a Sabbath day
Is lucky and bonny and wise and gay.

★ Scottish word for 'child'

This is an early Scottish version of a verse which many will recognise in differing versions as a children's nursery rhyme. There is no tradition that we know of which suggests that Wednesday is an unlucky day to be born on, quite the contrary in fact. The word 'Wednesday' derives from 'Woden's day' (Woden being the sovereign god of the Teutonic peoples) and it has been said that the original meaning of this line was that Wednesday's bairn was a child of Woden – and therefore the inheritor of the wisdom, courage and mastery attributed to this deity. Woden has been compared to the Norse god Odin and the Roman god Mercury.

The days of the week in English were all named after such ancient gods:

Sun (deity) day
Moon (deity) day
Tiw's day (Anglo-Saxon god who carries a spear of judgement, of judicial power, and is identified with Mars, the Roman god of spring and battle)
Woden's day (see above)
Thor's day (Teutonic thunder god Donar / Thor, fearless traveller between heaven and earth, who is identified with Jupiter, the chief god of the Romans)
Frija's day (beautiful and clever wife of the Norse god Odin and often identified with fertility goddess Gefjon 'the Giver')
Saturn's day (the hard-working agricultural god of the Romans, a vine-grower, a sower and a harvester, the bringer of prosperity in the course of time)

The sentiments of the verse above suggest that the gods of prehistory are still willing to endow those born on 'their' day with some of their qualities (see page 3). Among some Hindu communities of India it is considered most fortunate for a girl to be born on a Sunday, and for a boy to be born on a Wednesday.

Two verses to be said the night before the birthday

> When I have said my evening prayer,
> And my clothes are folded on my chair,
> And mother/father switches off the light,
> I'll still be __ years old tonight.
> But from the very break of day,
> Before the children rise and play,
> Before the darkness turns to gold,
> Tomorrow, I'll be __ years old…
> __ kisses when I wake,
> __ candles on my cake.

A goodnight kiss for the five year old
To send him/her to sleep and to dreaming.
And blessings on the six-year-old
Who'll climb out of bed in the morning.

Birthday songs

> Happy birthday to you
> Happy birthday to you
> Happy birthday, dear _____
> Happy birthday to you!

Love it or loathe it, this extraordinary ditty is the most widely known song in the world. It has crossed cultural, political and religious boundaries to be sung today on every continent. Its strident melody, unsubtle rhythm and one-track text has captured the hearts of birthday enthusiasts in almost every corner of the globe.

Now follows a suggested second helping to aid digestion and prevent you growing too weary of the first course:

> May the angels bless you
> In all that you do,
> May the stars up in heaven
> Shine down upon you!

Some say the tune was written by Wolfgang Amadeus Mozart; be that as it may, what we *do* know is that in 1853, in Louisville U.S.A., concert pianist Mildred Hill and her sister Patty collaborated in composing a song for Patty's kindergarten work. The tune was the one we know so well but the words were as follows:

> Good morning to all,
> Good morning to all,
> Good morning, dear Teacher!
> We come to your call.

We wish you a happy birthday

We may never know exactly when the inspirational metamorphosis came about to move this humble kindergarten refrain to the top of the global charts. However, should one, on a rare occasion, ever crave an alternative song which is almost as easy to learn and almost as linguistically unchallenging, then we recommend the following adaptation of a well-known Christmas song:

> We wish you a happy birthday, we wish you a happy birthday,
> We wish you a happy birthday and a long life to come.
> Your friends are all here to raise you a cheer.
> We wish you a happy birthday and a life full of fun.

ADAPTED FROM TRADITIONAL CAROL

We wish you a happy birthday, we wish you a happy birthday, we wish you a happy birthday and a long life to come. Your friends are all here to raise you a cheer. We wish you a happy birthday and a life full of fun.

Here is an adaptation of a popular German song that can be used as a round. The last verse would only be sung at the birthday party.

Birthday song

WORDS: ANN DRUITT   MUSIC: TRADITIONAL SWISS/GERMAN

-------- has a birth- day,   Sing goodbye to ---- years old,

Sing hello to ---- years old,   -------- has a birth- day!

_____ has a birthday
Sing goodbye to ___ years old
Sing hello to ___ years old
_____ has a birthday!

_____ has a birthday
Candles on the cake for tea
Clap your hands and sing with me
_____ has a birthday!

_____ has a birthday
Morning birds all sing this song
Sing you joy the whole year long
_____ has a birthday

_____ has a birthday.
Friends have come from far and near,
Bringing news for all to hear
_____ has a birthday!

Young children would enjoy the following song, especially if it was sung while moving around a circle holding hands, stopping only to clap and cheer!

The birthday child could stand in the middle of the circle if he wishes. Many small children do not relish this solitary exposure but would be happy to be there together with a friend.

Why is this a happy day?
    Because it's _____'s Birthday.
Why do we all sing and play?
    Because it's _____'s Birthday
So girls and boys who gather here
    to wish our friend a joyful year,
Join me now to clap and cheer,
    because it's _____'s Birthday!

Why is this a happy day?

WORDS: ANN DRUITT   MUSIC: KATHRIN IRWIN

Why is this a hap- py day? Be- cause it's *--------'s Birth- day.

Why do we all sing and play? Be- cause it's *--------'s Birth- day. So

girls and boys who ga- ther here to wish our friend a joy- ful year,

Join me now to clap and cheer, be- cause it's *---------'s Birth- day!

* rhythm can be changed to fit name, i.e.

Pet- er   Jane   E- mi- ly   Al-ex-an-der

177

Here is a Norwegian birthday song that is often used in the classroom. It takes the form of a ring game where the birthday child stands as the class moves around him in a circle, acting out the words of the song.

The second verse ends with the birthday child choosing a partner and dancing along with the whole class.

1st verse:

Happy the one who has the birthday.
We all gather round to greet you.
We stand in a ring and want you to play,
So watch us in all that we do:

For we curtsey and we bow and turn around,
Stamp and hop and dance our feet right off
   the ground,
Wishing you a happy birthday
And many more of them to follow!

Norwegian birthday song

WORDS ADAPTED BY ANN DRUITT   NORWEGIAN FOLKSONG

Hap- py the one who has   the birthday. We all   gather round to
We stand in a ring and want   you to play, So   watch us in all   that

greet   you.   For   we   curtsey   and   we   bow and turn around,
we   do:

Stamp and   hop and dance our feet right off the ground,   Wishing you a   happy

birth- day And many   more   of   them to   fol- low!

2nd verse:

Hurrah! our flags are waving with glee
So now is the time to praise you
Yours is the day so joyful may you be
We hope all your wishes come true.

Look around the ring and tell me who you see –
Who do you want to dance with? Will you
    dance with me?
Now everyone is dancing, hopping, skipping,
    prancing
Yes! We'll be friends tomorrow

Some family traditions require the birthday child to remain in his bedroom first thing in the morning and wait until he is summoned to the birthday table.

The song below suggests a lovely way to begin the special day by being led to the celebration by someone carrying a candle. (This 'light guide' could even be dressed as the birthday fairy or the birthday angel.)

If the celebration takes place later in the day then the birthday child might be asked to wait somewhere before being summoned.

> Softly softly waken,
>   waken to your special day.
> Let the candle lead you,
>   lead you on your way.

Softly waken

Words: Ann Druitt

Music: Christine Fynes-Clinton

Sof-tly sof-tly wa-ken, wa-ken to your spe-cial day.

Let the can-dle lead you, lead you on your way.

Here are two songs which can be elaborated into four-part rounds. Children of nine years and older will be more able to rise to this challenge and could also add their contribution on e.g. recorder or violin.

A star shines bright upon this day.
    Altho' the night has flown away.
The star beams falling to the earth,
    scatter their light on your day of birth.

The birth star

WORDS: ANN DRUITT   MUSIC: KATHRIN IRWIN

A star shines bright up- on this day. Al- tho' the night has flown a- way. The

star beams fal- ling to the earth, scat- ter their light on your day of birth.

Now we sing to celebrate your day of birth
    and to wish you joy and long life on earth.

Celebration song

GERMAN TRADITIONAL

Now we sing to ce- le- brate your day of birth and to

wish you joy and long life on earth.

Chapter 15

STORIES

It's not that age brings childhood back again. Age merely shows what children we remain.

Goethe

Story telling

Before literacy became widespread, it was common for people everywhere to tell stories to each other, not always to children. The magic of a story is enhanced when the teller has close contact with an audience and is aware of its reactions. If a story cannot be learned by heart then it is helpful if the text becomes familiar enough to allow the reader to lift her eyes frequently and communicate directly with the listeners, assessing their mood at the same time.

For children's stories, a style of speaking which is not over-dramatic but simply allows the story plot itself to unfold leaves children free to exercise their own imagination and to colour the various stages of the plot with as

much drama as they, personally, can handle. An adult mimicking the roar of a wolf may sometimes be more frightening to a child than the roar heard imaginatively; conversely, it may well be dismissed as a poor imitation.

Almost every nation in the world has its rich store of fairy tales or folk tales which are hundreds, if not thousands of years old. Their appeal has not diminished and they make wonderful stories for children of all ages. If you intend to use these at a party, we particularly recommend the collections which profess to stay as close to an original source as possible, avoiding embellishments and any attempt to 'retell' the story 'for the modern child'.

When making a choice of story, be guided by the child's own development, e.g. a child of three to four years has a short attention span and will be happier with a story of up to five minutes. Children under five years love stories with repetition and especially those that build up and then unbuild again e.g. the English tale *The old woman and the pig.*

By the age of five a child is able to cope with a more complicated storyline and will be happy to listen to such classics as *Mother Holle, Briar Rose, Snow White and Rose Red,* from the collection by the Brothers Grimm. This collection is widely known and could satisfy the needs of children ranging from three years to about ten years, but a child of seven or more is quite ready to absorb stories from many different lands. That said, it seems most natural that among the very first stories for young children should be those from the land or the culture with which they are most familiar.

Tip: Use only those stories with which you, personally, feel comfortable. Stories which present graphic descriptions of witches or dragons are best left until a child is about nine years old.

Preparation story

(For children aged 2¹/₂ to 5 years)
The excitement evoked by an approaching birthday can overwhelm some youngsters and the result may be wild or unusual behaviour or physical symptoms such as headache, stomach ache or a slight fever.

There are some adults and older children who really enjoy surprises, but it is a mistake to think that everyone will enjoy them, and small children much prefer sameness. Too much uncertainty about what a birthday may or may not bring can disturb a young child's security and create inner tension. A preparatory story will help to dispel anxiety and reinforce the secure base that every child needs. It will also help her to digest all the novelties of the day (including the gifts) and not be dazed by the flow of unusual events.

We recommend the use of an 'everyday story', i.e. one that simply recounts the real, ordinary happenings of a day in a particular child's life. A parent who is closely involved with the daily life of a child will find such stories easy to compose and tell. They can be used at bedtime or cuddle-time, and most pre-school children will listen attentively and with deep satisfaction. (They are also exceptionally useful as stories to prepare a young child for such things as a first visit to the dentist, a holiday trip, moving house, etc.)

A story that looks back on the day will describe the day's events accurately but briefly, without too much detail and, most important, in the right order. It can begin with waking in the morning and end with going to sleep at night. A story that looks forward must only include details over which the parent has some control, so references to the weather or other imponderables are best avoided. When the day to which the story refers actually arrives, the child will be anticipating that all the details of the plot will also become a reality. It is no good dressing the hero in a check jacket if, when the big day comes, his only check jacket is in the wash!

Children below the age of three and a half will be delighted with a story about a child who bears their name; older children may prefer a more subtle approach. In this case describe the character as a 'little boy' or girl, or use a name similar to the child's own name.

The story below is intended to be used only as a framework upon which parents could build an appropriate story for their child. It needs to be told in a quiet, undramatic style.

*O*nce upon a time, there was a little boy called Jack. One morning he woke up, climbed out of bed and took off his pyjamas. He put on his jeans and a clean, red T-shirt and opened his bedroom door. Outside was a trail of golden stars leading down the stairs. He followed the trail and it stopped at the breakfast table. A candle was shining by his plate and on his chair lay a small parcel tied with gold ribbon. Inside was a pearly seashell.

'Happy Birthday Jack!' said his father and gave him a big hug. They ate melon and banana for breakfast and some warm bread with honey. Afterwards Jack was allowed to snuff the candle.

Then Jack cleaned his teeth and went off to visit his friends at playgroup. They all sang Happy Birthday to him. When he came home he ate soup and salad and helped to clear the table. His mother asked him to colour some paper plates ready for the birthday tea party, so he fetched wax crayons and coloured one for each of his friends. Then he put on his new trainers and opened the front door to the visitors. Jack's uncle brought him a big yellow ball and his cousin gave him a kaleidoscope. Everyone played Follow-my-Leader and danced in a big circle singing 'Happy Birthday, dear Jack!'

Mother brought in the birthday cake and asked Jack to blow out the candles. The whole party had cake and strawberries and ice cream to eat.

'There's one more present for you, Jack' said mother and they went together to look in his bedroom. What should they find there but a tepee for Jack to play camps!

After all the guests had gone home, Jack had a bath with bubbles and was tucked up in bed. His father told him a story, kissed him good night, and Jack went to sleep.

If such a story captures a child's imagination it is most likely that he will feel inclined to re-enact the plot, and do all the things that Jack did; he may even receive the gifts in the story as if they were his own wishes come true. It is often a good idea to include an unusual word in a child's story. Words have a music and fascination of their own, independent of their meaning. If a child were to ask 'What's a kaleidoscope?' for example, one could allow the mystery of the word to live until the gift materialises. The magic of a story is preserved by answering 'I wonder, it must be a lovely gift...'

The great white egg

This story is suitable for the birthday of a young child. It could be told as a bedtime story on the eve of the birthday and again on the day itself after the celebrations are over. It could also be used as part of a celebration at nursery school or kindergarten.

The details of the story (name, sex, birth month) would be changed to suit the child concerned; mention of family members would need to be checked (obviously only older siblings would be there to greet the child). Particular family memories, for instance the weather conditions on the day, or night, of birth, could also be added. Any images suggested by the child's name and appropriate to the story may be included – if the child was called Jasmine, then maybe the scent of summer flowers would follow her down the mountainside, or if the child's name was Peter, he might feel the hard rock beneath his feet as he ran...

*O*nce upon a time, a great white bird opened her wings and flew. She flew among the tiny stars, she flew among the big stars, she flew to the great white moon. And *from the great white moon her wide, white wings took her down, down, down, down to the earth. There she made a nest on top of a great white mountain, and in the nest she laid a great white egg.*

Each day, when the sun came up and warmed the great white egg, a crack appeared in the shell. Each day, when the time was right, the crack widened and out stepped a child of the stars and ran down the mountainside to find a home in the village below. Late one night in the month of November, a beautiful child stepped through the widening crack and all the shadows on the snow vanished and the mountainside was radiant with light. Down this path of light ran the little girl (yes, it was a little girl!). She ran so fast one might have thought she flew. When she drew near to the village below, she saw that all the people were singing and rejoicing. Among the crowd there were faces that she recognised.

'There's my mother!' she cried, 'There's my father – and my sister and brother!'

They came to her with open arms and welcomed her with smiles.

'What's your name, my little one?' asked her mother.

'Lucy,' the shining child replied.

'Then come home with us, Lucy,' said her father, 'for there is a great feast awaiting for you.'

And so there was.

Every year after that, on a day in November, a feast is prepared and candles are lighted to remind us of the starlight on the mountain and the gift of the great white moon bird, and the day that Lucy first stepped down to the earth.

The golden tower

(A birthday story for children aged seven and above)

In the heart of the Land of Forever there stands on a high hill a castle with a golden tower. The king of the land lives in this castle and our story is about one of his sons.

When this young prince was approaching manhood, the king gave him the key to the golden tower and permission to visit its rooms whenever he wanted. In the tower, at the top of a winding, golden stair, were twelve rooms. Each room had a wide window which looked out on a different part of the kingdom. All the windows were coloured: one was rose pink, another aquamarine, a third was gold, and so on, but the window that the young Prince liked best was made of every colour you could imagine. Each day he would visit the tower and sit in the rooms one at a time, but in the room with the many-coloured window he stayed for a long time.

The view from the window was of a land the Prince did not know. When he gazed through red glass he saw a noble queen walking in a beautiful garden, but she was dressed in grey and weeping bitterly. He looked through green glass and saw a meadow outside city walls, where an old shepherd carried heavy stones to build a shelter for his sheep. Every day the prince watched as the shepherd completed his task by evening, but when the morning sun rose the stones were scattered in all directions and the shepherd had to begin the task again. The view through the deepest blue glass was also puzzling. Here the hills were scorched black by fire and day after day the people of the land walked among the ashes searching for food and wood for the home fire.

One day the young prince went to the king and said 'Father, the time has come when I must leave our golden home and make my way

184

in the world, for I have seen a kingdom which is in great need.'

The old king sighed, 'Have you only looked through the many-coloured window, my son? Have you not seen the noble cities that lie beyond the rose window, or the crystal seas which lap the shores beyond the gold window? These are more beauteous lands by far!'

'Yes, Father, I have seen them all,' replied the prince 'and they are fine indeed, but my mind is made up and I ask for your blessing.'

The king smiled upon his son and blessed him and hung a sword with a golden hilt at the young man's side. Then he gave him a cloak of invisibility and a snow-white tablecloth sewn by the queen's own hand. 'Keep these safe in your knapsack' said he, 'until their help is needed.'

It was a long journey to the many-coloured land and when the young prince arrived he was as dusty and as down-at-heel as any traveller could be. The evening was drawing in when he came to the blackened country that he had seen through the deep blue glass. There, at the edge of what was once a forest, he met a woodcutter returning to his hut. 'You look as hungry as the rest of us, traveller,' said the woodcutter cheerfully, as he dropped his small bundle of sticks by the door. 'Come along in and share my last crust of bread, for if it's not gone today it will certainly be gone tomorrow!'

While the woodcutter lit a fire with the twigs, the young prince opened his knapsack. 'To share someone's last crust of bread is a great honour,' he said, 'I must at least share what I have.' He brought out the snow-white tablecloth and spread it on the wooden table. The woodcutter was delighted. He broke the dry crust in half, put the two pieces on a board and brought it to the table. No sooner had the board touched the cloth than it disappeared and in its place was a rich banquet of every food one could wish for. The prince and the woodcutter were startled but soon recovered themselves and made a merry meal of it before they slept.

The following morning, the prince said 'Tell me, my friend, why is the land hereabouts so blackened and laid waste?'

'Where have you come from, traveller,' exclaimed the woodcutter, 'that you haven't heard about the curse of the dragon? Each night he roams the hills and his fiery breath burns trees and scorches the crops. He will have blighted our lives for one whole year come tomorrow, and we villagers face starvation for sure.' The prince grieved at his distress and gave the woodcutter the magic tablecloth, entrusting him to see that the village was never without food. That done, he went on his way.

Close to the city wall the fields were still green and a bird sang in a bush. The prince stopped to listen. At that moment, an old shepherd struggled past across the meadow with a large rock in his arms. 'Good day, old man!' called the prince, 'you need some help with that.' He quickly took the rock on his own shoulder and carried it to where the shepherd was rebuilding his shelter. Together they worked and by the time the sun was high in the sky the shelter was complete. The shepherd thanked him and invited him to share a piece of bread and cheese.

'Old man,' said the Prince, 'why are the rocks from your shelter scattered over the field each day?'

The shepherd sighed and told his story: 'You have heard that a dragon's curse lies upon this land; each night his belly aches, so each night he comes to destroy the shelter and take one of my creatures for his supper. Mine was the largest flock in these parts, but now only three sheep and four lambs have I left. They too will soon be taken, I fear, and my grandchildren will have no milk.'

The prince drew the invisible cloak from his knapsack, 'Throw this garment over the shelter tonight, it will keep you and your little flock safe.'

Sure enough, when the dragon came roaring for his supper not one stone of the shelter could be seen, and that night the beast returned hungry to his lair.

Early the following morning the prince arrived at the city gates. There stood guards with shining helmets and long lances. 'I wish to speak to the queen,' announced the prince. The guards laughed loudly and slapped their thighs, 'Ah, but does the queen wish to speak to you, laddie?' said one. 'Be off with you and beg somewhere else!' grunted another, and shook his lance.

'You must let me in, for I am a king's son' said the prince. Again the guards laughed, but the prince drew his sword and handed it to them. They gazed at the golden hilt and tested it with their teeth, 'Never seen anything like it' they whispered to each other. They opened the gates and allowed the young man to enter. He made his way through the streets to the castle, accompanied by two guards. The children pointed at him, 'Look at his big sword!' they cried, 'Is he going to fight the dragon, then?' and they laughed and clapped and shouted 'Hooray for the dragon slayer!'

The prince was shown into the royal garden where the queen spent her days. He knelt before her saying: 'My lady, I have come because I know you are in distress and my journey is devoted to bringing comfort to this land. Tell me why you are so sad.'

'Young man', said the queen, 'they say you are a king's son and by your bearing you seem so to be. Maybe it is you who will help us in our great need. Come, sit by my side and I shall tell you our story. That scourge of our kingdom, the dragon, demands that a young maiden of fifteen years old is given to him each month, or else he will destroy the whole city and everyone in it. The maidens are chosen by lot, and now it has come about that the one to be given to the dragon this day is our only daughter, the fairest maid in the land.' The queen wrung her hands. 'If you will fight the dragon' she said at last, 'and win, the king will give you our daughter's hand in marriage.'

'Then I shall fight', said the prince, 'and perhaps I shall win.'

The Prince asked for the help of all the strong men in the city. He sent half of them to dig a deep pit beyond the city gates, and the other half to the king's gardens where grew a mighty ash tree. From the tree they cut poles more than twice the height of a man, and four cartloads of brushwood. The poles were laid across the pit and the brushwood placed on top to make a thicket. Towards evening, the young princess came out of the city gates to await the coming of the dragon.

They did not wait long. The beast flew down from the hills and made straight for the princess, his heavy body setting the ground atremble as he ran. The citizens and guards fled to the castle, slamming the gates behind them, but the fair princess stood quietly, alone and without fear.

The young prince waited by the brushwood thicket that lay in the monster's path, and he held up the golden hilt of his sword which glittered and flashed in the light of the setting sun, half blinding the dragon. Enraged, the beast roared as he lunged towards the prince and towards the hidden pit. With a dreadful crash the scaly body disappeared into the ground. The prince strode forward and struck one blow with his sword, which broke the dragon's left wing. Then the beast cried to the prince in a human voice and said: 'Do not kill me! I can be useful to you. Let me be your trusted servant!' And he changed himself into a strong, black horse and served the prince faithfully from that day on.

The city gates opened and out came the king and queen. Trumpets sounded and the citizens leaped for joy. The king gave the hand of his daughter to the prince and their marriage was celebrated there and then.

They lived long and happily. In time the prince became king and ruled over a land that would never again live in fear of the dragon. And if the new king has not died, then he is ruling still.

The two best friends

This story was told to a four-year-old girl whose brother had been enquiring loudly about a certain minor malformation with which the little girl was born. For a time it became a birthday story. The story could be adapted to individual situations of a similar nature; the 'two friends' could of course be boys.

O*nce upon a time there were two angels in heaven who were the very best of friends. Every day they sat together, they sang together and they played together; they even looked like each other. Now there came a day when the keeper of the rainbow bridge called the two friends to him and said, 'I understand that one of you is ready for the journey down to earth, to live in a house with a family. Is that so?'*

'Yes!' said one angel, 'She's ready and I'm going to be guardian.'

The other angel smiled and nodded. 'Very well,' said the keeper of the rainbow bridge, 'follow me and I will show you where to go.' They reached the gate of the bridge and there the keeper solemnly said 'And now the guardian will take her friend's wings away and keep them safe.' So this was done.

The guardian angel asked the keeper 'May I please go a little way with my friend across the bridge?'

'You may only go halfway, and then you must say farewell,' said the keeper.

Hand in hand, the two friends walked together along the shining bridge. 'You look just like a little girl now, without your wings,' said the guardian angel, 'and I am going to watch over you every day of your life.'

'When I come back to heaven will we still play together and sing together and be friends?' asked the little girl.

'Of course we will,' said her guardian.

'But I'm afraid you won't recognise me when I come back, because I shall be an old lady!'

'I know what to do,' said her friend, and she gave the little girl a kiss on her (part of body). In exactly that place a (individual description) appeared. 'Now,' said the guardian angel, 'even when you are an old, old lady, I shall always be able to recognise you as my own dear friend.'

George goes to market

(for children aged four to seven years)

An ideal 'winding down' story. The episodes occur with rhythmic repetition, knitting together and unravelling in a way that sets the whole world to rights.

Once upon a time there was a farmer and his wife. They had a son called George. One day his mother said: 'George, today you shall take this basket of eggs to market. Be sure not to break any and bring me back six new pennies.'

George set off down the hill to the village. On the way he met the shepherd, who was counting his sheep:

'One-erum, Two-erum
Cock-erum, shu-erum,
Sith-erum, sath-erum,
Wineberry,
Wagtail,
Tarrydiddle,
Den!

Hullo there, my boy! What fine eggs! May I buy one for my breakfast?'

'Oh no,' said George, 'I must take them to market.'

'Never mind,' said the shepherd, 'I have plenty of bread and cheese – come, have some with me.'

When they had eaten breakfast George walked on towards the river. On the bank he met a fisherman. 'Good day,' said George.

'It certainly is a good day,' replied the fisherman, 'I've caught three big fish already, and the sun is not yet high in the sky. Those are fine eggs you have there, may I buy one for lunch?'

'Oh no', said George, 'I must take them to market.'

'Never mind,' said the fisherman, 'I can have fish for my lunch... now shhh! Be very quiet or you'll scare the fish away.'

George lay quietly on the grass and watched the ripples in the water. The sun was warm on his neck. Then he remembered his errand. He whispered 'Goodbye!' to the Fisherman, and set off over the bridge.

Near the village was a smithy. Benjamin the blacksmith was a big man. His face was red and cheery and he wore a large leather apron. This was the day for making horseshoes and he stood by the hot fire singing to the beat of his hammer:

'Bang! Bang!
Hear the iron clang!
Hear the hammer's joyful clatter,
Bang! Bang! Bang!

Din! Din!
Hear the hammer ring!
See the golden sparks a-flying,
Din! Din! Din!'

He winked at George and looked into his basket. 'What do I see there? Eggs! May I buy one for lunch?'

'Oh no,' said George, 'I must take them to market.'

'Never mind,' chuckled Benjamin, 'my good wife has made me something most delicious today. Sit down and join me!'

So George ate lunch with the blacksmith. Then he thanked him and walked on towards market.

Passing the tailor's shop he saw the tailor on his hands and knees on the floor. 'Good afternoon,' said George, 'can I help you? Have you lost something?'

'That's most kind of you,' said the tailor 'I seem to have mislaid my thimble – it's not in its box, it's not on the table, but it must be somewhere!'

So George and the tailor hunted the thimble. High and low they searched, in every nook and cranny. Then George began to laugh: 'Why, Mr. Tailor, the thimble is on your finger!'

'Bless my soul! So it is!' said the tailor, squinting through his spectacles, 'What a remarkably observant child you are!' He patted George on the head and peered into his basket, 'I say!' he exclaimed, 'Are those fresh eggs? Could I have one for my tea?'

'Oh no,' said George, 'I must take them to market.'

'Never mind, never mind,' said the tailor, 'I believe I have an egg somewhere, if only I could find it…. Now run along, little boy, I have work to do.'

Further down the street George heard a rapping noise:

Tap, tap, tap,
Rappety tappety tap.
Tappety rappety,
Rappety tappety,
Tap, tap, tap!

In the cobbler's shop sat the cobbler hard at work, with his little hammer tap-tapping on the sole of a large, black boot. 'Hullo!' he said in surprise, 'What are you doing with a basket of eggs, are you hoping I shall buy one?'

'Oh no,' said George, 'I must take them to market.'

'Never mind,' said the cobbler, 'I have no money to spend until these boots are finished. When my customer pays me then I shall be able to buy supper for my children. Now, off you go – I've no time for a chat!'

The cobbler's little hammer started tapping and George walked on.

The last shop in the street was the bakery. There stood the baker, pondering. Seeing

George he clapped his hands. 'Are those fresh eggs in your basket?'

'Yes,' said George, 'I must take them to market and bring back six new pennies for my mother.'

'Oh my,' said the baker, 'you're too late, the market packed up some time ago.' George's face fell. 'Cheer up, son,' said the baker, 'I need some eggs to make a birthday cake. I haven't any pennies but I'll give you the biggest loaf in my shop. I'm sure your mother will be pleased with that!' George took the big loaf and set off wearily for home.

At the cobbling shop a voice was sighing 'Oh dear, oh dear!'

'What's the matter?' asked George.

'My customer didn't come for his boots,' complained the cobbler, 'and I have no money to buy food for my children.'

'Take this loaf,' said George, 'the baker gave it to me for my mother, but she wants six new pennies.'

'Why, thank you!' said the cobbler, 'and I shall give you a pair of fine green boots. They were left behind in my shop, and I'm sure your mother will be pleased with them.'

George took the boots and walked up the street.

Outside the tailor's shop George met the tailor tiptoeing about in his stockinged feet. 'Bless my soul!' he exclaimed when he saw George, 'What are you doing with my boots?'

'I think you left them at the cobbling shop by mistake,' said George, 'and the cobbler gave them to me for my mother, but she really wants six new pennies.'

'Well now, isn't that fortunate?' said the tailor, taking the boots, 'because I seem to have lost my carpet slippers! I must give you something for your trouble – I know, two splendid leather patches for your trousers. I'm sure your mother will be pleased with these!' George took the patches and went on his way.

At the smithy, Benjamin the blacksmith was looking at his bellows. 'I've more horseshoes to make today,' he complained to George, 'but there's two big holes in my bellows. If my bellows don't blow, my fire doesn't burn, then I can't work.'

'Will these help?' asked George and handed him the patches, 'The tailor gave them to me for my mother, but she really wants six new pennies.'

'Just the thing!' said Benjamin, 'I'll mend my bellows with those in no time! But now I must give you something in exchange.' He picked up a bucket, 'I've just mended this, I'm sure your mother will be pleased with a bucket.' George took the heavy bucket and trudged along towards the river.

He crossed the bridge and saw the fisherman on the riverbank beside a large pile of fish. 'Hullo again,' he called to George, 'see what a good catch I made today – I have so many fish, I can't carry them all home.'

'Take this bucket!' said George, 'the blacksmith gave it to me for my mother but she really wants six new pennies.' The fisherman was delighted and gave George some fish to take home to his mother. George put the fish in his basket and began to climb the hill.

He reached the shepherd's hut where the shepherd greeted him with a smile: 'Hullo, my friend, have you had a good day?' George told him the story of his day and how he had come home without the six new pennies for his mother. 'Cheer up,' said the shepherd, 'you're tired and you're hungry, and so am I. How many fish have you got there?' And he counted them shepherd-fashion:

> 'One-erum, two-erum,
> cock-erum, shu-erum,
> sith-erum, sath-erum,
> wineberry,
> wagtail,
> tarrydiddle,
> den!

'Plenty for us both. I'll cook them for supper and then you'll feel better.' They shared a tasty supper and soon it was time to go. The shepherd gave a large bag to George, saying 'Take this home with you. I'm sure your mother will be pleased with that.'

George took the bag home to where his mother was waiting. 'Mother,' said George, 'I haven't brought you six new pennies, but I have brought you this.'

George's mother opened the bag and exclaimed joyfully 'Why, George! How did you know I wanted the pennies to buy sheep's wool for spinning? Aren't you just the cleverest boy in the whole wide world!'

Chapter 16

BIRTH AND STAR WISDOM

There was a star danced and under that star was I born
Shakespeare, *Much Ado About Nothing*

Astrological qualities

In ancient epochs, in the event of a royal or noble birth, the accurate time and date would be required for casting an astrological chart, or horoscope. Such a chart would indicate the positions and the relationships of the sun, the zodiac and significant planets at the moment of birth; astrologers maintain that this chart can, when interpreted correctly, indicate a person's character and destiny. Astrologers flourished in the royal courts of Europe in the sixteenth century and ensured that birth charts were drawn for most royal infants. Even today, it is common practice in some parts of the world to draw

up a horoscope at each birth; the chart can then be referred to when choosing a name for the child, and later when selecting a spouse or business partner, or fixing the date and time of important personal events.

One may treat astrology seriously or dismiss it as outdated superstition, or indulge in it as a harmless pastime. Nevertheless, it has to be recognised that the wisdom of the starry heavens and its connection with our earthly lives and loves is one of the oldest sciences and continues to exercise its fascination on many of us.

For the purposes of astrology, the year is divided into twelve sections, each under a 'sign' bearing the name of a constellation of the zodiac. Each sign is traditionally endowed with certain symbolic qualities.

Ten planets have been accorded an association with the twelve signs and are said to bring specific forces or 'life functions' with them. These functions express themselves through the 'channel' of the sign and are, consequently, modified or enhanced by the sign's own nature.

Astrologers take into account other factors which influence the birth chart namely: the four elements; the three qualities – enterprising, intense, adaptable; the positive and negative archetypes which affect the ability to express or repress the self.

In Wales it was held that children born when the moon was new would be eloquent; those born during the last quarter would be gifted with a good intellect.

We include below a brief indication of the characteristics connected with each sign and the governing planet(s), together with some traditional associations. These may be a help (or an amusing diversion) in the task of choosing a gift or greeting, designing an invitation, or selecting a theme for an inspirational birthday event.

To find your own 'star sign' or 'birth sign', simply locate the section of the astrological year that coincides with your birthday. The astrological year begins in March.

ARIES (RAM)

21 March – 19 April

Glyph:	V	(Ram's horns – thrusting, pushy)
Influenced by:		Fire; enterprise; self-expression
Nature:		Objective, urgent, assertive, free
Body area:		Head (headstrong, headfirst)
Hobbies:		Competitive/hazardous sport; anything using cutting tools
Plants:		Poppy, thistle, fern, gorse, wild olive, alder, pomegranate, dogwood
Colours & Gems:		All shades of red; bloodstone, ruby, diamond, emerald, amethyst
Life function:		Activity with enterprise, assertiveness, physical energy
Organs & Metals:		Gall function and red corpuscles of the blood; Iron
Planet:		**MARS** (Roman god of spring; later, the god of battle)

Symbol:

(old form)
Cross (matter) above circle (divine spirit) – accent on physical

(form now)
Arrow suggests initiatory nature; cipher for male gender

TAURUS (BULL)   20 April – 20 May

Glyph:	(Full face and horns of this uncompromising animal)
Influenced by:	Earth; steadfastness; self-restraint
Nature:	Productive, enduring, receptive, practical
Body area:	Neck, throat
Hobbies:	Gardening, painting, sculpture, music, sedentary pursuits
Plants:	Daisy, dandelion, lily, willow, blackthorn, hawthorn, elder
Colours & Gems:	Green, blue, pink, orange; lapis lazuli, emerald, rose quartz, sapphire
Life function:	Uniting through sympathy, feeling, evaluation
Organs & Metals:	Kidneys; copper
Planets:	**VENUS** (Roman goddess of fruitfulness, love and beauty)
Symbol:	Circle (divine spirit) above cross (matter) – accent on wholeness; cipher for female gender

GEMINI (TWINS)   21 May – 20 June

Glyph:	(Roman numeral for 2 – shows essential duality of sign)
Influenced by:	Air; adaptability; spontaneity
Nature:	Quick-witted, changeable, communicative
Body area:	Lungs, arms
Hobbies:	Fencing, agile and dextrous games, travel, languages, socialising
Plants:	Tansy, yarrow, privet, hawthorn, oak
Colours & Gems:	Yellow, light green; agate, citrine, amber
Life function:	Communication through nerve and mental response
Organ & Metal:	Lungs; quicksilver
Planet:	**MERCURY** (Swift-footed messenger of the Roman gods)
Symbol:	Half-circle (mind) poised above circle (spirit) and cross (matter)

CANCER (CRAB)   21 June – 22 July

Glyph:	(said to indicate nourishment, motherhood, regeneration)
Influenced by:	Water; enterprise; self-restraint
Nature:	Sensitive, protective, outgoing, tenacious
Body area:	Breast, rib-cage, stomach
Hobbies:	Sailing, swimming, collecting, knitting, sewing, music, painting
Plants:	Water lilies, bulrushes, heather, cedar, lime, oak, holly
Colours & Gems:	Green, purple, pastels, white; emerald, agate, moonstone, pearl, peridot
Life function:	Rhythm through response, reflection, assimilation
Organ & Metal:	Brain; silver
Planet:	**MOON** (Personified by the Romans as fertility goddess Luna)
Symbol:	Incomplete circle of mind/evolving spirit – conscious/unconscious

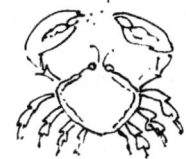

LEO (LION)   23 July – 22 August

Glyph:	(said to be from the Royal Arms of the fabled Empire of the Sun)
Influenced by:	Fire; steadfastness; self-expression
Nature:	Impressive, authoritative, generous, warm-hearted, regal
Body area:	Heart, spine
Hobbies:	Amateur acting, theatre and film, spending money
Plants:	Sunflower, chamomile, lavender, holly, hazel, almond, apple
Colours & Gems:	Blue, white, gold, scarlet; onyx, beryl, tiger's eye, yellow topaz, ruby
Life function:	Self-integration
Organs & Metals:	Heart; gold
Planets:	**SUN** (Personified as Greek god Apollo, symbol of light and truth)
Symbol:	Circle of eternity with seed potential within; sign for human ego

VIRGO (VIRGIN)   23 August – 22 September

Glyph:	(depicts serpent's coil ending with female indication or 'ear of wheat')
Influenced by:	Earth; adaptability; self-restraint
Nature:	Analytical, practical, efficient, perfectionist
Body area:	Abdomen, metabolic system
Hobbies:	Writing, gardening, research, reading, detailed construction, charity work
Plants:	Wintergreen, sage, privet, hazel, almond, apple, grapevine, blackberry
Colours & Gems:	Indigo, dark violet, silver, grey; sardonyx, carnelian, peridot, amethyst, pyrite
Life function:	Communication through nerve and mental response
Organ & Metal:	Lungs; quicksilver
Planet:	**MERCURY** (Swift-footed messenger of Roman gods)
Symbol:	Half-circle (mind) poised above circle (spirit) and cross (matter)

LIBRA (SCALES)   23 September – 22 October

Glyph:	(depicts yoke/beam of balance, bringing two things together in balance)
Influenced by:	Air; spontaneity; self-expression
Nature:	Harmonious, relating, mentally active
Body area:	Hips, lumbar spine, endocrine system
Hobbies:	Sunbathing, body care, painting, dancing, happy and lazy pastimes
Plants:	Pansy, primrose, violet, strawberry, grapevine, blackberry, ivy
Colours & Gems:	Dark violet, green, strong pink, primaries; crysolite, peridot, opal, jade
Life function:	Uniting through sympathy, feeling, evaluation
Organ & Metal:	Kidneys; copper
Planet:	**VENUS** (Roman goddess of fruitfulness, love and beauty)
Symbol:	Circle (divine spirit) above cross (matter) – accent on wholeness; cipher for female gender

194

SCORPIO (SCORPION)   23 October – 21 November

Glyph:	(Depicts serpent's coil ending with male indication)
Influenced by:	Water; intensity; self-restraint
Nature:	Penetrating, intuitive, emotional, deep
Body area:	Genitals, nose
Hobbies:	Boxing, water sports, the arts
Plants:	Root vegetables, ivy, bulrush, broom, furze
Colours & Gems:	Violet, red, black, grey; beryl, aquamarine, ruby, garnet, carnelian, opal
Life functions:	Activity through enterprise; transforming through elimination/renewal
Organs & Metals:	Gall, mental and regenerative functions; iron, plutonium
Planets:	**MARS** (see Aries) **PLUTO** (Greek god of the underworld/unconscious)
Symbol:	Initials of Percival Lowell 'discoverer' of Pluto

SAGITTARIUS (ARCHER)   22 November – 21 December

Glyph:	(Arrow that shoots freely afar)
Influenced by:	Fire; adaptability; spontaneity
Nature:	Free, exploratory, energetic, idealistic
Body area:	Thighs, upper arm, muscles
Hobbies:	Sport, hiking, riding, serious study
Plants:	Asparagus, chestnuts, bulrush, elder
Colours & Gems:	Rosy lilac, orange, denim blue, beige; topaz, turquoise, amethyst, citrine
Life function:	Expansion through material growth and soul development
Organ & Metal:	Liver; tin
Planet:	**JUPITER** (Roman supreme god, seer and guardian of justice and virtue)
Symbol:	Half-circle (mind) above level of cross (matter)

CAPRICORN (GOAT FISH)   22 December – 19 January

Glyph:	(Indicates horned goat with fish tail)
Influenced by:	Earth; enterprise; self-restraint
Nature:	Prudent, rational, disciplined, practical
Body area:	Knee, skin
Hobbies:	Practical work, serious reading, solitary pursuits
Plants:	Poisonous hemlock, burdock root, yew, elder, birch
Colours & Gems:	Dark colours, pale magenta, blue, orange; chrysoprase, turquoise, agate
Life function:	Formative through restraint, discipline
Organ & Metal:	Spleen; lead
Planet:	**SATURN** (Roman god of agriculture; Greek god of Time the Reaper)
Symbol:	Cross (matter) takes precedence over half-circle (mind). Human spirit must penetrate physical limitations

AQUARIUS (WATERMAN)   **20 January – 18 February**

Glyph:	(Ancient depiction of water, sometimes as two serpents)
Influenced by:	Air; steadfastness; spontaneity
Nature:	Detached, unconventional, progressive, communicative
Body area:	Shin, ankles
Hobbies:	Photography, archaeology, astrology, writing
Plants:	Dandelion, frankincense, myrrh, birch, rowan
Colours & Gems:	Pink, electric blue, silver grey; jacinth, garnet, sapphire, amber
Life functions:	Forming through restraint; deviating through invention, drastic change
Organs & Metals:	Spleen, pineal gland; lead, uranium
Planet:	**SATURN** (see Capricorn); **URANUS** (To the Greeks the starlit sky, husband and son of Gaia the earth)
Symbol:	Two curves of soul parted by cross of matter

PISCES (FISHES)   **19 February – 20 March**

Glyph:	(our physical and spiritual selves, separate yet joined)
Influenced by:	Water; adaptability; self-restraint
Nature:	Impressionable, dreamy, intuitive, spiritually seeking
Body area:	Feet
Hobbies:	Art, music, poetry, dancing, fishing
Plants:	Moss, ferns, seaweed, ash, alder, pomegranate, dogwood
Colours & Gems:	Rose red, orange, mauve, sea-green; amethyst, opal, jade, pearl, bloodstone
Life functions:	Expansion through understanding; refining through dissolution, subtlety
Organs & Metals:	Liver, thalamus; tin, neptunium
Planet:	**JUPITER** (see Sagittarius); **NEPTUNE** (Roman god of the sea)
Symbol:	Half circle (mind) transcends physical; Trident/Chalice of Holy Grail

The virtues of gemstones, plants and colours

The wearing of precious or semi-precious stones as symbols of beneficent influence can be traced right back to Biblical times. Judaic tradition describes, in the book of Exodus (Chap. 39), the jewelled breastplate of Aaron the high priest of the Israelites. The twelve stones, set in four rows on the breastplate, were associated with the twelve tribes of Israel. Twelve stones reappear in the Christian tradition, set in the foundations of the golden city of the New Jerusalem, described in the book of Revelations (Chap. 21). By virtue of the number twelve, these stones found association also with the signs of the zodiac and the months of the year.

It may once have been considered fortunate to wear the gem of the current month, but certainly by the early nineteenth century in Europe and elsewhere it was a widespread custom (for those who could afford it) to wear the gem of one's birth month all the year round. Stones have long been considered to be of medicinal value, healing conditions of the soul as well as the body. They are thought to be able to ward off unfavourable influences as well as confer beneficial ones. A selection of stones, plants and colours are listed below with some of the virtues traditionally attached to them:

Stone	Virtue	Helpful for
Bloodstone	courage, flexibility	stomach, liver, kidneys and excessive bleeding
Blue sapphire	clear thinking, hope, protection	cleansing, harmonising
Agate	health, good fortune, long life	emotional cleansing
Emerald	fidelity, prosperity	eyes, intelligence, memory
Onyx	health, friendship, mutual love	hearing, teeth, bones
Carnelian	true love, protection against evil *(said to have been set in the betrothal ring of the Virgin Mary)*	fertility, arthritis, rheumatism, depression, kidneys, healing of bones
Peridot	marital harmony, reduces anger; protection against harm, anxiety	skin, eyes, heart, spleen; overcomes hypochondria
Aquamarine	protects against perils at sea, endows with wisdom, courage and youthfulness	bodily vigour, throat, teeth, thyroid, jaw, stomach, calms hay fever
Topaz	emblem of true friendship, fidelity	metabolism, inner strength
Chrysoprase	fortitude, patience, love of truth	sore throat, peaceful sleep
Zircon *(Stone of virtue)*	prosperity, hardihood	allergies, stimulates dreaming
Amethyst	sincerity, authority, peace-making; inspires virtue and high ideals, conducive to meditation	protection against intoxication, insomnia, violent passions
Lapis lazuli *(Stone of heaven)*	prosperity, friendship	immune system, migraine, insomnia, vertigo
Ruby *(Stone of abundance)*	friendship, passion for life	fever, detoxification of body; heart, kidneys, depression

Stone	Virtue	Helpful for
Diamond (*King of stones*)	protection, ennoblement, purity, eternal love, repentance	clarity of mind, allergies
Garnet	will power, constancy, resurrection	circulation, cleansing of blood
Turquoise	happiness in love, secures fidelity in friendship	protection against injury; exhaustion, panic attacks
Opal	for those born in the sign of Libra: good fortune	memory, childbirth, infections, fevers
Tourmaline	hope, uprightness	energy flow
Moonstone	health, inspiration, longevity	balance, fertility
Pearl	forbearance, health, longevity	
Amber	equanimity, positivity	growth of teeth, stress
Tiger's eye	protects against fear	night vision, healing bones
Coral	patience	anaemia

Plant	Virtue	Colour	Virtue
Amaryllis	pride	fiery red	passion
Azalea	temperance	pink	romance
Chrysanthemum, white	truth	crimson	merriment
Ferns	sincerity	orange	prestige
Camellia, white	excellence in woman	soft yellow	mental activity
Lily	purity, modesty	lemon yellow	spirituality
Orchid	beauty in woman	green	lovableness
Hazel branch	reconciliation	olive green	melancholy
Rose	love	apple green	musicality
Sunflower	adoration	baby blue	kindliness
Violet, blue	fidelity	royal blue	loyalty
Rosemary	remembrance	navy blue	respectability
Jasmine, yellow	grace, elegance	greenish blue	self-confidence
Snowdrop	hope	white	drive for perfection
Olive branch	peace	violet	intuitiveness
Ivy	friendship	lilac	healing

Chinese animal years

Chinese astrology is based on a cycle of twelve years, each governed by its own animal symbol which is said to influence the personality and disposition of all those born in that year. These animals are considered to be bearers of great wisdom and to be of equal importance.

Legend recounts that long, long ago, a Chinese king invited all the animals to spend the New Year at his grand palace. Only twelve animals came, first the rat, then the ox and then the other ten animals in a certain order. In recognition of their presence, the king named a year for each of the twelve animals in their order of arrival.

The Chinese New Year begins on the second new moon after the winter solstice i.e. on varying dates between 21 January and 19 February, so people whose birthdays lie between those two dates will have to calculate carefully to discover in which animal year they were born.

The cycle of twelve years begins with the Rat and ends with the Boar. The cycle then repeats itself. The sequence of animals in recent years has been as follows:

23 January 1993 – 9 February 1994	Rooster
10 February 1994 – 30 January 1995	Dog
31 January 1995 – 18 February 1996	Boar
19 February 1996 – 6 February 1997	Rat
7 February 1997 – 27 January 1998	Ox
28 January 1998 – 15 February 1999	Tiger
16 February 1999 – 4 February 2000	Hare
5 February 2000 – 23 January 2001	Dragon
24 January 2001 – 11 February 2002	Snake
12 February 2002 – 31 January 2003	Horse
1 February 2003 – 21 January 2004	Goat
22 January 2004 – 7 February 2005	Monkey

Rat

Some characteristics: Charming, imaginative, opportunistic, touchy, critical
Career orientation: Business, journalism, photography
Compatible with: Dragon, ox, monkey
Incompatible with: Horse

Ox

Some characteristics: Quiet, practical, natural leader, demanding, self-important
Career orientation: Boss, surgeon, hairdresser
Compatible with: Rat, dragon, rooster
Incompatible with: Monkey, goat, tiger

Tiger

Some characteristics: Sensitive, ardent, stubborn, fault-finder, rebel
Career orientation: Explorer, actor, animal handler
Compatible with: Horse, dragon, dog
Incompatible with: Snake, monkey, ox

Hare

Some characteristics:	Happy, sociable, kind, careful, sometimes sentimental
Career orientation:	Nurse, social work, diplomat
Compatible with:	Goat, dog, boar
Incompatible with:	Rooster, rat, tiger

Dragon

Some characteristics:	Intelligent, influential, generous, straight, critical, tactless
Career orientation:	Business, politics, computer programming
Compatible with:	Rat, snake, rooster, monkey
Incompatible with:	Tiger, dog

Snake

Some characteristics:	Wise, charming, successful, parsimonious, humourless
Career orientation:	Psychology, teacher, writer
Compatible with:	Ox, rooster
Incompatible with:	Boar, tiger

Horse

Some characteristics:	Attractive, popular, independent, industrious, selfish, conceited
Career orientation:	Scientist, engineer, poet
Compatible with:	Goat, dog, tiger
Incompatible with:	Rat

Goat

Some characteristics:	Elegant, artistic, hard to get to know, pessimist, worrier
Career orientation:	Designer, architect, landscape architect, director
Compatible with:	Hare, boar, horse
Incompatible with:	Ox, dog

Monkey

Some characteristics:	Quick-witted, impish, popular, egoistical, manipulative
Career orientation:	Successful with most things
Compatible with:	Dragon, rat
Incompatible with:	Tiger

Rooster

Some characteristics:	Industrious, decisive, heroic fantasist, big spender, boastful
Career orientation:	Restaurateur, tour guide, entertainer
Compatible with:	Ox, snake, dragon
Incompatible with:	Hare

Dog

Some characteristics:	Trustworthy, champion of justice, quick learner, introverted, worrier
Career orientation:	Mechanic, secretary, vice-president
Compatible with:	Tiger, horse, hare
Incompatible with:	Dragon, goat

Boar

Some characteristics:	Reliable, obliging, honest, polite, independent, loyal, naive
Career orientation:	Sales, finance, publishing, mechanical engineering
Compatible with:	Hare
Incompatible with:	Snake, goat

Chapter 17

CALENDAR OF SAINTS

Even so we, in like manner, as soon as we were born, began to draw to our end.

Apocrypha 5.10

The historical sketch of the development of birthday celebrations (see pages 1–6) clearly shows that the influence of Christianity was decisive in Europe. The Roman Emperor Constantine's conversion to Christianity came as many of the principles which had guided the Greek and Roman world were ripe for replacement with new ideas. These new ideas brought the practice of emperor worship to an end and cast an air of disapproval over all festivities connected with natal anniversaries.

Christian baptism, however, required a Christian *name*. Over time, this was formalised into selecting a name from a Calendar of Saints, an 'official' list of Christian men and women whose lives were deemed worthy of imitation. It came to be expected of those who were baptised that they would honour their 'name day', i.e. the day dedicated to the saint whose name they were given.

Some of the traditions that arose in this connection nevertheless acknowledged a growing inclination to celebrate the person as well as the saint after whom he or she was named. For centuries the tradition of the name day managed to preserve a space in the year for confirmation of an individual's importance within the universal whole. Social conditions have, more recently, favoured the rapid growth of a secular birth anniversary festival, but people in many lands still observe a name day instead of, or as well as the natal day.

We offer here a Calendar of Saints in which the name of the saint is entered in the traditional way on the death-day, if it is known. (Christianity regards the death-day as a day of birth into heaven.) Where the death-day is not known, we have respected local or universal custom; in isolated instances a name is placed as near as possible to the customary date.

We have gathered together saints from across the world, including Celtic Christians, little-known local saints and even some who, like St. Faine, have been declared entirely mythical but have secured a place in country lore:

> 'Whether the weather be snow or raine
> We are sure to see the flower of St. Faine.'
> (Vibernum tinus)

This calendar is a very personal selection and is not intended to supplant any other of its kind.

JANUARY

1. FAINE; BASIL the GREAT
2. GREGORY NANZIENZEN
3. GENEVIEVE
4. ELIZABETH ANN SETON
5. SIMON the STYLITE
6. MELCHIOR; CASPAR; BALTHAZAR
7. RAYMOND of PEÑYAFORT
   LUCIAN; THORFINN; CEDD
8. SEVERIN of NORICUM
9. JULIAN of LE MANS
10. MARCIAN
11. SLAVIUS of AMIENS
12. BENET BISCOP
13. HILARY of POITIERS; KNUT
14. KENTIGERN; FELIX of NOLA
15. PAUL, hermit; ITA of KILLEEDY
16. PRISCILLA; FURSEY
17. ANTHONY of EGYPT
18. PRISCA
19. MARIUS & COMPANIONS
    WULFSTAN
20. FABIAN; SEBASTIAN
21. AGNES
22. VINCENT, deacon
23. JOHN the ALMSGIVER
24. TIMOTHY
25. Conversion of PAUL; HENRY SUSO
26. POLYCARP
27. ANGLA MERICI
28. PETER NOLASCO
29. FRANCIS of SALES
30. MARTINA; CHARLES, king
31. JOHN BOSCO; EDAN

FEBRUARY

1. BRIGID
2. THEOPHANES
3. BLAISE; ANSGA
4. VERONICA
5. AGATHA
6. PAUL MIKI & COMPANIONS
   DOROTHY of CAESAREA
7. MEL
8. JOSEPHINE BAKHITA
9. TEILO; APOLLONIA
10. SCHOLASTICA
11. PASCHAL
12. DAMIAN
13. CATHERINE of RICCI
14. VALENTINE
15. SIGFRID of VAXJO
16. JULIANA
17. REGINALD of ORLEANS
18. FLAVIAN
19. BONIFACE of LAUSANNE
20. WULFRIC
21. PETER DAMIAN
22. MARGARET of CORTONA
23. Raising of LAZARUS
    SERENUS
24. MATTHIAS
25. ETHELBERT of KENT
26. ALEXANDER of ALEXANDRIA
27. GABRIEL POSSENTI
28. OSWALD of WORCESTER
29. JOHN CASSIAN

MARCH

1. DAVID of WALES
2. SWITHBERT; CHAD
3. WINNOLD
4. CASIMIR
5. EUSEBIUS of CREMONA
6. PERPETUA & FELICITY
7. THOMAS AQUINAS
8. JOHN of GOD
9. FRANCES of ROME
10. JOHN OGILVIE
11. OENGUS
12. FINA; GREGORY the GREAT
13. EUPHRASIA
14. MATILDA; LEOBINUS
15. LONGINUS; EDWARD, boy king
16. HERIBERT
17. PATRICK of IRELAND
    JOSEPH of ARIMATHEA
18. CYRIL of JERUSALEM
19. JOSEPH of NAZARETH
20. CUTHBERT of LINDISFARNE
21. BENEDICT; NICHOLAS of FLÜE
22. LEA; NICHOLAS OWEN
23. SYBILLINA of PAVIA
24. GABRIEL, archangel
25. Annunciation to V. MARY
    DISMAS
26. BRAULIO
27. JOHN of EGYPT
28. SIXTUS III
29. RUPERT
30. ZOSIMUS
31. BENJAMIN; AMOS

APRIL

1. IRENE; CELSO
2. FRANCIS of PAOLA
3. RICHARD of CHICHESTER
4. ISIDORE; AMBROSE
5. VINCENT FERRER
6. WILLIAM of ESKILL
7. JOHN BAPTIST de la SALLE
8. PERPETUUS; DIONYSIUS
9. WALDEATRUDIS
10. FULBERT
11. STANISLAUS; LEO the GREAT
12. JULIUS I
13. HERMENGILD
14. JUSTIN
15. RAPHAEL, archangel
16. BENEDICT JOSEPH LABRE
17. ANICETUS
18. ELEUTHERIUS & COMPANIONS
19. ALPHEGE of CANTERBURY
20. AGNES of MONTEPULCIANO
21. ANSELM
22. CAIUS
23. GEORGE of LYDDA
24. FIDELIS
25. MARK, evangelist
26. CLETUS
27. PETER CANISIUS; TASSACH
28. ADALBERT
29. ROBERT of MOLESNE
    CATHERINE of SIENA
30. PIUS

MAY

1. PHILIP & JAMES the less apostles
2. ATHANASIUS
3. JOSEPH the WORKER; HELEN
4. MONICA; FLORIAN
5. ASAPH
6. PETRONAX; DOMINIC SAVIO
7. JOHN of BEVERLY
8. VICTOR
9. PACHOMIUS
10. COMGALL of BANGOR
11. MAMMERTUS
12. PANCRAS
13. SERVATIUS
    JULIAN of NORWICH
14. BONIFACE; CARTHAGH
15. SOPHIA; ISIDOR the FARMER
16. BRENDAN; NEPOMUK; HONORÉ
17. PASCHAL BAYLON
18. VENANTIUS
19. ALCUIN; DUNSTAN
20. BERNADINE of SIENA
21. HUMILITY
22. CONSTANTINE, emperor
    RITA of CASCIA
23. WILLIAM of ROCHESTER
24. DAVID of SCOTLAND
25. GREGORY VII; URBAN I
26. PHILIP NERI; VENERABLE BEDE
27. AUGUSTINE of CANTERBURY
    MARIANNE of JESUS
28. GERMANUS of PARIS
29. MARY MAGDALEN of PAZZI
30. JOAN of ARC
31. PETRONILLA

JUNE

1. NICODEMUS; JUSTIN
2. MARCELLINUS and PETER
3. CHARLES LWANGA & COMPANIONS
    KEVIN
4. CLOTILDA
5. BONIFACE of MAINZ
6. NORBERT; JARLATH
7. ROBERT of NEWMINSTER
8. PAUL of CONSTANTINOPLE
9. COLUMBA; WILLIAM of YORK
10. ITHAMAR
11. BARNABAS, apostle
12. JOHN SAHAGUN
13. ANTHONY of PADUA
14. ELISEO; BASIL the GREAT
15. VITUS; GERMAINE COUSIN
16. AURELIAN
17. BOTOLPH; NECTAN
18. ELIZABETH of SCHONAU
19. JULIANA FALCONIERI
20. OSANNA of MANTUA
21. ALOYSIUS GONZAGA
22. JOHN FISHER; PAULINUS of NOLA
    ALBAN
23. AUDREY
24. Birth of JOHN the BAPTIST
25. WILLIAM of VERCELLI
26. RUDOLPH
27. LADISLAUS of HUNGARY
    CYRIL of ALEXANDRIA
28. IRENAEUS
29. PETER, apostle
30. PAUL, apostle

JULY

1. OLIVER PLUNKETT
2. OTTO
3. LEO II
4. ELIZABETH of PORTUGAL ULRICH
5. CYRIL & METHODIUS; PHILOMENA
6. THOMAS MORE
7. APOLLINARIS
8. KILIAN; WITHBURGA
9. VERONICA GIULIANI
10. FORTUNATUS
11. BENEDICT; PIUS I
12. ANDREW of RINN; JOHN JONES
13. HENRY
14. CAMILLUS of LELLIS
15. SWITHIN; BONAVENTURE
16. MARY-MAGDALEN POSTEL
17. ALEXIUS
18. FREDERICK
19. MACRINA the YOUNGER
20. MARGARET of ANTIOCH
21. LAURENCE of BRINDISI
22. MARY MAGDALENE
23. VALERIAN; BRIDGET of SWEDEN
24. SHARBEL MAKLUF; DECLAN
25. JAMES, apostle; CHRISTOPHER
26. JOACHIM & ANNE; CHRISTIAN
27. PANTALEON
28. NAZARIUS & CELSUS
29. MARTHA; BEATRICE
30. PETER CHRYSOLOGUS; URBAN II
31. IGNATIUS of LOYOLA; GERMAN

AUGUST

1. PETER JULIAN EYMARD; WILFRED
2. EUSEBIUS of VERCELLI
3. ALPHONSUS LIGUORI
4. DOMINIC; JOHN VIANNEY
5. AFRA; OSWALD, king
6. SIXTUS II & COMPANIONS
7. CAJETAN
8. COLMAN of LINDISFARNE
9. EDITH STEIN; NATH; FELIM
10. LAWRENCE
11. CLARE of ASSISI
12. PORCARIUS & COMPANIONS
13. RADEGUND; HIPPOLYTUS
14. MAXIMILIAN KOLBE
15. STEPHEN of HUNGARY
16. JOACHIM; CHARLES INGLIS
17. HYACINTH
18. HELENA
19. JOHN EUDES; SEBALDUS
20. BERNARD of CLAIRVAUX
21. PIUS X
22. FILBERT
23. ROSE of LIMA
24. BARTHOLOMEW, apostle
25. LOUIS, king
26. ULFILAS
27. JOSEPH CALASANCTIUS
28. AUGUSTINE of HIPPO
29. JOHN the BAPTIST, beheaded
30. FELIX; FIACRE
31. AIDAN of LINDISFARNE

SEPTEMBER

1. GILES
2. VERENA
3. WILLIAM of ROSKILDE
4. ROSALIE of PALERMO
5. NATHANIEL
6. BEGA; ZACCARIA
7. MAGNUS
8. Birth of VIRGIN MARY
9. CIARAN; PETER CLAVER
10. NICHOLAS of TOLENTINO
11. DEINIOL
12. VICTORIA FORNARI-STRATA
13. MAURILIUS
14. CYPRIAN; JOHN CHRYSOSTOM
15. NOTBURGA
16. CORNELIUS; NINIAN
17. HILDEGARD of BINGEN; LAMBERT
18. TITUS; JOSEPH of CUPERTINO
19. JANUARIUS
THEODORE of CANTERBURY
20. EUSTACE
21. MATTHEW, evangelist
22. MAURICE; PHOCAS
23. ADAMNAN of IONA; EUNAN
24. LINUS
25. FINNBAR; CLEOPHAS
26. VINCENT de PAUL
27. COSMAS & DAMIAN
28. WENCESLAUS; LIOBA
29. MICHAEL, archangel
30. JEROME; THÉRÈSE of LISIEUX

OCTOBER

1. REMIGIUS
2. GUARDIAN ANGELS
3. THOMAS of CANTALUPE
4. FRANCIS of ASSISI
5. RAYMOND of CAPUA; PLACID
6. BRUNO; FAITH
7. MARK, pope
8. KEYNE
9. DENIS; JOHN LEONARDI
10. DANIEL; PAULINUS of YORK
11. ALEXANDER; Bd. JOHN XXIII
12. WILFRID; MÓIBHI
13. EDWARD the CONFESSOR, king
14. CALLISTUS
15. TERESA of AVILA
    THÉRÈSE of JESUS
16. GALL; HEDWIG
17. IGNATIUS of ANTIOCH; AUDREY
18. LUKE, evangelist; ISAAC JOGUES
19. PAUL of the CROSS; FRIDESWIDE
20. WENDELIN
21. HILARION; URSULA; CELINA
22. Bd. TIMOTHY GIACCARDO
23. JOHN of CAPISTRANO
24. RAPHAEL, archangel
25. CRISPIN & CRISPINIAN
26. THADDEUS, apostle; EVARISTUS
27. OTTERAN
28. SIMON & JUDE, apostles
29. CONRAD; ABRAHAM OF ROSTER
30. ALPHONSUS RODRIGUEZ
31. WOLFGANG

NOVEMBER

1. ALL SAINTS; BENIGNUS; SALAUN
2. ALL SOULS
3. WINIFRED; HUBERTUS
   MARTIN of PORRES
4. CHARLES BORROMEO
5. ELIZABETH & ZACHARIAH
6. ILLTUD; LEONARD of SUSSEX
7. WILLIBRORD; HILDA
8. ELIZABETH of the TRINITY; TYSILIO
9. THEODORE TIRO
10. LEO the GREAT; EDMUND RICH
11. MARTIN of TOURS
12. JOSAPHAT
13. NIKOLAUS I, pope; BRICE
14. DYFRIG
15. ALBERT the GREAT; MALO
16. MARGARET, queen of SCOTLAND
    GERTRUDE the GREAT
17. ELIZABETH of HUNGARY; HUGH
    GREGORY of TOURS
18. ODO of CLUNY
19. MECHTILD of MAGDEBURG
20. EDMUND, king & martyr
21. GELASIUS
22. CECILIA
23. COLUMBAN; CLEMENT I
24. VIRGIL; FLORA; COLMAN ELA
25. CATHERINE of ALEXANDRIA
26. LEONARD of PORT MAURICE
27. FERGAL; BARLAAM
28. CATHERINE LABOURÉ
29. RADBOD
30. ANDREW, apostle, of Scotland

DECEMBER

1. ELIGIUS
2. NICHOLAS FERRAR
3. FRANCIS XAVIER
4. BARBARA; JOHN DAMASCENE
5. CLEMENT of ALEXANDRIA
6. NICHOLAS
7. AMBROSE, bishop of MILAN
8. MARY & ANNE
9. PETER FOURIER
10. JOHN ROBERTS
11. DAMASUS I; DANIEL, stylite
12. JANE FRANCES of CHANTAL
13. LUCY; ODILIA
14. JOHN of the CROSS
15. MARY of ROSA
16. ADELAIDE
17. LAZARUS
18. FLANNAN
19. ANASTASIUS
20. FACHANAN
21. THOMAS, apostle
22. FLAVIANUS
23. JOHN of KANTY
24. IRMINA & ADELA
25. Birth of JESUS CHRIST
26. STEPHEN
27. JOHN, evangelist
28. HOLY INNOCENTS
29. THOMAS À BECKET
30. EGWIN
31. SYLVESTER

Appendix 1

BACK TO BASICS

To melt wax

Candle wax is available at most craft shops; follow manufacturer's instructions for preparation. Alternatively, recycle old candle stubs:

Process: Place wax or candle stubs in leak-free metal container set in pan of simmering water. (A cloth beneath container will protect pan.)

Protect working surface with thick newspaper.

Pour melted wax through an old nylon stocking stretched across shallow metal container (e.g. aluminium take-away dish) that is lightly oiled on the inside.

Allow wax to cool before disposing of stocking and removing block of wax.

Wrap wax in plastic to store.

WARNING

Follow above instructions carefully for a safe process. Wax is inflammable and must be removed from heat source if it begins to smoke.

If it should catch fire **do not use water** but smother flames with a pan lid.

Never leave melting wax unattended.

To transfer a pattern

Method I – Photocopying

Use a photocopying machine on which the pattern can be enlarged or reduced as required.

Position the photocopy on the appropriate paper or card, secure with paperclips and cut through both according to the pattern.

Method II – Tracing

Place transparent paper on top of pattern and trace using HB pencil. Turn tracing over and rest on sheet of white paper.

With soft lead pencil, draw heavy broad line along traced lines.

Turn tracing to right side, place over paper on which pattern is required and secure with paperclips.

With ballpoint pen, draw along traced lines once more, taking care not to shift the papers.

Method III – carbon paper

You will need:
Carbon paper
Tracing paper (any transparent paper)
Ballpoint pen or coloured pencil
Paperclips

Place transparent paper on top of pattern and trace.

Place carbon paper, carbon side down, over paper on which pattern is required.

Place tracing on top of carbon paper and secure the layers with paperclips.

Draw along lines of pattern with ballpoint pen.

To cut circles of tissue paper

You will need:
Sheets of tissue paper
Piece of card, sharp scissors
Pair of compasses and pencil

Arrange sheets of tissue paper, folding them if necessary, to make twelve layers. Check all edges are neatly aligned.

Using compasses, draw circle on card of diameter required for circles of paper.

Cut out circle of card and place it on the twelve layers of paper, about 1cm from edge:

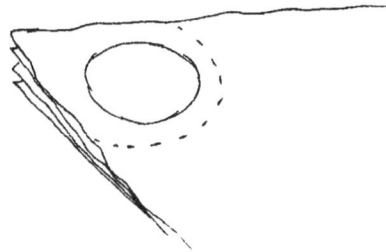

Grip card and layers of paper firmly between finger and thumb and cut paper as indicated by dotted line. Now the pile is easier to handle.

Continue to grip card and paper firmly together while trimming tissue to circumference of card.

With practice and a good pair of scissors, it will be possible to increase the layers of tissue paper cut at one time.

Coloured muslin cloths

Wherever children are busy and creative these cloths will have a multitude of uses and we heartily recommend them to every family. Indeed, they make the perfect present for an infant, ready to bless the years ahead with many hours of fun and imaginative play.

When birthday time comes round the versatility of these cloths make them a valuable resource. They can be used for dressing-up games or simple scenery for puppet shows. They can be hung behind the birthday table or draped over windows to quieten the atmosphere for story time at the end of the party. They create a circle of colour on which to play Spin a Bottle (see page 72) or a meandering birthday path (see page 28) from the child's room to the breakfast table.

Such a cloth, arranged over the hair under a simple crown, will transform the birthday child into a prince or princess; under its magic touch an ordinary chair becomes a grand throne and a corner of the living room becomes a secret treasure-house of gifts.

You will need:
Pieces of cotton gauze, butter muslin or mull
    (1 metre square is a useful size for
    dressing up, 2–3m lengths are good for
    making 'camps')
Red, blue and yellow, hot or cold fabric dyes.
    Dip the material according to the
    manufacturer's instructions.

Fabric dyes are easily obtainable but they are often labelled with fanciful names. Ignore these and select shades that correspond most closely to the basic artist's colours: lemon yellow, golden yellow, prussian blue, ultramarine, crimson red and vermilion.

Once you have yellow, blue, and red cloths, you can have fun making other colours by careful mixing of dyes. To avoid 'muddy' mixtures, follow these guidelines: for a clear green, mix lemon yellow and prussian blue; for a good purple, choose ultramarine blue and crimson red; for a shining orange, mix vermilion red with golden or lemon yellow.

Remember that yellow, red and blue together always make brown. Browns can vary greatly – experiment by mixing red and green, or yellow and purple, or vermilion and blue. Each combination will give you a different shade of brown, some warmer, some cooler, from which to make your choice. Generally, blue makes the shade cooler and red will warm it.

To make the activity more economical, buy a large quantity of cloth and share with friends. Set aside time for the dyeing when younger children are out of the way, and allow adequate working space. You will never regret dyeing more than you think you need! Once you are comfortable with the dyeing process, try obtaining many shades of colour on one length of cloth by gradually strengthening the dye.

With this technique it is possible to make a rainbow veil. Take a long piece of cloth and, working along the length, dip sections into different colours to make the sequence – red, orange, yellow, green, blue, deep blue-purple, lighter red-purple. Batik dyes work particularly well for this. In order to merge one colour gradually into another the dye needs to be graded using, for example, three red dye baths which become progressively lighter (less concentrated), then become orange by adding a small amount of yellow, and so on.

Supplies and sources

Most of the craft materials referred to in this book can be obtained at a good crafts suppliers. Below are some useful sources of particular items (mainly UK suppliers)

◇ Packs of A4 size gold card and crêpe paper: Woolworths stores

◇ Packs of A4 size coloured card and tissue paper: WH Smith stores

◇ Art and craft materials:
Mercurius United Kingdom
6 Highfield, Kings Langley
Herts. WD4 9JT, UK

◇ High quality natural materials and most of your craft requirements:
Myriad Natural Toys
Buckman Building
43 Southampton Rd.
Ringwood
Hampshire BH24 1HE
UK
www.myriadonline.co.uk

◇ Coloured modelling wax and beeswax crayons:
www.peanutbutterkisses.com/stockmar

◇ Art and craft materials (USA):
www.art-makes-sense.com

Further Reading

◇ *The Children's Party Book,*
Anne and Peter Thomas,
Floris Books, Edinburgh (1998)

Patterns

Birthday crown

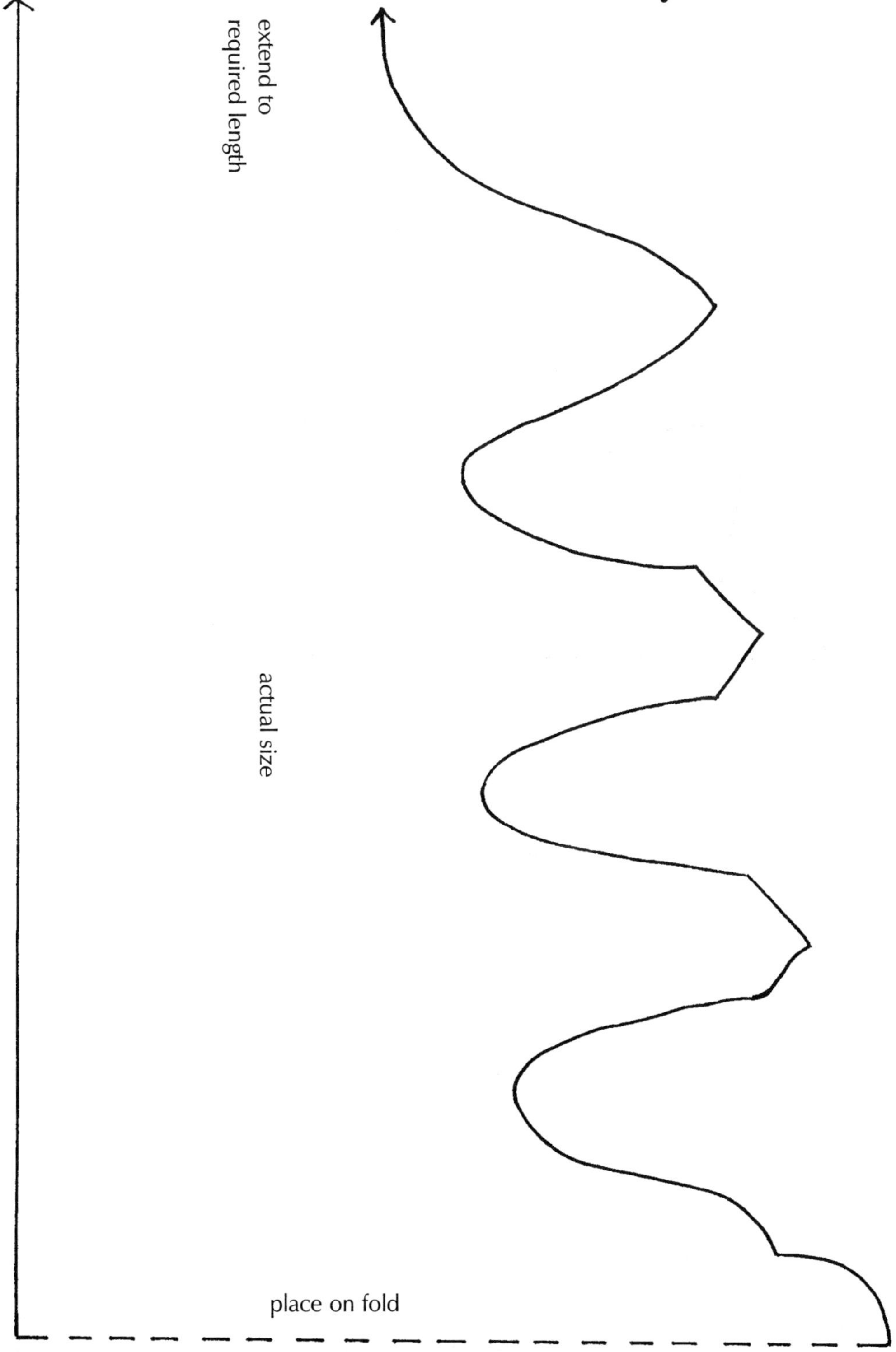

extend to
required length

actual size

place on fold

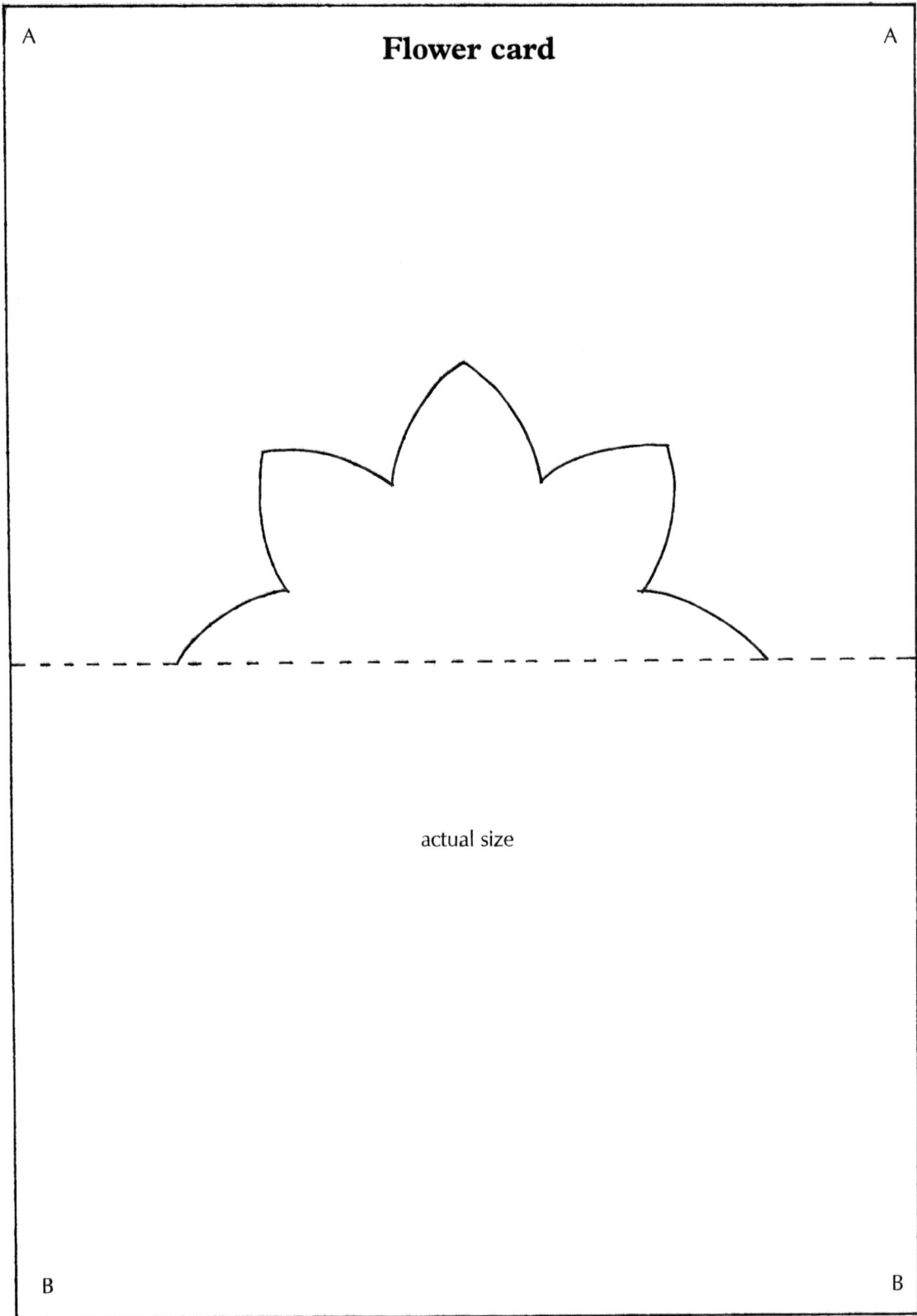

Flower card

A   A

actual size

B   B

Windflower

Humspinner

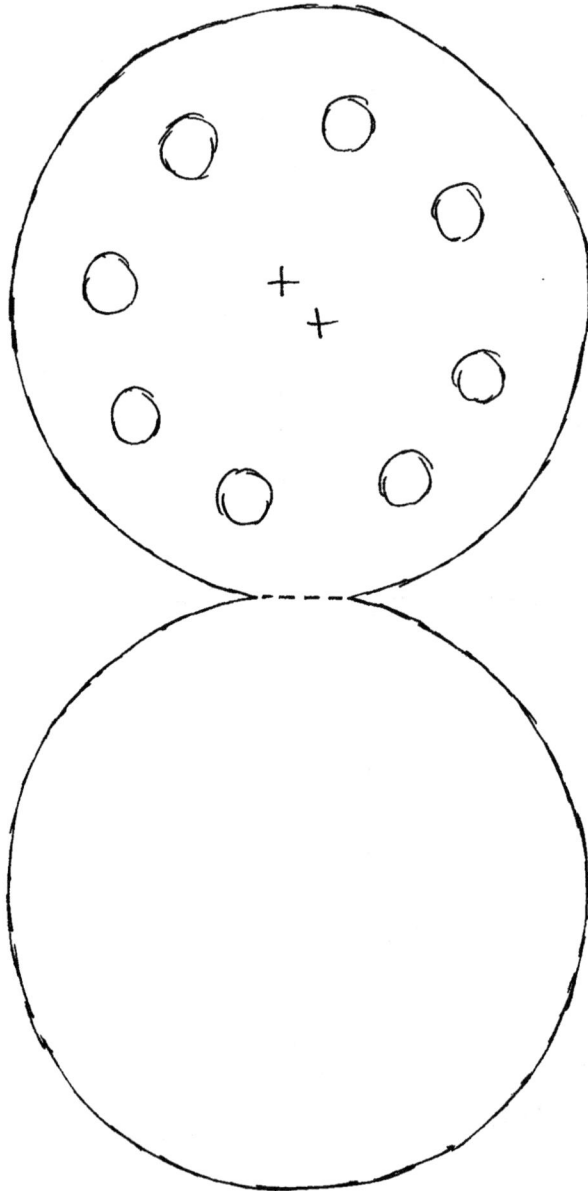

actual size

Kazoo

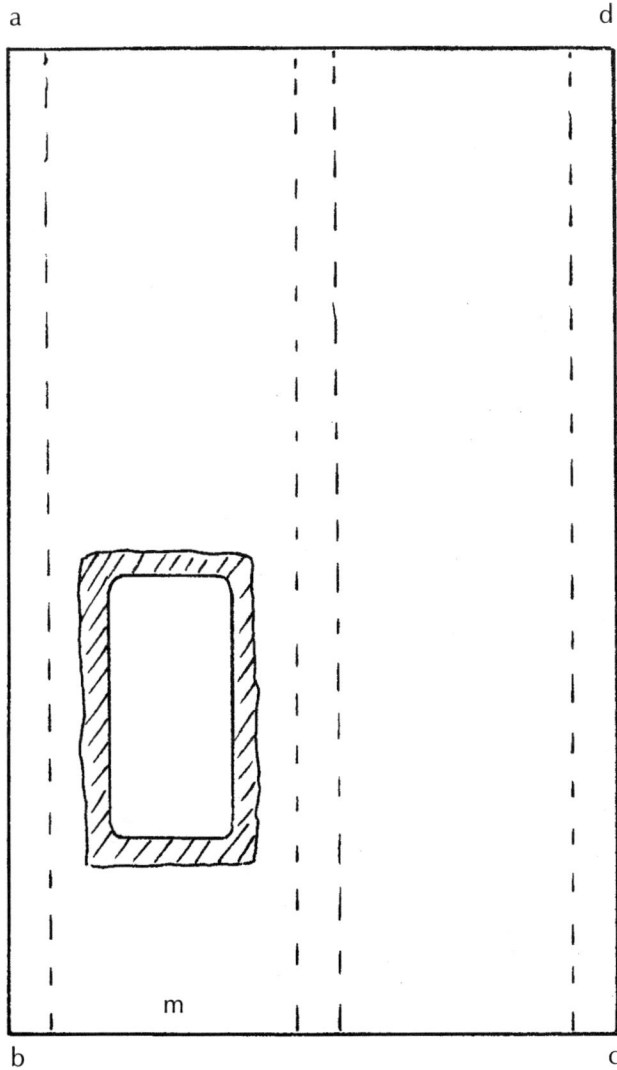

actual size

Croaker

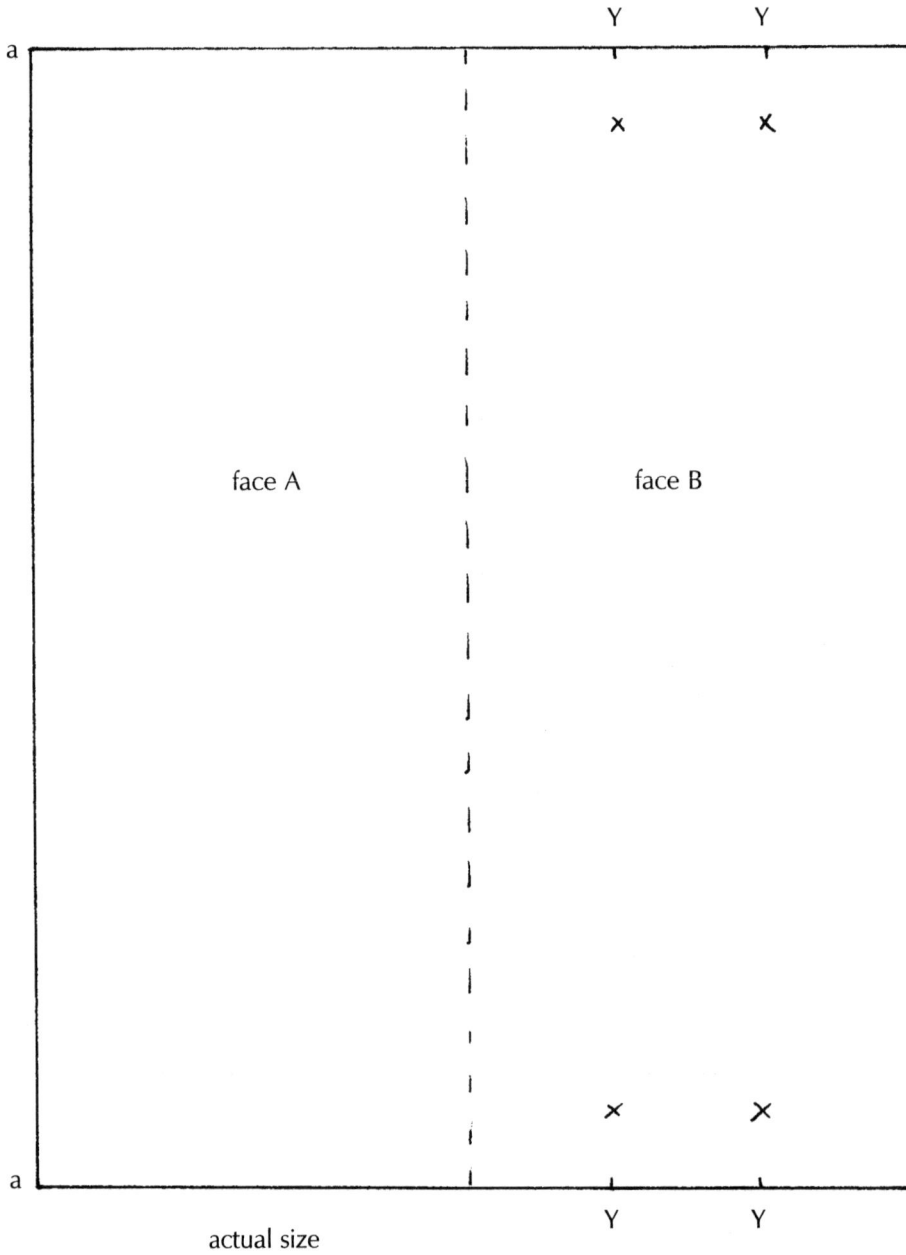

actual size

Star

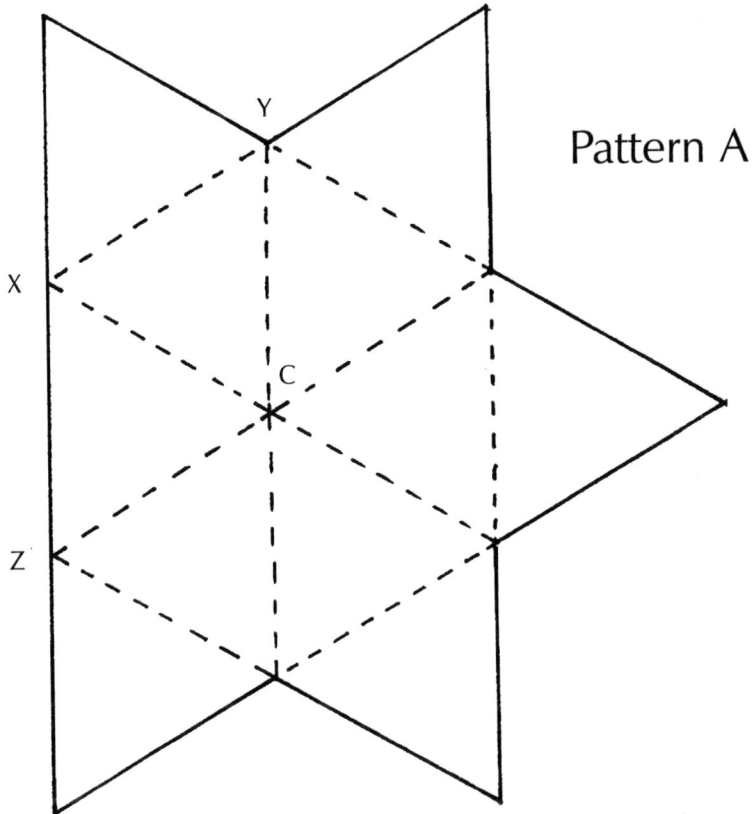

Pattern A

actual size

Pattern B

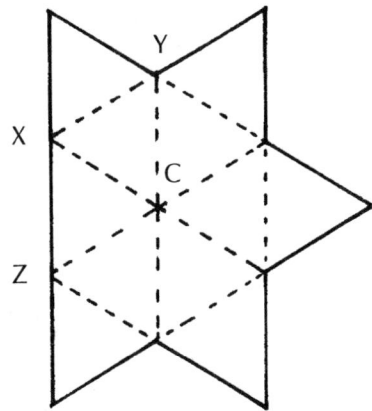

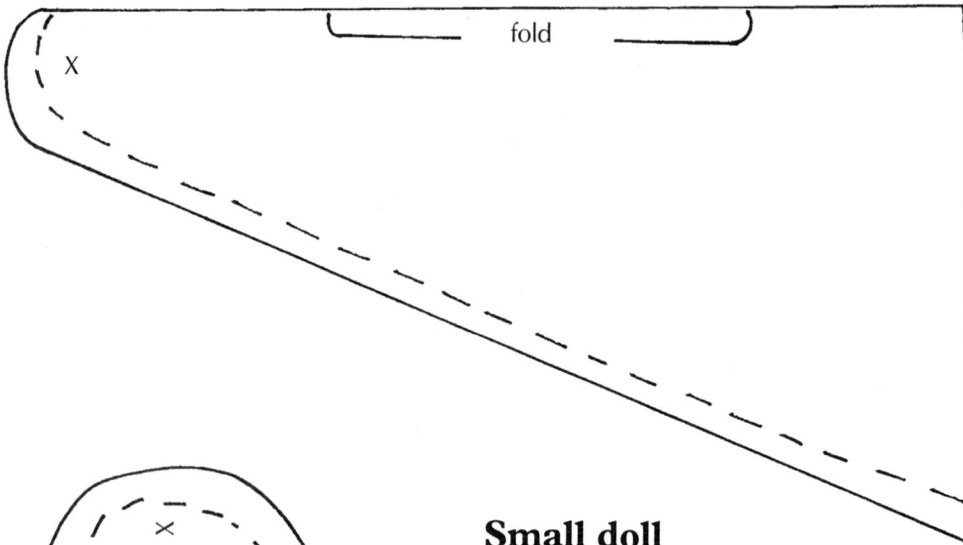

fold

Small doll

actual size

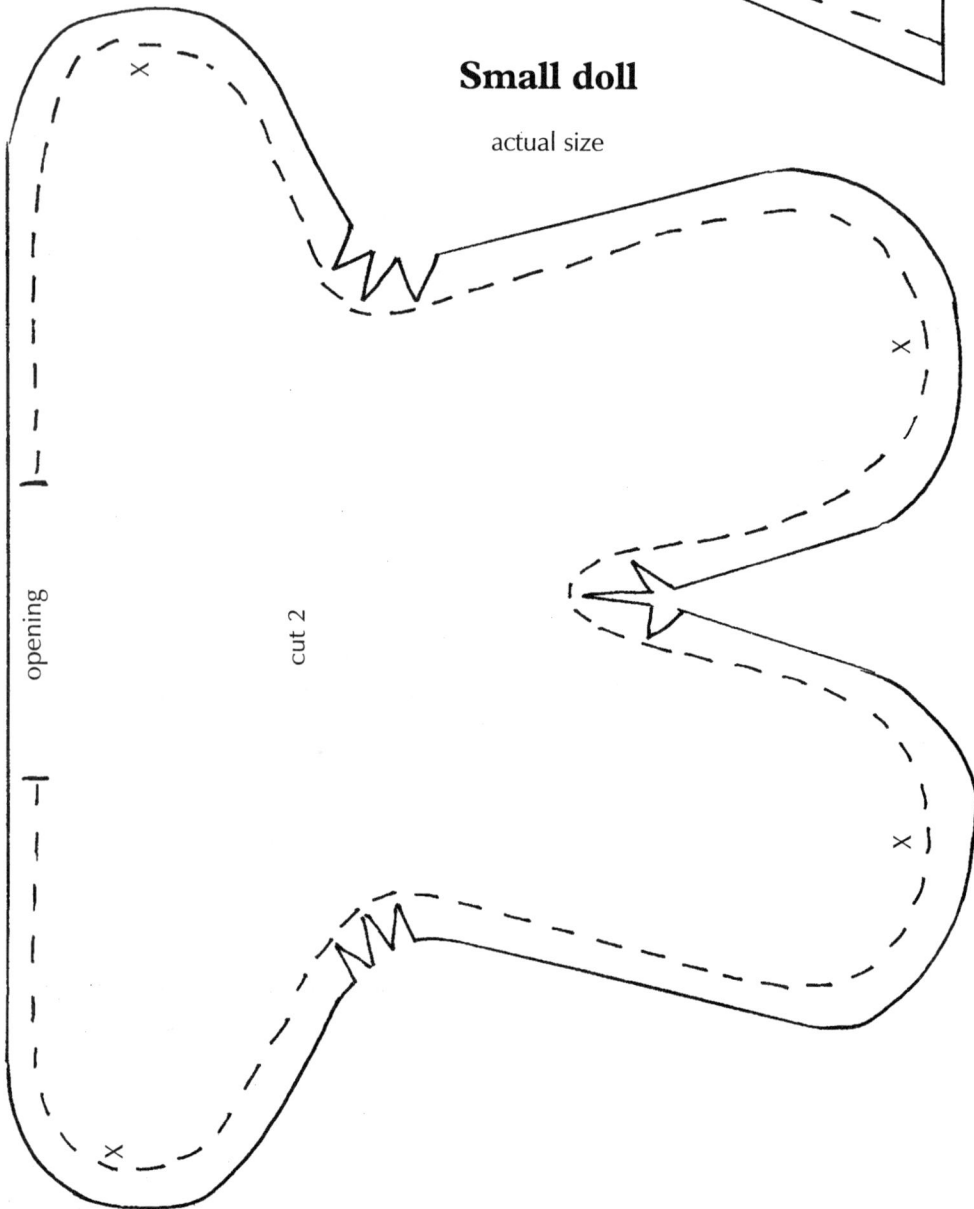

opening

cut 2

Star Boy

cut 4

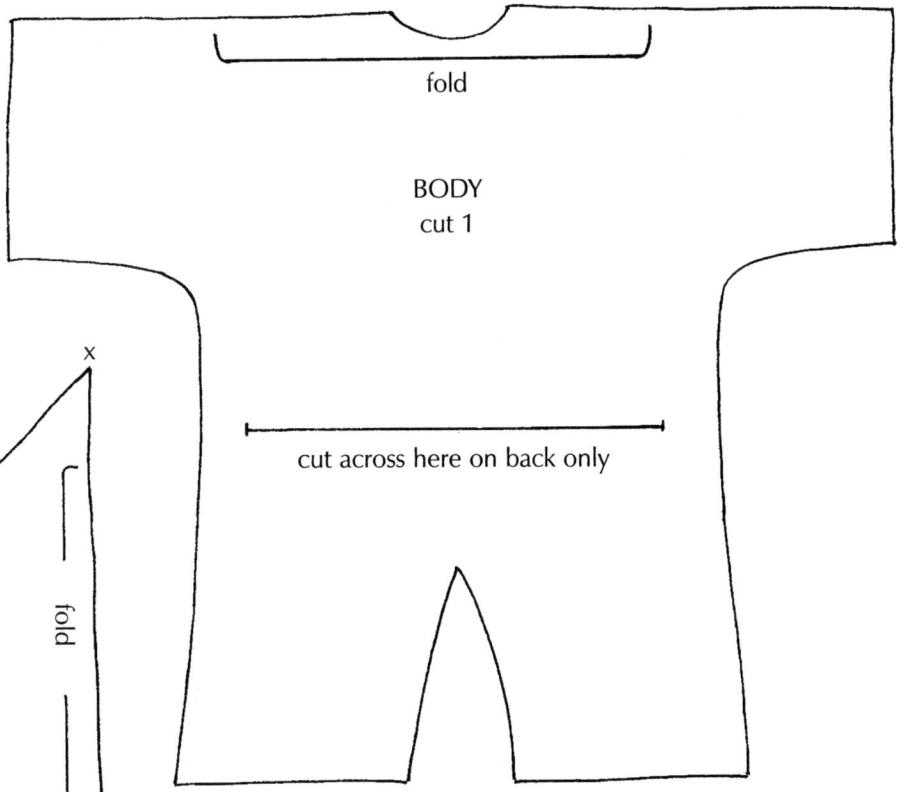

fold

BODY
cut 1

cut across here on back only

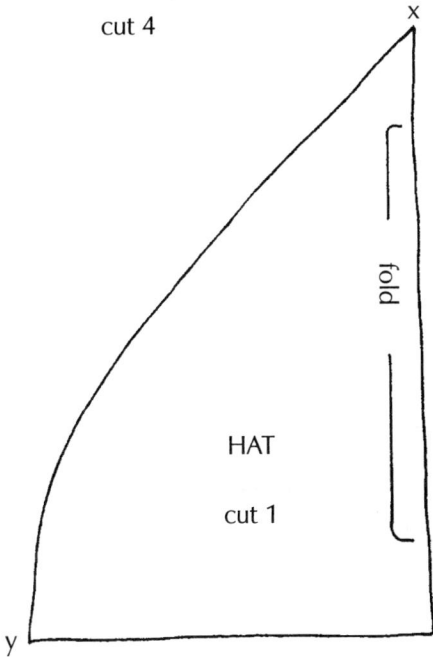

x

fold

HAT

cut 1

y

actual size

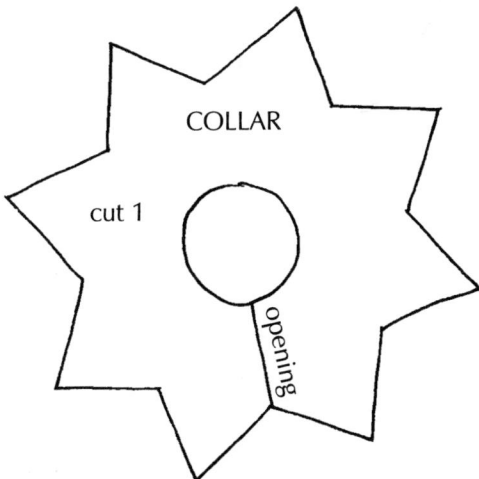

COLLAR

cut 1

opening

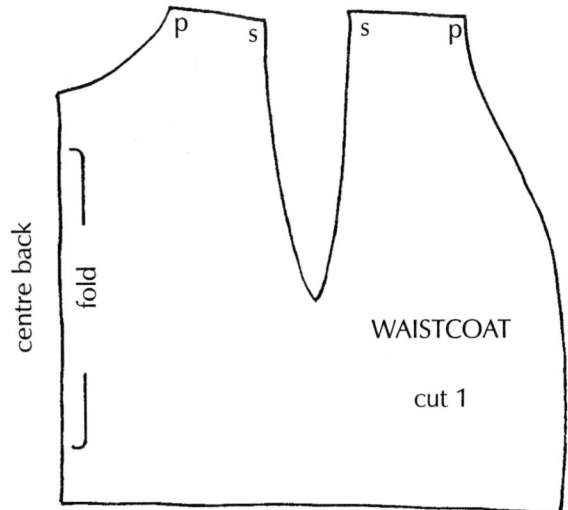

p   s   s   p

centre back

fold

WAISTCOAT

cut 1

Jester

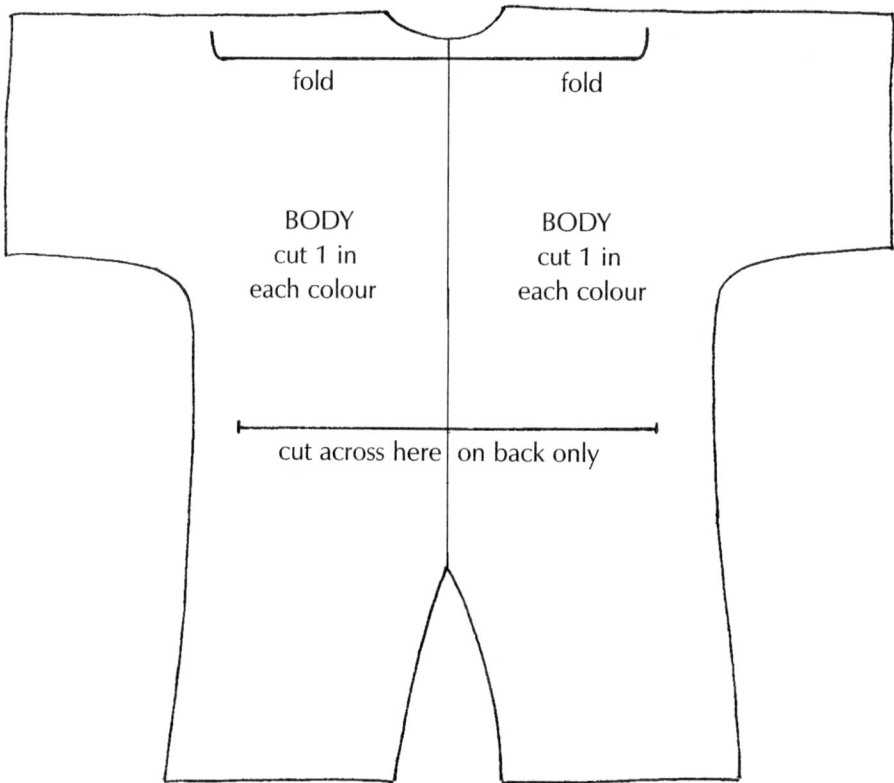

fold   fold

BODY
cut 1 in
each colour

BODY
cut 1 in
each colour

cut across here | on back only

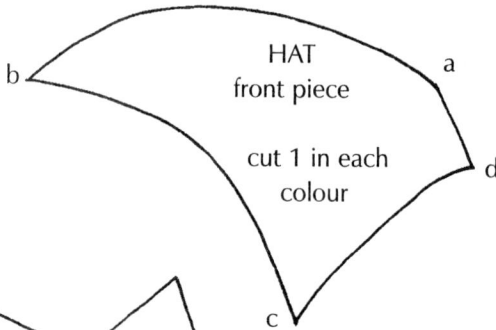

b

HAT
front piece

cut 1 in each
colour

a

d

c

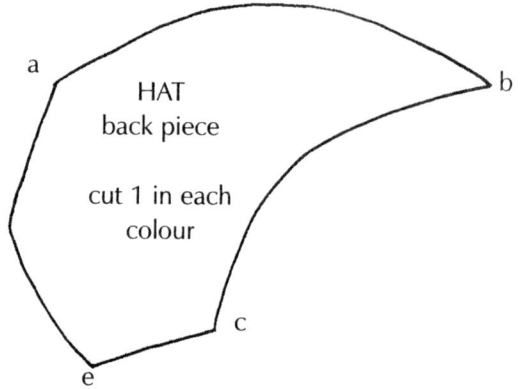

a

HAT
back piece

cut 1 in each
colour

b

c

e

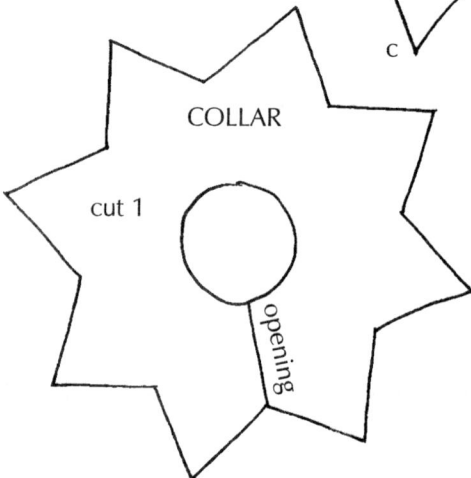

COLLAR

cut 1

opening

actual size

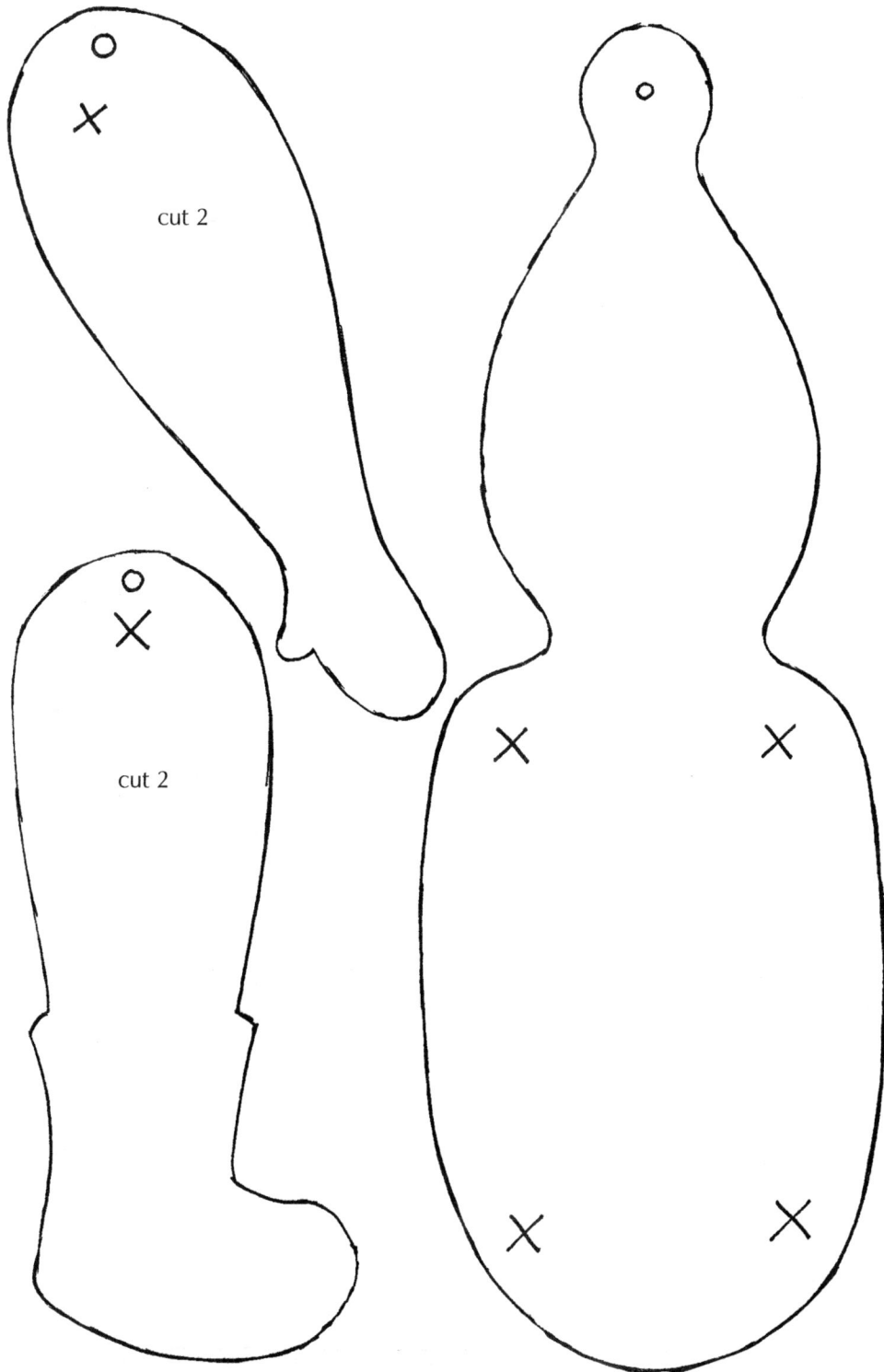

Jumping Jack

cut 2

cut 2

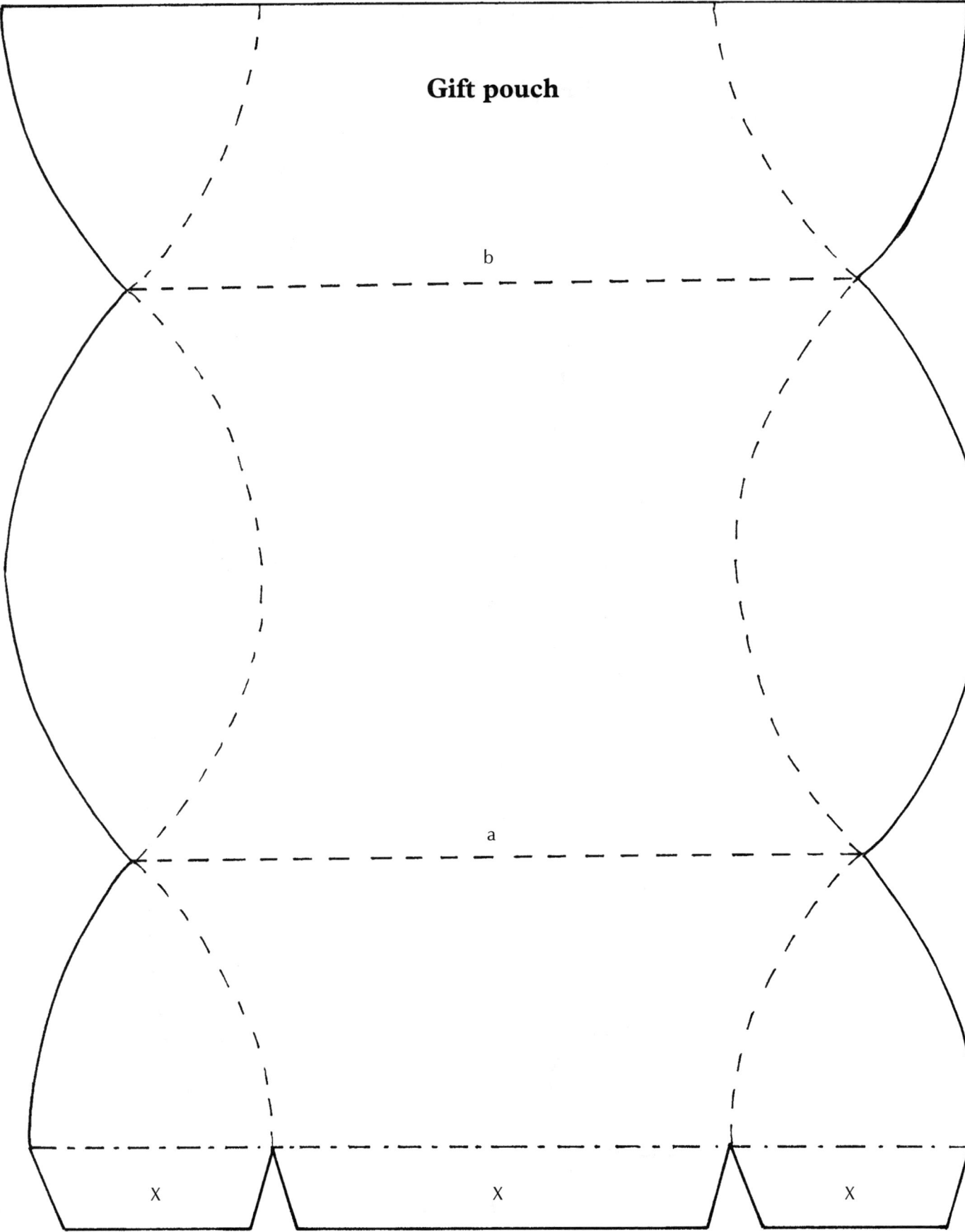

Gift pouch

b

a

X X X

Flap lid box

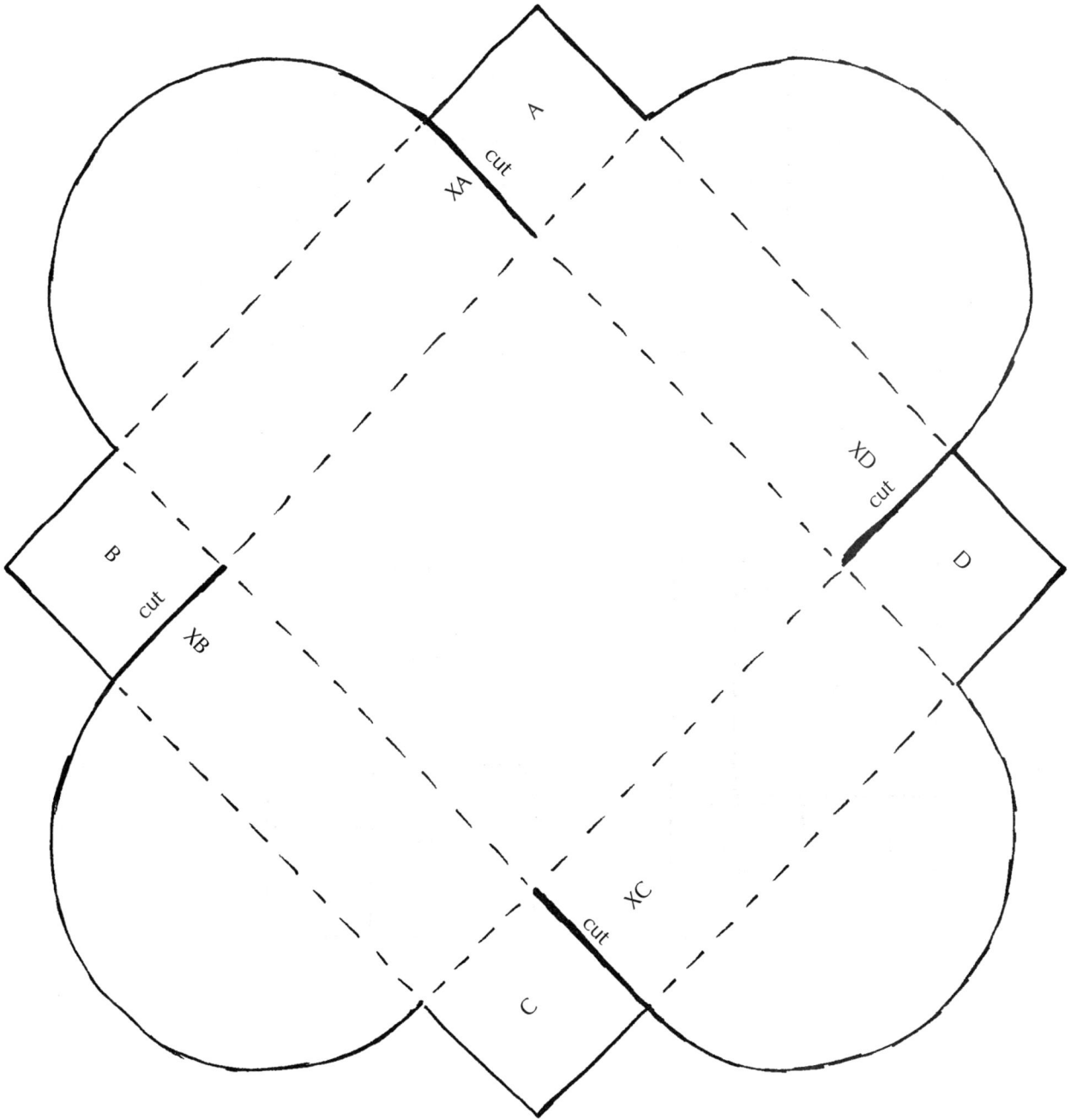

A

XA cut

B cut XB

XD cut

D

XC cut

C

Layout plan for seven gift boxes

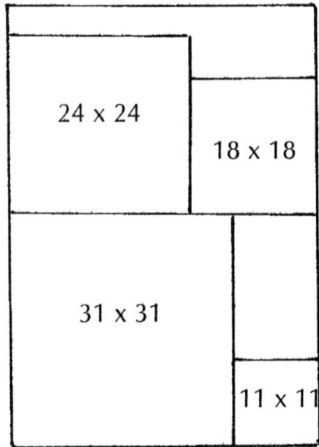

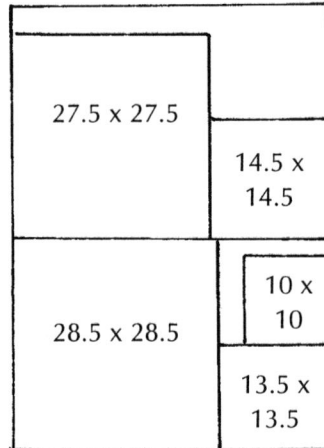

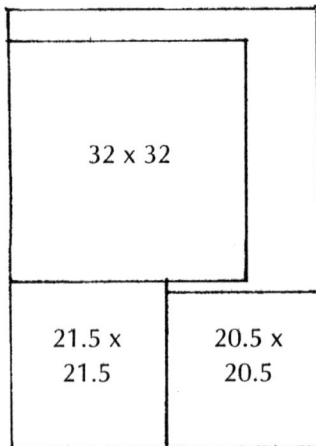

24 x 24	
	18 x 18
31 x 31	
	11 x 11

27.5 x 27.5	
	14.5 x 14.5
28.5 x 28.5	10 x 10
	13.5 x 13.5

32 x 32
21.5 x 21.5 · 20.5 x 20.5

paper size A2

measurements in centimeters

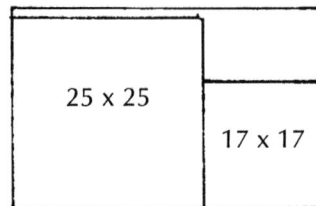

25 x 25	17 x 17

Appendix 2

CONVERSION CHARTS

Oven temperature conversions:

Gas Mark	Fahrenheit (°F)	Centigrade (°C)
1	275	140
2	300	150
3	325	160
4	350	180
5	375	190
6	400	200
7	425	220
8	450	230

Some weight conversions:

	Metric	American
Butter, margarine	250g	1 cup
Flour	125g	1 cup
Granulated sugar	125g	1 cup
Icing sugar	150g	1 cup
Ground nuts	250g	1.33 cup
Grated carrots	250g	1.5 cup

Fluid volume conversion:

250ml 1 cup

Abbreviations:

tsp   teaspoon (5ml)
tbsp tablespoon (15ml)

Glossary for American readers:

British term	American term
Baking parchment	Baking paper
Biscuit	Cookie
Blu-tack	White-tack
Cake tins	Cake pans
Caster sugar	Finely granulated sugar
Conker	Fruit of horse chestnut tree
Crockery	Dishes
Demerara sugar	Brown granulated sugar
Fringe	Bangs
Hundreds and thousands	Sprinkles (coloured)
Icing sugar	Powdered sugar
Jelly	Jello
Mobile phone	Cell phone
Oversewing	Neaten edge with stitches
Plait	Braid
Rucksack	Backpack
Shuttlecock	Badminton birdie
Sovereigns	Coins of great value
Stockinette	Thin cotton sock / T-shirt material
Sultanas	Seedless raisins
Sweets	Candy
Take-away	Take-out
Zest	Finely grated lemon peel

About the Authors

Ann Druitt

Ann made her first installation at about the age of five using moss, candlewax and spent matches. Much later she trained as an artist, studied Steiner Education and divided her time between teaching, writing, bringing up her four children and messing about with a wide variety of materials.

Christine Fynes-Clinton

Christine brought up her four children while opening her home to a succession of teenage boarders. She works as a music teacher and doll-maker and enjoys running workshops on festivals and family life.

About the Illustrator

Marije Rowling

Depending on the moment, Marije is a 'Mum', 'Homemaker', 'Art teacher' or 'Artist' – for at any time one of these descriptions may become more appropriate than the others! The 'red thread' connecting them is her attempt to be creative in all four areas of her life.

Index

Other books from Hawthorn Press

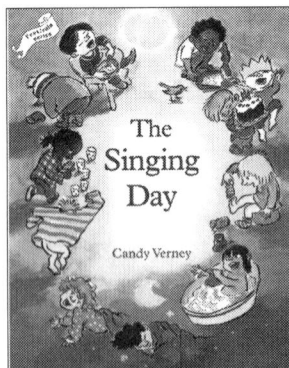

The Singing Day

Songbook and CD for singing with young children

Candy Verney

Singing with babies is one of the joys of being a parent. It is a lifetime gift from you that children love. This easy to use songbook and CD offer practical help for singing with young children from birth to 4 years old. *'Opens our eyes to all the opportunities for singing that arise in a child's day, giving encouragement as well as practical tips.'*

Caroline White, Stream of Sound Choir

The Islamic Year

Surahs, Stories and Celebrations

Noorah Al-Gailani and Chris Smith

Celebrate the Islamic Year in your family or at school! You are invited to explore Muslim festivals with this inspiring treasury of stories, surahs, songs, games, recipes, craft and art activities. Folk tales illustrate the core values of Islamic culture with gentle humour and wisdom. *The Islamic Year* is beautifully illustrated with traditional patterns, maps and pictures drawn from many parts of the Muslim world, and Arabic calligraphy.

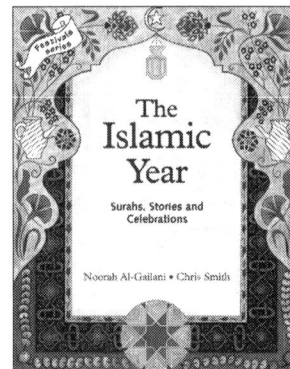

240pp; 250 x 200mm
paperback; 1 903458 14 5

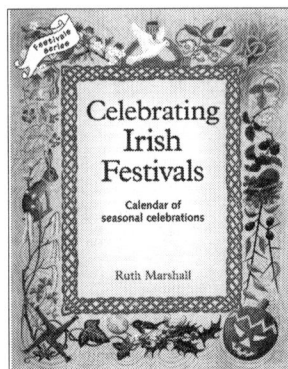

Celebrating Irish Festivals

Calendar of seasonal celebrations

Ruth Marshall

If you are interested in Irish traditions, need a family or school resource, then here is an inspiring treasury of stories, beautiful illustrations, poems, traditions, food, activities, games, dances and songs. Reaching back to the ancient festivals of Imbolc, Bealtaine, Lughnasadh, Samhain, and to Celtic Christianity – Ruth Marshall also offers new ways for engaging children. *'A comprehensive calendar of festivals that children will cherish.'*

Irelands Own, Summer 2003

224pp; 250 x 200mm; paperback; 1 903458 23 4

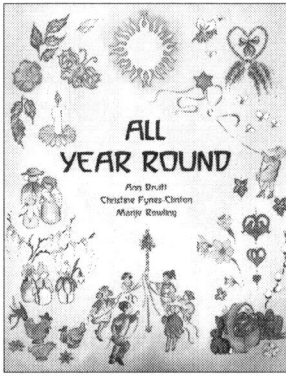

All Year Round

Christian calendar of celebrations

Ann Druitt, Christine Fynes-Clinton, Marije Rowling

All Year Round is brimming with things to make; activities, stories, poems and songs to share with your family. It is full of well illustrated ideas for fun and celebration: from Candlemas to Christmas and Midsummer's day to the Winter solstice. Observing the round of festivals is an enjoyable way to bring rhythm into children's lives and provide a series of meaningful landmarks to look forward to. Each festival has a special

320pp; 250 x 200mm; paperback; 1 869 890 47 7

The Children's Year

Seasonal crafts and clothes

Stephanie Cooper, Christine Fynes-Clinton, Marije Rowling

You needn't be an experienced craftsperson to create beautiful things! This step by step, well illustrated book with clear instructions shows you how to get started. Children and parents are encouraged to try all sorts of handwork, with different projects relating to the seasons of the year. Here are soft toys, wooden toys, moving toys such as balancing birds or climbing gnomes, horses, woolly hats, mobiles and dolls. Designs and patterns for children's clothing are included, using natural fabrics. Over 100 treasures to make, in seasonal groupings.

192pp; 250 x 200mm; paperback; 1 869 890 00 0

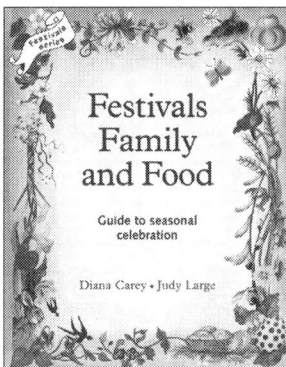

Festivals, Family and Food

Guide to seasonal celebration

Diana Carey and Judy Large

This family favourite is a unique, well loved source of stories, recipes, things to make, activities, poems, songs and festivals. Each festival such as Christmas, Candlemas and Martinmas has its own, well illustrated chapter. There are also sections on Birthdays, Rainy Days, Convalescence and a birthday Calendar. The perfect present for a family, it explores the numerous festivals that children love celebrating.

'It's an invaluable resource book'   The Observer
224pp; 250 x 200mm; paperback; 0 950 706 23 X

'Every family should have one'   Daily Mail

Festivals Together

Guide to multicultural celebration

Sue Fitzjohn, Minda Weston, Judy Large

This special book for families and teachers helps you celebrate festivals from cultures from all over the world. This resource guide for celebration introduces a selection of 26 Buddhist, Christian, Hindu, Jewish, Muslim and Sikh festivals. There are stories, things to make, recipes, songs, customs and activities for each festival, comprehensively illustrated. You will be able to share in the adventures of Anancy the spider trickster, how Ganesh got his elephant head and share in Eid, Holi, Wesak, Advent, Divali, Chinese New Year and more.

'The ideal book for anyone who wants to tackle multicultural festivals.'

Nursery World

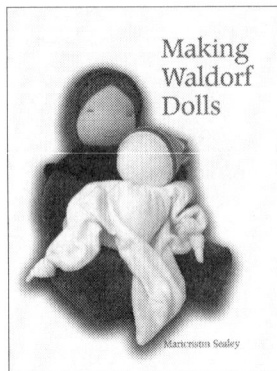

224pp; 250 x 200mm
paperback
1 869 890 46 9

Making Waldorf Dolls

A Waldorf doll-making handbook

Maricristin Sealey

Children treasure handmade dolls. Making a simple doll for a child is a gift for life. Formerly 'Kinder Dolls', this comprehensive, well-illustrated book shows how to create unique, handcrafted dolls from natural materials. The designs will inspire both beginners and experienced doll makers alike.

'A valuable primer, full of practical tips, simple designs and clear, easy to follow instructions.'

Sara McDonald, *Magic Cabin Dolls*

160pp; 246 x 189mm; paperback; 978 1 903458 58 7

Games Children Play

How games and sport help children develop

Kim John Payne

Illustrated by Marije Rowling

Games Children Play offers an accessible guide to games with children of age three upwards. These games are all tried and tested, and are the basis for the author's extensive teacher training work. The book explores children's personal develop-ment and how this is expressed in movement, play, songs and games. Each game is clearly and simply described, with diagrams or drawings, and accompanied by an explanation of why this game is helpful at a particular age. The equipment that may be needed is basic, cheap and easily available.

192pp; 297 x 210mm; paperback; 1 869 890 78 7

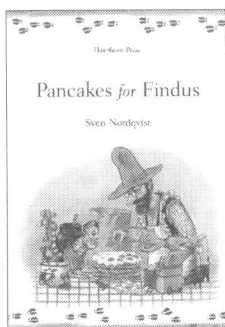

Pancakes for Findus

Story book for 4–8 year olds

Sven Nordqvist

This is the first of a series of stories about the adventures of Farmer Pettson and his cat Findus. The story tells of the mishaps that occur when Pettson tries to bake a pancake birthday cake for his cat. Set among the forests, fields and meadows of rural Sweden, every picture tells a story, revealing a fascinating, magical world of tiny creatures.

'It's not often that we come across books with such immediate and lasting appeal as Sven Nordqvist's 'Findus' series.
Philip Pullman

28pp; 297 x 210mm; hardback; 978-1-903458-79-2

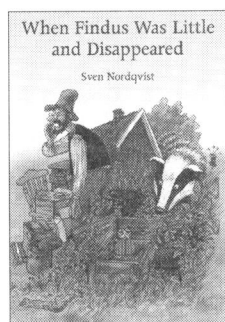

When Findus was Little and Disappeared

Story book for 4–8 year olds

Sven Nordqvist

This is the second in the Findus and Pettson series about Farmer Pettson and his cat Findus. Pettson recounts the story of how Findus came into his life, and what happened the day Findus disappeared then reappeared with a little help from the 'muckles'.

'The stories are ingenious, the characters are quirky and original, and the illustrations are absolutely delightful … I can't recommend them highly enough. Hurrah for Findus!'
Philip Pullman

28pp; 297 x 210 mm; hardback; 978-1-903458-83-9

Baking Bread With Children

Warren Lee Cohen

From our Crafts series, this book has everything you need to share the magic of baking with children of all ages. The recipes are cleverly seasoned with stories, songs and poems to make the whole process really enjoyable for everyone. Warren Lee Cohen has over 20 year's experience of baking bread with children and adults, building bread ovens and teaching bread workshops.

'Baking bread at home with children is a wonderful thing to do. This delightful book provides the ideal guidelines and inspiration. I strongly recommend it.'
Mollie Katzen, *Moosewood Cookbook*

128pp; 250 x 200mm; paperback; 978 1 903458 60 0

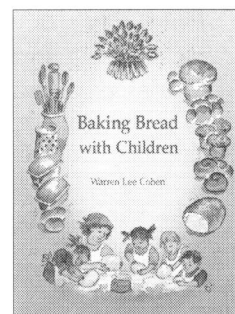

Now You See It...

String Games and Stories Book 2

Michael Taylor

String Games are fun, inviting children to exercise skill, imagination and teamwork. They give hands and fingers something clever and artistic to do! Following the success of *Pull the Other One!*, here are more of Michael Taylor's favourite string games, ideal for family travel, for creative play and for party tricks.

136pp; 216 x 148mm; paperback; 1 903458 21 8

Storytelling with Children

Nancy Mellon

Telling stories awakens wonder and creates special occasions with children, whether it is bedtime, around the fire or on rainy days. Nancy Mellon shows how you can become a confident storyteller and enrich your family with the power of story.

'Nancy Mellon continues to be an inspiration for storytellers old and new. Her experience, advice and suggestions work wonders. They are potent seeds that give you the creative confidence to find your own style of storytelling.'

Ashley Ramsden, Director of the School of Storytelling, Emerson College

192pp; 216 x 138mm; paperback; 1 903458 08 0

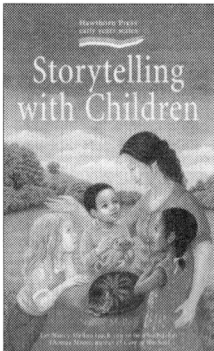

The Winding Road

Family treasury of poems and verses

Compiled by Matthew Barton

Celebrate each age and stage of your child's life with this poetic travelling companion. *The Winding Road* offers over 200 poems on the theme of childhood and growing up by writers ancient and modern — from Gaelic blessings to Navajo prayers, from William Blake to Eleanor Farjeon and Billy Collins. This rich treasury of poems, verses, blessings and meditations reflects a child's journey from baby to teenager, from first milestones to leaving home.

'What pleasure awaits those who not only dip into this book at random, but who also search for the particular poem or verse which has personal meaning….'

Jamila Gavin, author of *Coram Boy*

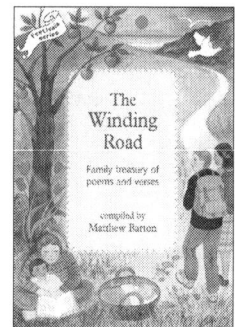

224pp; 210 x 148mm
paperback
1 903458 47 1

Set Free Childhood

Parents' survival guide to coping with computers and TV

Martin Large

Children watch TV and use computers for five hours daily on average. The result? Record levels of learning difficulties, obesity, eating disorders, sleep problems, language delay, aggressive behaviour, anxiety – and children on fast forward. However, *Set Free Childhood* shows you how to counter screen culture and create a calmer, more enjoyable family life.

'A comprehensive, practical and readable guide … the skilful interplay between academic research and anecdotal evidence engages the reader.'

Jane Morris-Brown, *Steiner Education*

240pp; 216 x 138mm; paperback; 1 903458 43 9

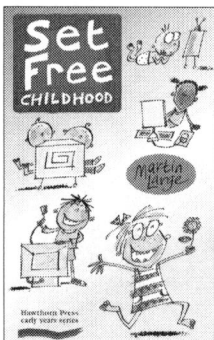

Ordering Books

For further information or a book catalogue, please contact:

Hawthorn Press
1 Lansdown Lane, Stroud
Gloucestershire, GL5 1BJ, UK
Tel: +(44) (0) 1453 757040
Fax: +(44) (0) 1453 751138
E-mail: info@hawthornpress.com
Website: www.hawthornpress.com

If you have difficulties ordering Hawthorn Press books from a
bookshop, you can order direct from:

BookSource
50 Cambuslang Road, Glasgow, G32 8NB
Tel: (0845) 370 0063
Fax: (0845) 370 0064
E-mail: orders@booksource.net